The Scar of Revolution

For Mark and Isabelle,
very warmly

Irena Grudzinska Gross

Atlanta, April 1992

The Scar of Revolution

Custine, Tocqueville, and the Romantic Imagination

Irena Grudzinska Gross

UNIVERSITY OF CALIFORNIA PRESS

Berkeley / Los Angeles / Oxford

University of California Press
Berkeley and Los Angeles, California

University of California Press
Oxford, England

Copyright © 1991 by The Regents of the University of California

Library of Congress Cataloging-in-Publication Data

Grudzinska Gross, Irena.
    The scar of revolution : Custine, Tocqueville, and the romantic
imagination / Irena Grudzinska Gross.
        p.   cm.
    Includes bibliographical references and index.
    ISBN 0-520-07351-7 (alk. paper)
        1. Custine, Astolphe, marquis de, 1790–1857.   Russie en
1839.   2. Custine, Astolphe, marquis de, 1790–1857—
Journeys—Soviet Union.   3. Soviet Union—Description and
travel.   4. Tocqueville, Alexis de, 1805–1859. De la démocratie
en Amérique.   5. United States—Politics and government.
6. United States—Social conditions—To 1865.   7. Democracy.
8. Romanticism—France.   9. France—History—Revolution,
1789–1799—Influence.   I. Title.
DK25.C973G78   1991
321.09'4—dc20   91-9336
                                                                     CIP

Printed in the United States of America

1   2   3   4   5   6   7   8   9

The paper used in this publication meets the minimum requirements
of American National Standard for Information Sciences—
Permanence of Paper for Printed Library Materials, ANSI Z39.48-
1984 ∞

Contents

Preface

In 1831 the young French aristocrat Alexis de Tocqueville traveled to America to observe the working of the democratic political system. Eight years later another French aristocrat, Astolphe de Custine, traveled to Russia to observe the working of autocracy. The two men wrote renowned accounts based on their travels. Although they set off in opposite directions, they left from the same historical and intellectual place: postrevolutionary France. The common point of departure was as important to their works as their destinations, and there is a symmetry between the two men and their works. "As a venture into the world of political speculation, Custine's journey to Russia was a counterpart of Tocqueville's nine-month voyage to America."[1]

Tocqueville's *De la démocratie en Amérique* is *the* nineteenth-century book about the United States, and Custine's *La Russie en 1839* is *the* nineteenth-century book about Russia. The greatness of Tocqueville is generally recognized, whereas Custine's perspicacity is obscured by the length of his work and by the low respect in which literature of travel is held. Yet his work is truly remarkable. The famous nineteenth-century Russian writer Alexandr Herzen considered it the most revealing and true book about Russia ever written. The striking similarity between *La*

1. Daniel J. Boorstein in his Foreword to the 1989 Doubleday edition of Custine's *La Russie en 1839*, titled in English *Empire of the Czar: A Journey Through Eternal Russia* (New York: Doubleday, 1989), xiii. All quotations from Custine are taken from this edition; passages omitted from that version have been translated from the original and are indicated by volume and page of the 1843 edition of *La Russie en 1839*.

Russie en 1839 and *Democracy in America* is that the two writers were able to capture the functioning of the political systems of the countries they visited. The originality of Custine's analysis lay in his ability to understand that repression in Russia was not only enforced by the central authority but was exercised by all the members of the society against whoever was weaker. He showed that authoritarianism pervaded the simplest relationships from top to bottom of the social scale. It was this understanding of Russian society that enabled Custine to predict with such accuracy the coming of the Russian Revolution.

Both Tocqueville and Custine saw revolutions as a result of social malfunctioning: and while Tocqueville analyzed the Old Regime to find the reasons for the French Revolution, Custine analyzed the Russia of his epoch in order to see its future. Where traditional writers see a breakdown between old regimes and regimes constituted after a revolution, Custine and Tocqueville constructed analytical frameworks that revealed continuity of these regimes. Both men were "strange" liberals, conservative democrats. The juxtaposition of Custine to Tocqueville shows how European thinkers evolved at this concrete point in history and how *our* opinions about the borderlands of European civilization came to be.

This study proposes a reading in the history of European culture: it follows Custine and Tocqueville in their intellectual and poetic reactions to Russia and America, to the French Revolution, and to the advancement of equality, and it seeks sources of these reactions in the situation of their country and social class. The interworking of cultural tradition, personal history, and experience of foreign reality is discussed through an analysis of Custine's *La Russie en 1839* and Tocqueville's American travel accounts and diary. The two areas of interest are the formulation of modern West-European self-consciousness with its mental geography and the functioning of tradition in descriptions of cultural difference. Custine and Tocqueville are read through their readings and analyzed in the context of cultural and historical memory they shared. America and Russia are, together with Custine and Tocqueville, the main protagonists of this book.

The problem of understanding foreign cultures is at the center of this study. "It is only in the eyes of *another* culture that foreign culture reveals itself fully and profoundly," wrote Mikhail Bakhtin.

A meaning only reveals its depths once it has encountered and come into contact with another, foreign meaning: they engage in a kind of dialogue,

which surmounts the closedness and one-sidedness of these particular meanings, these cultures.

But the way we address these cultures is not arbitrary. "We raise new
questions for a foreign culture," Bakhtin continues,

ones that it did not raise itself; we seek answers to our own questions in it; and
the foreign culture responds to us by revealing to us its new aspects and new
semantic depths. Without *one's own* questions one cannot creatively understand
anything other or foreign (but, of course, the questions must be serious and
sincere). Such a dialogic encounter of two cultures does not result in merging or
mixing. Each retains its own unity and *open* totality, but they are mutually
enriched.[2]

Custine and Tocqueville went to Russia and America and described
these countries with hitherto unmatched perspicacity. They were able to
do this because they "engaged in a dialogue" with the new cultures and
brought to them their own questions—questions that were serious,
sincere, and urgent. They asked what the essence of Europe was;
whether violence in history was unavoidable; and whether equality was
compatible with individual freedom. These questions were imposed on
them by the traumatic experience of their country in the French Revolution, and both writers analyzed the countries they visited in its light.
The historical and personal trauma of the French Revolution influenced
Custine's and Tocqueville's understanding of foreign cultures, and, in
turn, these cultures explained for them the Revolution itself.

"In the realm of culture, outsideness is a most powerful factor in
understanding," wrote Bakhtin (p. 7). The two men were outsiders in
America and Russia, and that allowed them to see "new meanings and
semantic depths" in these cultures. But since the Revolution had un-
seated the already-weakened aristocracy to which they belonged, they
felt outsiders in their own country as well. Published in 1843, *La Russie
en 1839* opens with a one-hundred-page memoir about the sufferings of
the Custine family during the Revolution, and this serves as a setting
and frame for Custine's experience and analysis of Russia. Tocqueville's
family also suffered in the Revolution, and his *Democracy in America* has
been described by François Furet as a "theory of family experience."[3]

2. M. Bakhtin, "Response to a Question from *Novy Mir*," in *Speech Genres and Other
Essays*, trans. Vern W. McGee (Austin: University of Texas Press), 1–9; 7.
3. François Furet, "The Conceptual System of *Democracy in America*," *In the Workshop
of History*, trans. Jonathan Mandelbaum (Chicago: University of Chicago Press, 1984),
167–196; 171.

Also, both men used in their thinking the Romantic vocabulary of the time (drawing, especially, on that of François-René de Chateaubriand), which was itself shaped, in part, in response to the social plight of aristocracy during and after the Revolution. In fact, Chateaubriand was the writer who captured most successfully the postrevolutionary mood and provided several generations with the vocabulary in which to express it.

Though older than Custine and Tocqueville, Chateaubriand belonged to their historical milieu. Further, he had ties with the families of both men: he was a lover of Custine's mother and became a sort of spiritual father to Astolphe, and he was a relation of Tocqueville's. The sister of Tocqueville's mother was married to Chateaubriand's older brother; the couple perished in the Great Terror. Their children were brought up together with Alexis and his two brothers. Chateaubriand's most important works about the United States were published at the beginning of the century, before Tocqueville was born; and by the time young Tocqueville went to America Chateaubriand's vision of that country was already an integral and important part of French culture. "The greatest of all French writers"[4] put a definitive stamp on the Romantic vision of America—a stamp stronger than that left by the most influential political theories of the time. It was not only France's vision of America that was altered by Chateaubriand: the character of René and of other protagonists in his early American writings were powerful and influential expressions of the entire "mal du siècle." Whereas Custine was conscious of Chateaubriand's influence—one may say he even aspired to it—Tocqueville never thought of himself as René. His work, however, is imbued with a vision of America that came directly from Chateaubriand. Chateaubriand's America and the figures populating its landscape shaped Custine's and Tocqueville's poetic unconscious. René is the protagonist of Custine's travels to Russia and Tocqueville's American travel accounts.

René was an embodiment of several problems shared by Tocqueville and Custine. One was the "outsideness." Like René facing the Indian chief Chactas and exile in America, both writers examined other nations in order to define their own identity, in terms not only of nationality but of class. (They examined other nations also to discover, in these nations' present, signs of the future of French society.) They were both

4. As François Furet wrote in "From Savage Man to Historical Man: The American Experience in Eighteenth-Century French Culture," from his *In the Workshop of History*, 153–166; 166.

acutely aware of the declining role of the French aristocracy and tried to reformulate its social responsibilities. The aristocracy's function would cease to be primarily political and military and become intellectual and spiritual instead. In their work and life, both writers tried to fulfill this role, and they succeeded brilliantly.

Another important characteristic the two writers shared with Chateaubriand was their Catholicism. This was a matter not only of faith but also of perspective: they saw the world—the political and geographic world—through the vocabulary of the Catholic tradition. Custine's rejection of Russia was formulated in terms of a tradition that goes back to fifteenth-century travel reports of the papal nuncios. Tocqueville, too, drew on the Catholic tradition in his description of America; his imagery goes back to the sixteenth century and the Catholic efforts at dealing with the discovery of the New World. In both cases, the Catholic tradition is implied or hidden in what seemed to be rational and conscious political choices.

Catholicism, "outsideness," and René-like attitudes were the elements of the Romantic world-view. Both authors felt a tragic conflict between the freedom of the individual and the logic of history; both were aware of the tension between what has to be and what is longed for. Nostalgia was the dominant emotional tone of Custine's journeys, but also a strong undertone in Tocqueville's American fragments. *La Russie en 1839* and *Democracy in America* were written at the height of French Romanticism. Yet both authors were strongly attached to the ideals of Enlightenment. Tocqueville strived for the systematicity of a Montesquieu, while Custine operated on the basis of eighteenth-century classifications and definitions. In fact, the two men complement each other in their two ways of being Romantic. Custine is an extroverted Romantic who hides his intelligence behind the Romantic pose of a lonely and rejected "traveler." Tocqueville is an intellectual Romantic who hides his Romanticism behind a clear and orderly brilliance.

Custine's *The Empire of the Czar* was a sort of enhanced travel diary—personal, emotional, impressionistic, anecdotal; Custine talks directly about history, about himself, about the country he visits, about his emotions, and about many of his literary sources. This direct relationship with the narrating protagonist, however stylized or removed from the author, makes the cultural reconstruction simpler. As for Tocqueville, a unique insight into his way of thinking is offered by comparing several texts and testimonies about one episode in his and Gustave de Beaumont's American journey: an emotional excursion to Lake Oneida.

The texts are: Tocqueville's short travel account "Voyage au Lac Onéida," two entries in his American notebooks, and a letter to his sister-in-law; and Beaumont's novel *Marie ou de l'Escalvage aux Etats Unis,* a letter to his sister, and a drawing. In comparing these, a poetic, unthought-through vision of America appears, which then can be traced in Tocqueville's political treatise *Democracy in America.* Because this study follows the way in which various areas of culture are interconnected, it moves between primary and secondary texts and brings in several other sources both written and visual. On the map of European mental geography, no borders of genre or canon need be respected.

Acknowledgments

I would like to thank most cordially many people who helped me at various stages of making this book come to be. They are Jan T. Gross, Stanley Holwitz, Florence Stankiewicz, and Jonathan Schell, as well as Helen Solanum, Roman Laba, Tony Judt, Marina Beer, Patricia Hilden, Timothy Reiss, Lucyna Gebert, Dalia Judovitz, Amy Lang, Ewa Wolynska, Dorinda Evans, Darra Goldstein, Walter Adamson, Zygmunt Gross, and Stanislaw Baranczak.

I would also like to acknowledge the generous help of Emory University, which granted me four consecutive Summer Faculty Development Awards (1987–1990), and Andrew Mellon Foundation, whose Faculty Fellowship allowed me to spend 1986–1987 academic year in the libraries (and classrooms) of Harvard University.

December, 1990   Irena Grudzinska Gross

Introduction: Two Frenchmen

On February 22, 1841, Astolphe de Custine decided to write a long-overdue letter to his friend, Baron August Varnhagen von Ense. At that time Custine was preparing his book *La Russie en 1839*, but the letter does not mention work. It describes the agitated social life of a rather unhappy man. After complaining about the indifferent frivolity of "what they call here the world," Custine goes on to tell two real-life love stories, one involving his Italian "valet de chambre," Antonio, and the second his Polish house-guest, Ignacy Gurowski. Perhaps because it had Italians of the lower classes as its protagonists, the first story was strongly stylized, with an invocation of the letter Amélie wrote to René in Chateaubriand's novel *René*. The love of the Spanish *infante* for Gurowski was recounted simply as amusing gossip. Other Parisian news included a curious episode: a reading "chez Madame Récamier" of Monsieur de Chateaubriand's account of his travels to Prague. An old and ailing Chateaubriand was so moved by his own recollections (read aloud by somebody else) that twice he had to leave the room. It was here, too, that Astolphe de Custine met Alexis de Tocqueville, a portrait of whom ends this part of the letter.[1]

"[Most] geniuses of my times," writes Custine before mentioning either Chateaubriand or Tocqueville, "seem to me composed of misery,

---

1. Custine and Tocqueville may have met at Madame Récamier's before. Custine was writing letters to her already in 1834, and in 1839 his tragedy *Béatrix Cenci* was read in her salon. Chateaubriand made her invite Tocqueville in 1835 to a reading of *Mémoires d'outre-tombe*.

drolleries, and superior capacities; I would not want to pay for their qualities with their faults." The marquis obviously put himself in a lower category. After a few rather critical words about Chateaubriand comes a portrait of Tocqueville. It consists of a presentation of his superior capacities and his flaws.

He is thin, short, still young, and looks sickly; there is something about him both of an old man and of a child; he seems the most naive among those who are ambitious: his manner is charming but lacks sincerity; his mouth is old and unpleasantly shaped; his color is bilious. His physiognomy would captivate me more if it disturbed me less; one can see that he will voice many opinions and that his opinions are weapons to attain his objectives. Here you have the new star on our political horizon as I've seen him. . . .[2]

When the two writers met at Madame Récamier's, Tocqueville's reputation was on the rise, and he was held in high intellectual esteem. His masterpiece, *De la démocratie en Amérique,* the reason for his success, was the fruit of a strenuous visit to the United States spanning May 11, 1831 to February 20, 1832. The book's first two parts were published in 1835 and met with an immediate, "universal and resounding" success, not only in France but abroad as well.[3] The next two volumes appeared five years later and were received with curiosity and respect. The French intellectual establishment recognized in the young author (only thirty years old in 1835) a writer deserving to become a member of the Académie des Sciences Morales et Politiques (1838) and of the Académie Française itself (1841). Considering that the book was also successful with the general public, one could scarcely hope for a better reception. "Everybody knows what Monsieur Royer-Collard said after having read *Democracy:* 'Since Montesquieu nothing like it has appeared,' " wrote Gustave de Beaumont. "Twenty years later, the same words were repeated by the famous historian de Barante" (p. 35). These were only two among many lavish encomiums Tocqueville's work received. Tocqueville was a famous and respected man.

From the descriptions of his contemporaries, however, a rather unflattering picture emerges. There was something slightly unpleasant in the way he looked and behaved. "He is a man of the intellect [un

2. Marquis Astolphe de Custine, *Lettres à Vernhagen D'Ense,* Présentation de Roger Pierrot (Genève: Slatkine Reprints, 1979), 419 and 420–421. The letter is a long one: it occupies pp. 407–422. All translations are mine unless indicated otherwise.
    3. Gustave de Beaumont, *Notice sur Alexis de Tocqueville* (Paris: Calmann Lévy, 1897), 36 and 38. Beaumont was a very close friend of Tocqueville, and the two went together to America. In this study I often quote Beaumont echoing Tocqueville's words.

homme de tête], who has little natural vitality," Heinrich Heine wrote, "and his conversation has a sort of cold brilliance, as if it were of carved ice."[4] A friendly Charles de Rémusat described Tocqueville in terms almost identical to those used by Custine: "He was a short man without affectation, but sickly; with a pleasant-looking and regular face, shadowed by a mass of brown, curly hair that preserved in him an air of youthfulness; his immobile, sad physiognomy was more expressive when he conversed." His paleness announced future illnesses and made people think that he was "bilious, envious," which was not the case: "he was just a bit defiant, often suffering, often discouraged about himself."[5] The tendency to melancholy and withdrawal was noticed also by his devoted friend Beaumont, who stressed many times in his *Notice sur Alexis de Tocqueville* the extreme physical weakness and aloofness of the sickly man, but insisted that whenever Tocqueville was involved in anything that was of importance to him, he showed the most constant "male" energy and persistence. Tocqueville was a reserved man, not given to effusion. He was therefore difficult to like but very easy to respect.

If the descriptions of Tocqueville were not very flattering, those of Custine were downright negative. Fifteen years older than Tocqueville, the marquis was neither liked nor respected. His many talents and his well-documented generosity were, for his contemporaries, overshadowed by his homosexuality.

"At the home of the Comtesse Merlin one day," wrote Philarète Chasles in his *Mémoires,*

I saw a robust, rather stout man come in. . . . .[6] "The poor Marquis," she said to me, "he is charming, but I could not ever touch him. His very hand disgusts me." "Why?" [I asked.] "It does not grip, it clings." "But he speaks beautifully; his talk is like fireworks." "Oh, but it's built on sand," she said. "At bottom, there is such sadness in him, such black depths."

"In fact," Chasles continues, "He was such an extraordinary,

unhappy person—one who submitted with bowed head to public scorn, and who was . . . loyal, generous, honest, charitable, eloquent, spiritual—almost a philosopher; a person of distinction, almost a poet . . . such was this fervent

4. Heinrich Heine, *Allemands et Français* (Paris, 1868), 313; quoted after Luc Monnier, Introduction to vol. 12 of Tocqueville's *Oeuvres Complètes* (1964), 8.
5. Charles de Rémusat, *Mémoires de ma vie,* quoted in ibid. by Monnier, p. 8.
6. He was "gourmand" and "gourmet," wrote V.-F. Lambinet in his *Balzac mis à nu . . . ,* quoted in Julien-Frédéric Tarn, *Le Marquis de Custine* (Paris: Fayard, 1985), 255.

Catholic, this sensual mystic, this subtle, poetic, high-minded talent; yet he was lost in vice . . . his strict conscience bowing beneath the burden of his shame . . . a pariah who hung his head before a society which perhaps was worth less than he was. . . .

Custine's biographer Julien-Frédéric Tarn, who was admiring of his subject, finds this portrait "one of the fullest and most exact portraits drawn by a contemporary: all that's missing is the context."[7]

That the meeting between Custine and Tocqueville resulted in a mordant little portrait is very understandable. At Madame Récamier's, Tocqueville must have paid little attention to Custine, who had not yet published the work that brought him success, *La Russie en 1839*. In any case, Tocqueville probably would not have appreciated Custine's thinking-by-association or his highly personal style of writing, and, had he read it, he certainly would not have liked Custine's "refutation" of *Democracy in America*. Custine criticized Tocqueville's notion that it was Providence that found its expression in democracy and that democracy was linked to Christianity's equality of all souls. In the marquis's opinion, political systems had nothing to do with God. As for his own convictions, he remained firmly aristocratic, professing a theory that each system tends to produce its opposite and that history oscillates between monarchy and democracy. Yet he gave high praise to Tocqueville's style and intelligence and used a sentence from his book as the epigraph of the very work in which he criticized him.[8] The similarity of concerns made the difference of opinion secondary. Besides, Custine was not attached to this little political theory and did not return to it in his other works.

There was, in fact, much that the two men had in common. They belonged to the same caste—landed aristocracy—and, although Tocqueville was younger and had not lived through the ordeal of the French Revolution, both men were severely affected by it. Alexis de Tocqueville was born into a family that paid a heavy price in the Revolution. His eminent great-grandfather Chrétien-Guillaume de Malesherbes; his grandfather and grandmother Lepelletier de Rosambo; his maternal great-grandaunt Marquise de Sénozan; his mother's sister and her husband—the older brother of François-René de Chateaubriand—all perished in the Terror. Tocqueville's parents were married in 1793, at

7. Philarète Chasles, *Mémoires,* 2 vols. (Paris, 1876–1877), 1: 308, ff. Quoted in Tarn, pp. 217–218.
8. Astolphe de Custine, *L'Espagne sous Ferdinand VII* (Paris: Ladvocat, 1838); "Postscriptum," 2: 347–361.

the height of the Revolution. Arrested shortly thereafter, they witnessed a "daily roll call of the condemned, [in which] most of [their] family was taken off to the scaffold."[9] Like Delphine de Sabran, Custine's mother, Tocqueville's parents awaited execution every morning and were saved only by the fall of Robespierre. Hervé de Tocqueville left the prison prematurely old, while "his wife's health was impaired and she never recovered her emotional stability."[10] The couple took the orphaned children of the older Chateaubriand, and young Alexis de Tocqueville grew up with his cousins. Chateaubriand writes about it in his *Mémoires d'outre-tombe* while describing his visit to Verneuil, the château of the late Marquise de Sénozan. It was there that Hervé de Tocqueville brought up his three sons and the two Chateaubriand orphans. "Everywhere, it was the inheritance of the scaffold," Chateaubriand writes. "There [in a happy place of spoiled childhood], I saw my nephews grow up with their three cousins de Tocqueville." "Alexis de Tocqueville," Chateaubriand continued, "travelled in civilized America, while I visited her forests."[11]

Custine's family on his father's and his mother's side was equally distinguished. Among his ancestors he counted saints, military leaders, and administrators. Born in 1790, he belonged to the first generation that grew up in the postrevolutionary era. The Revolution was a catastrophe for the Custine family. Custine's father, Armand de Custine, and Custine's grandfather, the General Adam-Philippe de Custine, joined the revolutionary side yet were guillotined during the Terror. His mother spent nine months in prison, daily expecting to be executed. A faithful nanny saved Astolphe, passing him off as her own child. His childhood and early youth were spent with his mother. In the years 1811–1814, the mother and son lived abroad, traveling often. The return to his native France and his participation, in 1815, in the Vienna Congress—his only attempt at public service—convinced young Custine that in postrevolutionary France there was no useful role for a proud person of his social origin. The rest of his life was spent in an effort to overcome his social isolation.

The predicament of social isolation was felt by many in his milieu, but in Custine's case it was aggravated by what George F. Kennan has called his "lurid behavior," that is, his homosexuality. Custine tried to

9. See the excellent *Tocqueville: A Biography*, by André Jardin, trans. Lydia Davis and Robert Hemenway (New York: Farrar, Straus, Giroux, 1988), 37.

10. André Jardin, p. 8.

11. Chateaubriand, *Mémoires d'outre-tombe* (Paris: Gallimard, 1951), 2: 745.

lead a respectable life—he married and had a child—but his young wife and infant son died within a few years of the marriage. His homosexuality, presumably a source of great torment for this profoundly devout Catholic, was publicly revealed in a scandal in 1824, when he was thirty-four years old. The marquis was found beaten and half-naked on the road to Saint-Denis—attacked, it was later revealed, by a group of soldiers, one of whom had had an amorous rendezvous with him. That revelation closed to him for a while the doors of French aristocratic salons, or at least made him often unwanted.[12] Custine had written poetry, letters, and travel accounts since his early youth; he now devoted himself entirely to literature and to attempts at becoming part of the milieu of Balzac, Stendhal, Chopin, and other writers and artists. He found himself between the two societies, "neither of which suited him, but in both of which he tried to keep his position."[13] A well-to-do patron of the arts, he was also the author of four novels, a play, and several volumes of travel writings and letters. When he was twenty-seven years old, he wrote in a letter to Rahel Varnhagen that for years he had been searching for his talent but had not found it. "And yet I feel," he said, "that there is in me something that needs to come out."[14] Although he perhaps never knew it, he found his special voice in the book about Russia, without which his life and work would have remained unknown—a footnote for pedants.

12. Tarn writes that Custine's correspondence attests that "le Faubourg Saint-Germain, contrairement à une légende bien ancrée, n'a pas tardé à lui faire des avances, sans pour autant cesser de jaser" (p. 243).

13. Tarn, p. 243.

14. In a letter of January 27, 1817, to Rahel Varnhagen, quoted after Tarn, p. 717.

PART ONE

Custine in Russia

1

La Russie en 1839

Most travel accounts aspire only to be practical guides to a country or a city the reader may intend to visit. But some address contemporary problems and discuss the dilemmas of their own societies while comparing them to the visited ones. The Russian travels of Marquis de Custine are a classic example of this kind of writing.

La Russie en 1839 described and analyzed Russia but was also an inquiry into the most pressing and painful problems of postrevolutionary French society. It was written in the then popular form of letters sent by the author from Russia to his Parisian friends. Custine stayed in Russia for three months in the summer of 1839; he visited Saint Petersburg, Moscow, Zagorsk, Jaroslav, and Nizhni Novgorod. He had introductions to many illustrious people and spoke to some of the most interesting and important figures of Russian life—among them the tsar and the main "dissident," Petr Chaadayev. In the introduction to the book, he sets forth all its main ideas; then we follow his slow and reluctant journey from Paris to Saint Petersburg. The traveling itself and the description of what is seen are constantly mixed with quotations, reminiscences, comparisons, and elucidations. Before we get inside Russia, we read the hundred-page-long memoir about the history of the de Custine family during the French Revolution; on the boat to Saint Petersburg we witness the narrator's conversations with, among others, a Russian prince (very critical of his country) and a Russian spy. Before setting foot in Russia, we are well prepared for what we are going to see.

One of Custine's reasons for undertaking his journey was his desire to intervene on behalf of his friend, the young Polish aristocrat Ignacy Gurowski, whose family possessions had been taken over by the tsar. Custine's intervention was not successful, and many of his critics attributed the bitterness of his description of Russia to this fact. But the book itself offers sufficient reason for the most biting criticism of Russia and its system of government, and looking for hidden resentments is unnecessary.

Custine described cities, the court, several members of the tsar's family, the Russian landscape, architecture, people, customs, and the unusual means of transportation. Each of these topics was an occasion for him to think about the nature of political power, about social responsibility, and relations between the rulers and those they ruled. Questions of religion and its role in society absorbed him very much. The scenes and people of Russia prompted reflections on art, literature, beauty, culture, and love. Actual travel descriptions probably occupy only about one-third of the book; the rest consists of thoughts and reflections. All these elements are well blended into an organic whole: there is a tension in the book which keeps all the elements together. The reader shares Custine's worries and apprehensions and follows excitedly in his steps. The letters Custine writes need to be hidden; he is being followed; he falls mysteriously sick. His writing is full of dark hints, suspicions of conspiracy and plots; he sees violence everywhere. The book is lively, *engagé,* and full of passion.

La Russie en 1839 is recognized as the most important travel account of Russia ever written in French. It is a classic and forms part of the canon of conservative books about Russia: no description of Russia is possible today without acknowledging it, even if only implicitly. In the English-speaking world the book is less known. There were some English and American editions in the nineteenth century; later, in 1951, a short "cold-war" edition appeared in the United States. In France, too, several shortened editions were published, the last one by Gallimard in 1975. For this edition, Custine's work was chopped into pieces and arranged for publication by the historian Pierre Nora. These abridged editions omitted everything that the editors considered boring for today's reader: the family memoir (which opened the "voyage") describing terror and death during the French Revolution; digressions on the Catholic Church; quotations from books of Russian history; many descriptions of cities and countryside. The liberties that virtually all the editors take with the book reflect their idea of the genre as a loose compilation of various fragments rather than an organic whole. What results, usually, is a 250-page volume of aphorisms—portable, affordable, snappy, and succinct. It has but a distant resemblance to the original four volumes. The newest American edition is a beautifully illustrated one-volume reissue of the British anonymous translation that appeared in 1843, soon after *La Russie en 1839* was published. *The Empire of the Czar*, for such is the title of this translation, also is shortened, although only by approximately 15 percent.

For his description of Russia, Custine used several printed sources, as well as his interviews and personal impressions. His general point of view was not a surprise to his readers. Custine viewed Russia as an alien and dangerous country, and most of the French reading public saw the country in this light: his book was in part a forceful and original restatement of opinions they already expected and shared. A strong, coherent, conservative critique of Russia was thus formulated and introduced to the French-speaking part of Europe. Soon it was considered definitive and became widely known. The four-volume book became extremely popular, although the critics were not friendly toward the author. Julien-Frédéric Tarn, in his *Le Marquis de Custine ou Les Malheurs de l'exactitude* (a title, incidentally, that is intentionally reminiscent of Custine's novels), declares that in the first twelve years of the existence of *La Russie en 1839* (between 1843 and 1855) the book had many shortened editions and nineteen complete ones, twelve in French (of which six were pirated—unauthorized—editions in Belgium), three in German, three in English, and one in Danish.[1] According to Pierre Nora, Custine estimated the number of copies in foreign editions at 200,000 for the first ten years.[2] For that time, it was a spectacular success.[3]

1. Tarn, p. 532.

2. See Marquis de Custine, *Lettres de Russie: La Russie en 1839*, ed. and with Preface by Pierre Nora (Paris: Gallimard, 1975), 405.

3. The book had six press reviews in the Parisian press from May to September of 1843, and nine more from November to December of the same year after the second edition appeared. They were rather critical. In the next ten years, eight more reviews appeared. None of the reviews recognized the importance of the book. See Tarn, pp. 487–540. As George F. Kennan pointed out, some of the critics were in the pay of the Russians, and some were afraid of Russian protests or just unfriendly toward the author. See George Frost Kennan, *The Marquis de Custine and His "Russia in 1839"* (Princeton, N.J.: Princeton University Press, 1971).

2

The Romantic Self and Russia

Aloys

When in the early summer of 1839 Astolphe, Marquis de Custine, set off on his travels to Russia, he was, at the age of forty-nine, a mature man. He came from the very center of "civilization," and his tastes and likes—those of aristocratic French culture—were synonymous with "culture" itself. He was ready to judge—to like and to condemn. Yet at the same time he was a divided man, unhappy, unsure of his talents. His uncertainty belonged to a more general malaise: Romantic unhappiness. Probably the most important single influence on Astolphe's life and work, beside his mother's, was that of Chateaubriand. Later in his life, Custine wrote that the memory of Chateaubriand was "linked to the first lights of my thought."[1] A formidable man, and the most influential writer of his era, Chateaubriand's impact on the young marquis was truly formative. Custine remained "Chateaubriandesque" throughout his life: unhappy, unfulfilled, looking for inspiration, conservatively and profoundly Catholic, Romantic. When writing about Russia he ironically called himself "an aging René," applying to himself the name of the protagonist of Chateaubriand's short novel of that title. Published in 1802, *René* gave birth to several generations of similar literary heroes. They never aged—they died young, or, if they

1. Quoted in Tarn, p. 34, who wrote that Custine's political attitudes were incomprehensible "without René" (p. 35).

survived their defeat, they remained in an in-between, death-in-life state—*les morts-vivants.* Chateaubriand, unable to accept his old age, was planning to write a book about René growing old. But he did not do it, perhaps because in René and his brothers their youth was an ideological category, one of the many ways of being an outsider.

René and his literary descendants were products of the event that prevented them from living fully: the Revolution. At the time, Europe was full of *morts-vivants.* The isolated, destroyed young men first spoke in German (Goethe's Werther); then, after the Revolution, in French (René), in English (Byron's Manfred), and, later, in all European languages. Such a man was estranged from nature, society, and himself. He was a literary character but also a model for life: a ruined life or early death was the fate of Chopin, Novalis, Schubert, Byron, Keats, Shelley, Nerval, Hölderin, Kleist, and Chatterton, to name a few. Deviation in behavior became a norm—at least, a literary norm. Illness, death, and estrangement were the themes used in literature to show alienation, as were incompleteness, fragmentation, and ruin.[2] These young, aristocratic literary protagonists were themselves ruins—remnants of the *Ancien Régime,* representatives of a class that felt part of the past. In their books they were found dying, most often in exotic surroundings, of an unhappy, impossible love; themselves orphans, they were unable to marry and have children—that is, to become part of society. Custine's first novel, *Aloys ou Le Religieux du Mont Saint-Bernard* (1827), had just such a character for its protagonist.

Aloys was one of several psychological novels written by various authors at the time on the topic of impossible love. Madame de Duras began the series with her *Olivier ou le Secret,* written in 1825, as a challenge to other writers to follow her. The second in the series was another *Olivier,* written a year later, by Hyacinthe Thibaud de Latouche, and this was followed by Stendhal's *Armance.* All three novels, as well as *Aloys ou Le Religieux du Mont Saint-Bernard* (the title was taken from another novel by Madame de Duras), describe a situation in which a betrothed young man breaks his engagement a few days before the wedding ceremony and then dies or withdraws from public life. In none of the books are the reasons for this unhappy ending spelled out. Philippe Sénart, in his preface to *Aloys* (entitled melodramatically "Un Martyr du Ro-

2. See Thomas McFarland, *Romanticism and the Forms of Ruin: Wordsworth, Coleridge, and Modalities of Fragmentation* (Princeton, N.J.: Princeton University Press, 1981). Especially relevant is the Introduction, in which these "fragmented modalities"—incompleteness, fragmentation, and ruin—are proposed as fundamental for Romanticism.

mantisme: Custine"), assumes that all four books, *Aloys* included, were based on an actual engagement of Custine, which he broke in 1818, to Claire de Duras, daughter of Madame de Duras—author of the first *Olivier*.[3] If this is true, then the secret that prevents the happy ending in all of the books is not, as Stendhal explained in a letter about *Armance*, sexual impotence, but homosexuality. This, as if to continue the secret of the novels, is never stated by Sénart, only suggested.

Sénart points out many similarities between Custine, Aloys, and Octave, the protagonist of *Armance*. They are brothers, he says. "Strangers to their time, exiled within their country, these young aristocrats without homeland or state are banished forever. They would like to fight, they would like to serve, but their marked birth keeps them away from the world" (p. xv). In fact, the impotence of the protagonists is social as well as personal. Whatever the reason for the impossibility of their love—be it homosexuality (actually rather unlikely as a *literary* reason), incestuous passion (as in the case of *René*), sexual impotence (Stendhal), the death of the beloved (Tocqueville's "Journey to Lake Oneida" and Gustave de Beaumont's *Marie*), or love for the mother rather than the daughter (*Aloys*)—the new protagonist expresses a social predicament common to a generation—or to generations—of postrevolutionary European men of the higher classes. Young noblemen are such important figures in these novels because it was they who traditionally were political actors. Here we see them passive and suicidal, mortally injured by the Revolution.

The French Revolution was of course an enormously disruptive and violent event.[4] For Custine, the Revolution and its violence were so shocking because they spelled an end to an epoch of innocence. The Revolution took away his childhood, killed his father and grandfather, and destroyed the world of his ancestors. It was therefore vitally important to understand the Revolution and its reasons. All his life, Custine tried to come to terms with his private horror of revolutionary destruc-

3. Astolphe de Custine, *Aloys ou le Religieux du Mont Saint-Bernard*, presentation by Philippe Sénart (Paris: Union Générale d'Editions, 1971). This is also Tarn's opinion—Tarn, p. 83.
4. The cost of the Revolution depends on who does the counting. René Sédillot gives a number of 2 million dead by including the victims of the Napoleonic Wars. See René Sédillot, *Le coût de la Révolution française* (Paris: Librarie Académique Perrin, 1987), 28. Jean-François Fayard arrives at approximately 16,000 "judicially" executed during the Terror (1793–1794). In the preface to Fayard's book, Pierre Chaunu claims the number of victims of the Revolution (including the wars) to be higher than that of the French victims of World War I. See Jean-François Fayard, *La Justice révolutionnaire: Chronique de la Terreur*, Preface by Pierre Chaunu (Paris: Robert Laffont, 1987), 12–13, 259–270.

tion and violence, and to find a socially useful place for himself and his class. Perhaps his *La Russie en 1839* is such a powerful book in part because in it we see an aging René expressing his unhappiness and finally rendering public service. The book is gripping because it is a meeting place of personal grief with the unhappiness of an entire country.

The French Revolution and the Understanding of Russia

The young—and then the aging—René is in a sense the protagonist and hero of all of Custine's writings, and, indeed, of his life. René is the subject of his novels, letters, and of his travel writings. His voice is lyrical. He is not a man of action but of musings, premonitions, fears, and visions. But he is also a thinking man. His travels are his action. In all his books he presents a certain psychological and political *situation* that characterizes his class and his generation, and this functions as a vantage point in *La Russie en 1839*.

The literary protagonist—the defeated young nobleman—is a negative expression of the feudal need to serve: the denial of the present. Such negation, the rejection of the world-as-it-is, took many forms in Romanticism. One of them was an extravagant love of the Middle Ages and of history in general; another was the fondness for the Oriental. Travel in time and travel in space were, like death, forms of exile. The work of Custine, and of many of his contemporaries, is enclosed by and wavers between the two extremes of service or death.

Custine and his contemporaries expressed social isolation through the Romantic biographical model of a defeated hero. Although these heroes appear to die of an unhappy love, they are in a deeper sense crushed by history. And history, in addition to psychology, provided the language in which the radical alienation of the aristocracy was expressed. At the same time the use of history for this purpose was in itself an effort to *overcome* social estrangement. History was a place to travel to in search of reasons and explanations. When Custine went to Spain or Russia, he moved not only geographically but also in time. Following standard Enlightenment theories he believed that countries, like people, had developmental stages to go through: Spain was for him the medieval past—France's past—while Russia was an unnatural combination of old age in a young and developing giant. If one was to comprehend the present, one had to reach into history and see at what stage the country had arrived.

The problem that Custine investigated in his Russian travelogue was that of historical change associated, in his mind, with the Revolution and violent upheavals. The Revolution, he felt, was a new kind of change, and historical and travel writing was a place to assess it. Change, of course, is a natural subject of historical and even of philosophical inquiry. An attempt at reconciliation with death and ruin—with the inevitable end—is a basic underlying motive of much of Custine's writing, and of Tocqueville's political writing as well. Their class had no confidence in change, seeing it as more likely to bring disaster rather than improvement. In their works, a longing for lost unity and wholeness was combined with premonitions of doom. This type of longing, shared by several postrevolutionary generations, was a form of perception. Most Oriental travels, for example, were undertaken in search of the still-living past—for an unchanged biblical landscape, for the "immobile, dreaming Oriental woman" (Flaubert)—as if to reassure oneself that outside of the unrecognizable, fluid Western world some things remained stable. Stability was what Custine looked for in conservative Russia, while the younger Tocqueville tried to spot, in America, the direction of the change accepted as inevitable.

There are certain periods when historical inquiry becomes particularly poignant, and the time in which Custine was writing about Russia was one of them. While in 1811 only 3 million pages of historical works were published in France, in 1825 there were 40 million. Historical language was used to talk about contemporary politics, and the main event around which discussion crystallized was, of course, the Revolution. Liberal historians interpreted this series of events as logical steps in the people's striving for emancipation, while conservatives treated it as a violent disruption of a stable national life.[5] Custine's starting point was conservative: the Revolution meant disruption of an orderly historical cycle. He traveled to Russia in search of historical continuity: "I went to Russia to seek for arguments against representative government," he said. What he found, however, was only the semblance of order, and he returned "a partisan of constitutions" (Custine, *Empire of the Czar*, 16; see Bibliography).

The superficial order of Russian life covered up the change that was

5. Stanley Mellon, *The Political Uses of History* (Stanford, Calif.: Stanford University Press, 1958).

due not to the action of its people but to an individual's capricious will. Change came from the tsar, not from the people. Peter the Great single-handedly redirected the course of Russian life, and Custine, although a monarchist, could not accept it. The Revolution had taught him that social life is complex and cannot be reduced to any one element; history is not only about personalities, their will and their actions, but about a complicated interaction of individual will and social forces working as a system. Instead of the continuity and order he expected in Russian autocracy, he found tyranny, which he interpreted as another form of disruption. "In France," he wrote, "revolutionary tyranny is an evil belonging to a state of transition; in Russia, the tyranny of despotism is a permanent revolution" (p. 206). This might have been an echo of Sismondi's saying that "tyranny is a perpetual revolution,"[6] but it was his visit to Russia (where he felt the violence with which the social order was imposed and maintained), not anything he read, that made him understand the reasons for the French Revolution. And, conversely, the revolutionary experience offered itself as a paradigm to which Custine could refer the incomprehensible and unacceptable violence of the Russian regime. The Revolution provided concepts and a vocabulary into which Russia could be translated; the central notion of this vocabulary was that of violence. Russia explained the Revolution to Custine and was herself explained by the Revolution.

It is precisely for this reason that *La Russie en 1839* opens with a memoir about the de Custine family during the Revolution. The memoir sets a framework for an interpretation of Russia as a colossus that will soon become victim of its own lack of social justice. Politics, Custine declared, consisted of a mutual sense of obligation between the ruler and the people. That reciprocity was essential.

A fearful and mysterious relativeness of merits and of demerits has been established by Providence between governments and subjects, and . . . moments arrive in the history of communities when the State is judged, condemned, and destroyed, as though it were a single individual. (P. 385)

Having himself witnessed the end of a régime believed to be permanent, Custine knew very well that a political system could be abolished, that it was not divinely guaranteed, and that it continued only as long as it was *allowed* to continue. He blamed not only the rulers but also the

6. Quoted in G. P. Gooch, *History and Historians in the Nineteenth Century* (Boston: Beacon Press, 1959; first published in 1913), 160.

people for complicity in oppression and looked for signs of rebellion. The Russian people—alien as they were to Custine—were subjugated by unprecedented violence, and with equal violence, he thought, they would one day respond. The nobility did not fulfill its duty to defend the oppressed. Such a situation could not be maintained indefinitely. Custine felt in the people the future mob avenging by massacres centuries of meek acquiescence. "To whom will the people one day appeal against the silence of the great? What explosion of vengeance is being prepared against the autocracy by the abdication of such a cowardly aristocracy?" Russian history, as Custine saw it, was already a series of spasmodic interruptions, arbitrary crimes, capricious reversals. It lacked only one final, apocalyptic eruption. "Either the civilized world will, before another fifty years go by, pass anew under the yoke of barbarians, or Russia will undergo a revolution more terrible than the revolution whose effects are still felt in Western Europe" (p. 131). It was because he put together the beneath-the-surface violence of Russian life and his understanding of the Revolution that he was able to predict with such clarity the eruption of the Russian Revolution, *only* seventy-eight years away.

Violence in Russia

Nineteenth-century writers often accepted that history contained, among other elements, "demonic" social forces, and many delighted in the violent themes of history, showing a special predilection for gruesome detail. Stendhal, Shelley, and Custine himself were among many who wrote on the Italian family of Cencis; Cesare Borgia, Galeazzo Sforza, and Ezzelino da Romano were other popular "monsters" and "fiends" of historical poetry and prose. The depiction of cruelties accompanied another historical theme running through nineteenth-century literature: the struggle for freedom by peoples abused by tyrants (Masaniello, Rienzo, Sicilian Vespers). The literary treatment of these subjects followed the immense popularity of a few historical books about Italy or Rome: Gibbon's *The Decline and Fall of the Roman Empire* (1776–1788), Roscoe's *Life of Lorenzo de' Medici* (1795) and of *Leo X* (1805), and Sismondi's *History of the Italian Republics* (1809–1818).[7]

7. See C. P. Brand, *Italy and the English Romantics: The Italianate Fashion in Early Nineteenth-Century England* (Cambridge: Cambridge University Press, 1957).

Although Russia was a "literary" place, no Western writer described Romantic Russian heroes struggling against tyranny. It was not for lack of models, however. In the Decembrist uprising of 1825, young, idealistic noblemen—Romantic men of action—rebelled against the tsar. The uprising occurred in the year Madame de Duras was writing her *Olivier ou le Secret,* but these truly Romantic Russians failed to appeal to the literary imagination of the West weary at the time of even the slightest hint of regicide.[8] The implacable repression that followed the rebellion, and the sufferings of the defeated young men aroused therefore a limited amount of compassion. The Decembrists, certainly brothers—or at least cousins—of René, were not recognized as belonging to the family at all.

The most memorable character that remained in Western literature after the Decembrist uprising was the Faithful Wife who voluntarily followed her husband into his Siberian exile.[9] In France, that literary heroic character was modeled after Princess Trubeckoja: she was French, and her sacrifice made an enormous impression on French public opinion. Her behavior was described by such well-known authors as Alexandre Dumas père (in his *Le maître d'armes*) and by Alfred de Vigny (in *Wanda*). Custine devoted several pages to "so noble a victim of conjugal duty," treating her case as an illustration of the tsar-jailer's lack of magnanimity (p. 354). Princess Trubeckoja was not a new kind of protagonist in literature. In nineteenth-century iconography and literature, Slavic women had been portrayed as beautiful, long-suffering, and passive—as passive as René in his life-in-death state. The writers used this tradition to describe the sacrifice of the princess.[10]

A figure of a noble, passive beauty fitted well another literary image: love in Siberia. There was a large popular literature about unhappy love in exile—for example, the 1806 best-seller *Élisabeth ou les exilés de Sibérie* by Madame Cottin, which was later turned into a play by the most

8. The Decembrists' behavior, by contrast, was very dependent on Romantic literature. See Iurii M. Lotman, "The Decembrist in Daily Life (Everyday Behavior as a Historical-Psychological Category)," in *The Semiotics of Russian Cultural History* (Ithaca, N.Y.: Cornell University Press, 1985), 95–149.

9. In his study "The Decembrist in Daily Life," Lotman shows that this behavior came to be perceived as heroic thanks to Russian literary models: before the uprising the wives of exiles followed their husbands as a matter of course, and their behavior was found only natural by their society. Several aristocratic women voluntarily joined their husbands in exile for moral reasons rather than because of love (pp. 119–123).

10. In Benjamin Constant's novel *Adolphe*—another in the family of first-name psychological and (auto)biographical novels like *Aloys*—a René-like protagonist was unable to love a passive Slavic beauty.

popular melodrama-writer of the time, Pixérécourt, and then, in 1853, made into an opera with music by Donizetti; and there was Xavier de Maistre's *Prascovie ou la jeune Sibérienne* (1807). These books, which could be grouped under the title of one of them—*Les amants exilés en Sibérie*—had a family resemblance to two other popular categories: books about unhappy Poland and books about the crimes of the tsars.[11] The image that the French public received from this literary and theatrical output was only confirmed by the true story of Princess Trubeckoja. Custine himself was strongly influenced by all this "Russian vogue" and produced a short story—"Histoire de Telenef"—which he included in *La Russie en 1839*. In this story he combined, rather predictably but movingly, the themes of unhappy love, of the Russian peasants' servitude, and of Siberian exile.

Custine described with real horror and repulsion the immeasurable violence done to the Russian people. His descriptions are thorough and lavish more detail than perhaps was sane or necessary. (But is there any good, sane way of describing violence?) He feels and sees this violence wherever he goes. Standing in front of the Winter Palace in Saint Petersburg, he recounts the story of its renovation after an accidental fire.

In order to complete the work at the time appointed by the emperor, unheard-of efforts were necessary. The interior works were continued during the great frosts; 6,000 workmen were continually employed; of these a considerable number died daily, but the victims were instantly replaced by other champions brought forward to perish, in their turn, in this inglorious breach. . . . During frosts when the thermometer was at 25 to 30 degrees below 0 of Réaumur, 6,000 obscure martyrs—martyrs without merit, for their obedience was involuntary—were shut up in halls heated to 30 degrees of Réaumur, in order that the walls may dry more quickly. Thus, these miserable beings, on entering and leaving this abode of death—destined to become, thanks to their sacrifice, the home of vanity, magnificence, and pleasure—would have to endure a difference of 50 to 60 degrees. (P. 93; the difference is of 100 degrees Fahrenheit)

There are many similar passages in *La Russie en 1839*, quoted from historical sources or from conversation, or perhaps even imagined or

11. See Charles Corbet, *L'opinion française face à l'inconnue russe, 1799–1894* (Paris: Didier, 1967). France felt, for a short period, strong solidarity with Poland in her unsuccessful anti-Russian insurrections of 1830 and 1861; that solidarity produced many books, pamphlets, songs, and so forth. As for the other category—the "crimes of the tsars"—it probably started with the stories about the scandalous life of Catherine II. See Corbet, p. 27. Today, this tradition continues with an English edition of Alexandre Dumas père's *Voyage en Russie*, entitled *Adventures in Czarist Russia* (London: Owen, 1960), which took from the original only the stories of the excesses of the tsars.

transcribed—passages such as the report, offered in an appendix, of the prison stay of an unfortunate Frenchman, Louis Pernet, on whose behalf Custine intervened while in Russia. ("Imagination," Custine wrote, "serves to extend the sphere of pity, and to render it more active" [p. 570].) Pernet was for Custine an occasion to describe Russian prisons and the source of information registered with a very personal emphasis:

The first two days he was left *without food.* . . . The only sound that he heard was that of the strokes of the rod, which, from five o'clock in the morning until night, were inflicted upon the unhappy slaves who were sent by their masters to this place, to receive correction. Add to that frightful sound, the sobs, the tears, the screams of the victims, mingled with the menaces and imprecations of the tormentors.

"The rod," Custine explained,

is formed of a cane split into three pieces, an instrument which fetches off the skin at every stroke; at the fifth, the victim loses nearly all power to cry, his weakened voice can then only utter a prolonged, sobbing groan . . . [a] horrible rattle. . . . (Pp. 577–578)

In these passages, the suffering is described not generically but in concrete and piercing detail.

The personal way in which Custine described the oppression turned his travel book into an act of testimony. Alert to details, he understood the pervasive, banal, everyday character of injustice.

In Russia the desire for travelling fast becomes a passion, and this passion serves as a pretext for every species of inhumanity. . . . Yesterday evening . . . a child who drove us had been several times threatened with blows by the feldjäger [Custine's courier] for delays, and I participated in the impatience and wrath of this man. Suddenly, a foal, not many days old, and well known to the boy, escaped from an enclosure bordering upon the road, and began neighing and galloping after my carriage, for he took one of the mares that drew us for his mother.

The young coachman was forbidden to stop, and the foal ran all the long stage at the fastest gallop. For three full pages Custine describes the unhappiness of the boy and his efforts to liberate the colt, the suffering of the animal, and his own complicity in "the martyrdom."

At the moment of leaving the broken-down foal and the forlorn young postillion, I felt no remorse; it came only upon reflection, and especially upon recording the circumstances in writing: shame then awoke repentance. Thus easily may those who breathe the air of despotism be corrupted. What do I say?

In Russia, despotism is only upon the throne, but tyranny pervades the country. (Pp. 386–389)

This passage conveys in exemplary fashion the minuteness, the everyday character of oppression; it shows the wordless victims—children, animals—suffering because of "petty acts of unnecessary cruelty." Only while writing, while comparing the facts to the standards of his convictions, did the traveler understand his actions. It is his complicity in these petty acts, the temptation to practice them, and the contagion "with the contempt for the weak" that are so revealing.

Custine was one of these rare travelers who were able to *see* persecution on the face of every passerby. French historians Michel Cadot and Jacques Brenner attribute this attraction to Russian horrors to what they allege was Custine's sadomasochism.[12] But his reaction—whatever its psychological reasons—was well justified: he could not accept the senselessness of violence and the total impotence of the individual in Russia. To bear witness was the obligation dictated by his conscience. Custine was creating (and participating in) a then new tradition of testimonial writing about wars and revolutions as meaningless and brutal—writing in anguish but writing nevertheless, as if somehow to come to terms with the horrors. It was "apocalyptic" reporting about history, in which the writer defended his sanity and protested by recording human misery in all its detail. His writings ceased at that point to be Romantic self-expression and became a passage through which the voices of the oppressed could be heard. Hence Custine gave (among other examples) the description of workers dying in the excess of heat or cold rather than merely recounting the emperor's balls he witnessed. Hence the story of the martyred boy and a colt. The reaction of horrified disbelief, far from being abnormal, was perhaps the only healthy reaction to such events. That tradition of testimonial writing continues today with innumerable books about the "univers concentrationnaire" in the Soviet Union, Cambodia, China, and about the Holocaust and many "minor" apocalypses. Custine should be recognized as a classic of the genre.

The detailed recounting of pain, fear, and dying reclaims the dignity of the victim. The adding-up of degrees of temperature inside and outside the Winter Palace is an effort to redeem the misery of the workers, to show it in its concrete dimension. But at the same time

12. Michel Cadot, *La Russie dans la vie intellectuelle française (1839–1856)* (Paris: Fayard, 1967), 186.

Custine understood that the victims could also be blamed for their complicity, for their passivity, for their connivance with the oppressor. "Martyrs without merit" is his bitter phrase for the dying workers. "People and government . . . the Russians great and small . . . they are drunk with slavery" (p. 96). Not one single voice is heard opposing the despotism. "An oppressed people has always deserved the ills under which they suffer; tyranny is the work of the nation" (p. 131).[13]

The secret of Russia—the reason such an inhuman system survives for so long—lay, he thought, in her plans for the future.

That nation, essentially aggressive, greedy under the influence of privation, expiates beforehand, by a debasing submission, the design of exercising a tyranny over other nations: the glory, the riches which it hopes for, consoles it for the disgrace to which it submits. (P. 614)

Only this common goal could, in the eyes of Custine, unite the oppressed people behind their oppressor. Their complicity is turned against weak and enervated Europe, and all the internal Russian violence will spill out onto the conquered West. Both of his predictions— that of the Russian Revolution and of the Russian expansion—turned out to be right. It was only their violence and its capacity to engulf both revolution and expansion that surpassed his expectations.

13. The responsibility of a nation for its own independence was one of the reasons for Custine's limited sympathy for Poland. In letter 36, written after his return to France, Custine explained that he did not travel through Poland in order to avoid telling the Poles the truth. And the truth was that "an attentive observer can see, in the fate of individuals as well as of nations, the results of the development of their characters." Besides, since Poles, like Russians, were Slavs, they shared all the characteristics of the race; in the case of Poles, however, the servile, imitative nature of the Slavic race was mitigated by Catholicism.

3

Russian History: The Tangled Tradition

Herberstein

To understand the violence he saw (and felt in Russia), Custine turned to history. He found autocracy unacceptably, inexplicably oppressive. In search of some sort of explanation, he reached for a tradition that was close to him. The choice of this particular tradition, although predetermined, had profound consequences for Custine's vision of Russia. He found in it a confirmation of his rejection of that country and the arguments and vocabulary in which to express this rejection. It is worth taking a brief look at this tradition in order to see how Custine, by relegating Russia outside of Europe, tried to assuage his own fear of perpetual revolutionary violence.

In fact, Russia was for Custine a state of heightened violence. "This empire," he said in one of his most celebrated aphorisms, "immense as it is, is no more than a prison, of which the emperor keeps the key" (p. 237). "Tomorrow," he predicted,

in an insurrection, in the midst of massacre, by the light of a conflagration, the cry of freedom may spread to the frontiers of Siberia; a blind and cruel people may murder their masters, may revolt against obscure tyrants, and dye the waters of the Volga with blood; but they will not be any the more free: barbarism is in itself a yoke. (P. 608)

The question that needed to be posed was, What was the reason for this perpetual violence?

Custine phrased this question by quoting words written in 1549 by another traveler to Russia—or, rather, Muscovy—Sigismund von Herberstein.

"He [the tsar] speaks, and it is done; the life and fortunes of laity and clergy, of nobles and burghers, all depend on his supreme will. He is unacquainted with contradiction, and all he does is deemed as equitable as if it were done by Deity; for the Russians are persuaded that their prince is the executor of Divine decrees. Thus, *God and the prince have willed, God and the prince know,* are common modes of speech among them. Nothing can equal their zeal for serving him. . . . I cannot say whether it is the character of the Russian nation which has formed such autocrats, or whether it is the autocrats themselves who have given this character to the nation."

"It appears to me," comments Custine,

that the influence is reciprocal; the Russian government could never have been established elsewhere than in Russia; and the Russians would never have become what they are under a government differing from that which exists among them. (Pp. 94–95)

Custine introduced the author of his quotation as a "German diplomatist" (p. 95), "the Baron Herberstein, ambassador from the Emperor Maximilian, father of Charles V, to the Czar Vasili Ivanovich" (p. 94). And he agreed wholeheartedly with the bitter criticism he could discern in that quotation. "This letter, written more than three centuries ago, describes the Russians precisely as I now see them," he declared (p. 95). "This letter," however, was not a letter at all but a book, entitled *Rerum Moscoviticarum Commentarii* and published in Latin, in Vienna, in 1549. Custine did not read this book: "The following passage I have found in Karamsin [*sic*]," he conscientiously indicated (p. 94). Who was Siegmund (or Sigismund or Sigmund, as his name was sometimes written) from Herberstein? And why would Custine quote him?

The question of the responsibility for autocracy is particularly well formulated by Herberstein, but the weight of his quotation is greater than its meaning. By the very act of repeating Herberstein's words, and then commenting on them, Custine made himself part of a very concrete tradition of writing about Russia of which Herberstein's name was a sign. For the reader who did not know the tradition, Custine presented it before he used it. He introduced Herberstein to the readers, and, to indicate his reliability, he quoted him from still another source. To grasp the reason for this double quoting, and Herberstein's importance for Custine, as well as for the whole European tradition of writing about Russia, it is necessary to talk about the baron, his book, and its influence on later writers.

In *Rerum Moscoviticarum Commentarii* Baron von Herberstein reported on his two embassies to the court of the Grand Prince Vasili Ivanovich, undertaken in the years 1517 and 1526. His mission was to bring about the end of the war between Poland and Muscovy, so as to free the two countries to fight the Turks. The second voyage was partially successful, but Herberstein's true success was the book, which had many editions in Latin and in German.[1] The popularity of the book was due to its comprehensive and serious character, and to the novelty of its subject. It was also very well written.

Herberstein was born in Vipava, near Trieste, in 1486, and died in Vienna, in 1566. In Vipava he learned the local Slavic language, Slovenian, and later learned Russian and Polish as well. (It is quite unusual to find a report on Muscovy, Russia, or the Soviet Union by an author who understands Russian.) The son of an Austrian nobleman, he worked in his native language—German. He graduated from Vienna University, in 1502, having had a very thorough Renaissance education. His Latin and Italian were excellent, and he also knew French and Spanish. He was interested in the sciences and his education prepared him for a life of scholarship, but instead he became a diplomat for the Habsburgs. His missions to Muscovy were only two of several embassies he undertook. Written at the request of the monarch, his book was an act of public service: it was a report, initially addressed to the emperor, in which he rendered account of his actions and the knowledge he acquired as a result of his missions. In writing his book, he followed two traditions. The first was that of the Renaissance reports addressed to the prince, which were meant to form a basis for wise foreign policy, the most famous reports being the description of Germany by Niccolò Machiavelli, of Spain by Francesco Guicciardini, and of the Netherlands by Ludovico Guicciardini. The second tradition was that of reports written by papal and Venetian envoys and by merchants—the most famous of these, of course, being *The Travels* of Marco Polo.

In preparing for his difficult and perilous missions, as well as in his

---

1. Herberstein himself translated his book into German, but there were other more popular translations. See "Editor's Preface" to Sigmund von Herberstein, *Description of Moscow and Muscovy* (1557), ed. Bertold Picard, trans. J. B. C. Grundy (London: J. M. Dent and Sons Limited, 1969). This translation of selected passages was made from Herberstein's 1557 German text considered definitive by the editor.

writing, Herberstein used several books and reports that belonged to that second tradition. He read the report by Joannes de Plano Carpini, an Italian minorite who in 1245 went to the Mongolians on behalf of Pope Innocent IV. Two Latin versions of this report, one short and one long, were easily accessible.[2] He also used *Viaggio in Persia,* the report of the Venetian ambassador Ambrogio Contarini on his journey in 1474 through Germany, Poland, Kiev, and the Crimea to Persia. This work was published in 1482, in Venice, where many of the reports of travels to near and distant lands were printed at that time. Herberstein also read and quoted *Tractatus de duabus Sarmatiis* by the Polish prebendary Mathias Miechowski (1517), and the work of the bishop of Vienna, Johann Fabri, whose report, published in 1525, was a survey of the religious situation in Muscovy based on his conversations with Russian ambassadors to Spain. This last book was recommended to Herberstein by the then archduke, Ferdinand. All four of these works (Western sources of Herberstein's information) were written by Catholics, whose perspective on the "wrong" religion played a critical role in their interpretations. Herberstein was himself a Catholic and felt estranged from the exotic rites and religious customs of the Muscovites. Devoutly Catholic Custine was bound to reach for this tradition.

Herberstein also used other sources. He talked with his hosts and with the guides—more with the latter, because of the severe isolation the Muscovites imposed on their visitors. Several of his guides were Polish or Lithuanian Catholics, whose opinions must have influenced his writing. In the many years he spent researching his book, he corresponded with many scholars, several of whom were his "Polish friends."[3] And—what was unusual—he read and quoted written Muscovite annals of the monasteries, chronicles of the cities, and other reports. In that way, he preserved an enormous amount of information and became an important source for later Russian historians. It was in Nikolai Karamzin's *History of the Russian State* that Custine found his quotation.

But Herberstein was quoted by everybody, and for good reasons. The seriousness and thoroughness of his work was unique. In fact, he

2. See the Introduction to Sigismund von Herberstein, *Notes Upon Russia: Being a Translation of the Earliest Account of that Country, Entitled "Rerum Moscoviticarum Commentarii,"* trans. and ed., with Notes and an Introduction by R. H. Major, 2 vols. (New York: Burt Franklin Publisher, n.d.), xvi–xviii.

3. See Christine Harrauer, "Die Ziegenössischen Lateinischen Drucke der *Moscovia* Herbersteins und Ihre Entstehungsgeschichte (Ein Beitrag zur Editionstechnik im 16.JH)," in *Humanistica Lovaniensia* 31 (1982): 141–163.

became known as the "discoverer of Muscovy." He went to a country that was emerging from a long isolation under the Mongol occupation. It was a faraway country: Herberstein's mental map must have had Vienna as its political and Rome as its religious centers. Muscovy was a relatively unknown entity—it was not only distant but had a harsh climate, no roads, and a very unfriendly attitude toward foreigners. No adequate maps of Muscovy were available, and Herberstein went around collecting data, formulating definitions, and making geographical decisions.[4] One of the main determinations to be made was the geographic placement of Muscovy.

It is interesting to observe the terms in which Herberstein thought about Russia. He was moving from the center of the known world toward its borders. Certain places were too far away to be visited. "Siberia," he wrote, "is a land which borders upon Perm and Vyatka [now Kirov]. I have been unable to learn whether there are castles and towns within it" (*Description*, p. 36). He went as far as Tula, "the last place before the desert [wilderness]" (p. 24). Already in Nizhni Novgorod [now, but not for much longer, Gorki] "Christendom comes to an end" (p. 23). He devoted much attention to tracing the trajectory of the Tanais [Don], "that celebrated river which is called a frontier between Europe and Asia . . . if a line were drawn from the estuary to the source of the Tanais and projected northward it might be said that Moscow lies in Asia and not in Europe" (pp. 24–25). But the answer to the question whether Moscow, the capital of Muscovy, was in Europe or in Asia depended on more than geography. Herberstein thoroughly described the political and cultural map of the country and found it distinctly non-European. The state organization—the absolute power of one person, the submission of the Church to state authority, the state ownership of all property, the servile forms of address to the authority, the military customs—were more Mongol and Chinese than European. The calendar and the alphabet were also different. Coats and dresses,

---

4. Probably modeled on the Greek genre of the commentary to a map, his book methodically described the country, the people, the government, religious life, the economy, and customs. Herberstein's geographic description provided information for several new maps, which accompanied his book from the very first edition. He devoted much time and attention to finding and checking the geographical names, distances, and particulars of landscape (as well as the names of animals and plants). Given his historical and geographical interests, his knowledge of languages, of the systems of government—given his general culture—the Vienna University graduate was perfectly prepared to write a comprehensive work of discovery.

religious rites, and the seclusion of women reminded Herberstein of what he had read about Asia.

The comparisons of Muscovite customs to Chinese and Mongolian customs were not accidental. Comparison—this basic way of assessing foreign reality—is necessarily founded on difference, similar things being of no interest; but what really matters is how the difference is classified, compartmentalized, grouped. Herberstein, in trying to define Muscovy, had little doubt about its non-European nature. In fact, it was around this time—in the middle of the sixteenth century—that the opinion that Muscovy belonged to Asia became entrenched.[5] All the early "discoverers of Muscovy," that is, authors of the most widely read books about Muscovy—Herberstein, Giles Fletcher, Adam Olearius—called Muscovite society Oriental. This was stated, one might say, not as a judgment but as a fact. And yet there was still a certain hesitation in Herberstein's report. Russia was a Christian country and that made it part of the European family. The people there were Slavs, as they were in other parts of Europe. And there was no clear geographical boundary to divide Europe from Asia, certainly not before one got to the city of Moscow. If the customs were to change—for example if the hoped-for conversion to Roman Catholicism took place, the border of Asia could be pushed farther away from the center of Europe. For where Asia began, Europe ended. Herberstein traveled from the center of Europe toward the "desert," and he had to decide where the desert began.

He was not writing on a blank slate—although he was in some sense the first, there were several books and authorities that he had to take into account. As we have seen, he carried with him concepts and loyalties that came from his education, from his readings, and from his role as a diplomat. His book was a continuation of a tradition. But it was still possible to have placed the accents differently from the way he did. There were

5. In 1559, the Venetian humanist Giovan Battista Ramusio published an anthology of travels with a volume on Asia that contained reports of travels to Muscovy. Herberstein's report was included in this volume, together with works by Ambrogio Contarini, Iosaphat Barbaro, Alberto Campense, Paolo Giovio, and others. In another collection, by Manuzio, travels to Muscovy were printed in a volume devoted to visits to Persia and India. (See Arturo Cronia, *La conoscenza del mondo slavo in Italia: Bilancio storico-bibliografico di un millennio* [Venezia-Padova: Istituto di Studi Adriatici, 1958], 116.) Many of these travel reports were, in fact, written by people who went to Persia or India and crossed Muscovy on their way. Even today, Herberstein is considered a major contributor to the field of Asiatic geography and cartography. See Helmuth Grössing, *Humanistische Naturwissenschaft: Zur Geschichte der Wiener mathematischen Schulen des 15. und 16. Jahrhunderts* (Baden-Baden: Koerner, 1983), 186.

Catholic reports in which positive, acceptable sides of the new society were stressed. In 1525, a year before Herberstein's second voyage, the Dutch Jesuit Alberto Campense praised the Muscovites for their moral purity.[6] Another relatively positive report about Muscovy was Paolo Giovio's *Libellus de legatione Basilii magni . . . ad Clementem VII* (1525).[7] Both of these books had political objectives, and, in order to create a propitious atmosphere for anti-Turkish alliance with Russia, they were more generous to the Muscovites than was common. Both books had no actual journey to a distant, unfriendly country as their basis—a journey, one might add, the end of which left most travelers exhausted, bewildered, and hostile. Herberstein, although interested in the anti-Turkish alliance, was bothered by the Greek Orthodox rituals and truly repelled by the political tyranny, by the secrecy, by the fear and submission of individuals, by the isolation of foreign visitors, by the pomp at the court, by the seclusion of women. So when he placed Muscovy on the map, he located it—culturally as well as geographically—in Asia.

We have seen the sources of his book. Once written, it itself became a source, or rather *the* source for thinking about Muscovy. Indeed, it was because Herberstein firmly placed that country on the *mental* map of Europe that he was called a "discoverer" of Russia. His description was accepted as authoritative and therefore was quotable. And he was quoted, invoked as an authority, and simply plagiarized. Antonio Possevino, sent as Pope Gregory XIII's personal emissary, in 1581–1582, to arrange a truce (again!) between Ivan the Terrible and the Polish king Stefan Batory, used Herberstein as his source (and Johann Fabri, as well as Paolo Giovio and Alberto Campense). He also used Alessandro Guagnini who "republished Herberstein under his own name without mentioning the real author."[8] Possevino, then, not only

6. "The vices against nature are totally unknown to them," he wrote. (See Cronia, 136.) Herberstein, however, as well as Fletcher and Olearius, reported widespread sexual license, homosexuality, drunkenness, and thievery. Campense based his relatively positive description of Muscovy on information he received from his father and brother. He thought Muscovy would be useful in a proposed league against Turks (see Hugh F. Graham, "Introduction" to Antonio Possevino, S.J., *The Moscovia*, trans. with Introduction and Notes by Hugh F. Graham, Series in Russian and East European Studies, No. 1 [Pittsburgh: University of Pittsburgh Press, 1977], 142), and his writings were colored by this intention.

7. This, too, was not the fruit of personal experience but a compendium of information given by the Russian envoy (or translator) Dmitrii Gerasimov. See Possevino, 142, fn.

8. Walter Leitsch, "Herberstein's Impact on the Reports about Muscovy in the 16th and 17th Centuries: Some Observations on the Technique of Borrowing," in *Forschungen zur Osteuropäischen Geschichte*, 24 (1978): 163–177; esp. 171. During his lifetime

used Herberstein (doubly, if one counts the content of Guagnini's book) but also used Herberstein's sources, as if to knit them all together anew. All of these works belonged to the same tradition—that of the Catholic Europe—and the net of quotations was made wider and stronger by every follower and user.

Walter Leitsch has shown that for a hundred years after his journeys Herberstein remained the most influential authority on Muscovy. Another student of the period, Samuel H. Baron, has stated[9] that Herberstein's book was the basis for three of the most important early books about Muscovy: *On the Rus Commonwealth* by Giles Fletcher (1591), *The Travels to Muscovy and Persia* by Adam Olearius (1647), and Juraj Krizanic's *Politika* (1666). Giles Fletcher, the "discoverer of Muscovy" for the British,[10] plagiarized Herberstein with no acknowledgement at all of his enormous debt. S. Baron has counted 131 instances in which Fletcher used, with slight modifications, fragments from Herberstein. Several ideas of Fletcher's treatise were taken from Herberstein, although the strongly Protestant Englishman was more critical of the Greek-Orthodox Christianity and compared it to the papacy.[11] Fletcher's way of writing his book was typical. He stressed sources he had hardly used—Strabo, Bonfinius, Martin Kromer—and hid the work he had appropriated, that is, the Latin edition of Herberstein. For almost a century after its publication (in 1591), Fletcher's work was considered definitive, therefore it was quoted and used in other works. This was the reason it served as a source for John

---

Guagnini was accused of plagiarism by Maciej Strykowski, who claimed the book as his own! (Leitsch, 171–172). That may be a proof of the extent to which Herberstein's book became "common property"—a necessary, though often unacknowledged, component of all writing about Muscovy.

9. During a lecture in the Russian Center of Harvard University, in the spring of 1987.

10. Or the second "discoverer," after Richard Chancellor; see Giles Fletcher, *Of the Rus Commonwealth*, ed. and with an Introduction by Albert J. Schmidt (Ithaca, N.Y.: Cornell University Press, 1966).

11. Educated at Eton and King's College, he traveled to Russia in 1589. Throughout his journey he was badly treated by his hosts; he, too, was kept from contact with the natives (whose language he ignored). One would suppose that the social isolation in which Fletcher and most foreign visitors to Muscovy were kept might have increased the temptation of plagiarism; however, books about even such an open and well-known country as Italy show an equal degree of unacknowledged borrowings. Herberstein may have been especially tempting to plagiarize because he had more direct experience of Muscovite reality than was common: he knew the language and, while in Muscovy, he was relatively less isolated. Also, his book was comprehensive, intelligent, and well written, which, I am sure, had a lot to do with its attractiveness for other writers.

Milton's *A Brief History of Moscovia*, a secondhand treatise written in the 1630s.[12] In this way, Herberstein, although unacknowledged, entered the bloodstream of British culture.

Another Protestant writer to use Herberstein, and to use with him the entire Catholic tradition—Guagnino's rewriting of Herberstein, Giovio, Matthew from Miechow, Possevino—was Adam Olearius (1603–1671), who traveled to Russia in the years 1634, 1636, 1639, and 1643 and published the first version of his famous report in 1647. A 1627 graduate of the University of Leipzig, Olearius had a thorough education in philosophy, literature, mathematics, astronomy, and geography. His book was extraordinarily popular and very critical of Muscovy.[13] It was so critical, in fact, as to be found slanderous by Juraj Krizanic (1618–1683), the author of a strongly pro-Muscovite book called *Politika*. Born in Croatia, Krizanic went to Russia with the vision of unifying all Slavs. *Politika*, one of his many books, was written while Krizanic was in Siberian exile. It was a description of Muscovite society, composed in an invented Pan-Slavic language ("Common Slavic"). The objective of the book was to teach the ruler how to govern. The religion Krizanic foresaw as common to all Slavs was Roman Catholicism. He approvingly mentioned Herberstein, Possevino, Giovio, and Pernisteri,[14] who, since they were

members of the Roman Catholic faith . . . do not curse us [Slavs], do not shame us, and they do not exaggerate our sins. On the contrary, they praise what is good and tell honestly what they have seen. . . . As for Adam Olearius, Petrejus,[15] Jacob the Dane,[16] and the rest of the writers, they belonged to the Lutheran heresy, and as a result they have spoken libelously in accordance with their custom and teaching.[17]

12. See Albert J. Schmidt, "Introduction," in Fletcher, xxvi. Fletcher's work was known in a censored version, due to the pressure from British merchants afraid of possible limitations in their trade with the severely criticized Muscovites.

13. Adam Olearius, *The Travels to Muscovy and Persia*, trans., ed., and with an Introduction by Samuel H. Baron (Stanford, Calif.: Stanford University Press, 1967).

14. Phillipi Pernisteri, author of *Relatio de Magno Moscoviae Principe*, printed in Frankfurt in 1579.

15. Peter Petrejus, *Historien und Bericht von dem grossfürstenthum Mushkow*, 1620.

16. Jacob von Ulfeldt, *Hodoeporicon Ruthenicum; De bello Moscovito (Moscoviticum?) commentariorum libri*, 1581. Olearius used Jacob's book and plagiarized Petrejus, see S. H. Baron, Introduction to Olearius, 14.

17. See Iurii Krizhanich (Juraj Krizanic), *Russian Statecraft: The "Politika" of Jurii Krizhanich*, an analysis and translation by John M. Letiche and Basil Dmytryshyn (London: Basil Blackwell Publisher, 1985), 122. In fact, it is true that Protestant writers were more critical of Muscovy than Catholic ones because of the religious meaning they saw expressed in manners and everyday behavior.

So Krizanic, by his quotations, introduced the Catholic writings about Russia into Muscovite culture. Although there is no sure proof that his book was read by Russian rulers, an indirect influence is almost certain (Introduction to Krizanic, xiv–xv). This would be, then, still another way in which Herberstein's thought traveled to other countries.

Karamzin

When quoting the famous question by Herberstein— whether it was "the character of the Russian nation which has formed such autocrats or the autocrats themselves have given this character to the nation"—Custine was borrowing from the Catholic tradition of writing about Russia; yet Custine himself pointed to the fact that the quotation was not taken directly from Herberstein. As is typical of the progress of travel opinions, this one meandered to him by an indirect route—the already-mentioned *History of the Russian State* by Nikolai Karamzin. Herberstein's quotation came to Custine in French, translated from the Russian; but it must have been translated *into* Russian from the German translation or the Latin original and only then into French.[18] This multiple remove from the source did not alter the question's meaning: "Incertum est an tanta immanitas gentis tyrannum principem exigat: an tyrannide principis, gens ipsa tam immanis, tamque dura crudelisque reddatur."[19]

The ironic twist in this case comes from the fact that the quotation came to Custine via a Russian historian who wrote an apologia for Russian autocracy. In order to produce a respectable, quotable history of Russia, Karamzin had to quote—even if only to rebut—the Catholic tradition of writing about Muscovy. Hence, although Custine had not read Herberstein and had no idea what kind of book the baron's "correspondence" was, he picked up in this one sentence and proposed again

18. The first French translation (from the Latin) appeared only in 1965. See *La Moscovie du XVIe siècle: Vue par un Ambassadeur Occidental Herberstein*, Présentation de Robert Delort (Paris: Calmann-Lévy, 1965).

19. Sigismundi Liberis Baronis in Herberstein, *Rerum Moscoviticarum Commentarii* (Basilea: Ioannis Oporinus, 1551), 18. The two versions in English: from the Latin—"It is matter of doubt whether the brutality of the people has made the prince a tyrant, or whether the people themselves have become thus brutal and cruel through the tyranny of their prince" (*Notes upon Russia*, 1: 32); and from the German—"It is debatable whether such a people must have such oppressive rulers or whether the oppressive rulers have made the people so stupid" (*Description*, 43).

the question containing all the main elements of Herberstein's critique of Muscovy: the condemnation of the Russian system of government, the feeling of radical estrangement from both the autocratic rulers and the submissive people, and the puzzlement of a rational (that is, Western) man at the mysterious nature of that country. These themes became the main motifs of Custine's critique of Russia.

As can be seen from this example, Karamzin's history served the detractors of Russia. And yet he worked all his life for Russia's glory. His predicament may be taken as symbolic of a problem Russian culture had to face time after time: the tense (and subversive) relationship between the new and old. Acceptance of Western cultural forms—for example, of the Western way of dressing—implied criticism of the native culture. History, as written by Karamzin, was a Western genre: it contained the idea of historical progress and of the irreversibility of the movement of history.[20] He followed Montesquieu and British and Scottish models— the historians John Gillies, Adam Ferguson, and William Robertson. The leading Russian historians of the end of the eighteenth century were editing and commenting on medieval chronicles and not writing narrative, unified stories.[21] Karamzin, like Herberstein, was "the first." Some Western histories of Russia existed already and also served as models. Karamzin wanted to write a history based on primary sources, and the reports of foreign travelers were for that purpose priceless. Yet these sources were almost entirely critical of Muscovite society. To use them was to introduce into Russian historiography a constant tension—found also in other modernized or "Westernized" areas of social life—between the modern and the old, the native and the foreign. This tension is one of the central features of post-Petrine Russian culture.

Karamzin's life and work are good examples of this tension. Born in 1766 and educated in the provinces, he acquired an excellent command of German and French and a working knowledge of English. As a young man he traveled abroad, and in the years 1789–1790, while the French Revolution was changing forever the face of Europe,

20. Rather than history that was a "return to the past." See Iurii M. Lotman, "Binary Models in the Dynamics of Russian Culture," *The Semiotics of Russian Cultural History,* 30–66; see p. 64.

21. Richard Pipes, *Karamzin's Memoir on Ancient and Modern Russia: A Translation and Analysis* (Cambridge: Harvard University Press, 1959), 52–53. On Karamzin, see as well A. G. Cross, *N. M. Karamzin: A Study of His Literary Career 1783–1803* (Carbondale, Ill.: Southern Illinois University Press, 1971); and, especially, Andrzej Walicki, *A History of Russian Thought: From the Enlightenment to Marxism,* trans. Hilda Andrews-Rusiecka (Stanford, Calif.: Stanford University Press, 1979).

Karamzin visited Germany, Switzerland, France, and England. His most important literary work, apart from the *History of the Russian State,* was an account of his foreign travels (in which the Revolution is barely mentioned at all). First published serially in magazines founded by himself—the *Moscow Journal* and *Aglaia*—and later enlarged and rewritten, the *Letters of a Russian Traveller* was completed in 1801. Based on his travel diary but enriched by extensive readings in Western descriptive literature and rewritten through the years, *Letters* was the first travel memoir published in Russia, and one of the best prose works of Russian eighteenth-century literature. From 1803 until his death in 1826, Karamzin worked on his history of the Russian state in the official capacity of Historiographer of the Russian Empire. Between the years 1818 and 1829, twelve volumes of the history were published in Saint Petersburg, and it was there that the French translation used by Custine was prepared almost simultaneously.[22]

It has often happened that history has been written at the request of the king. In France, the legitimizing role of history was exploited by François I, the first absolutist monarch. The chronicles and genealogies written in Europe before his time also had the function of reconfirming the God-given nature of royal power. Even if the history was not contemporary, the mere act of establishing a royal genealogy contributed to the seeming legitimacy of the ruler's dynasty or system of government, and thereby to his glory. But the modern state needed more complex narratives. Louis XIV appointed as his historiographers two bourgeois (but excellent) writers, Boileau and Racine, and sent them to the battlefields of his campaigns to create a proper record of his glory. History in which the king—the one who *made history*—was its object and recipient at the same time was difficult to write. Racine, who classified that kind of history as *éloge,* was unable to write it, partly because his archives were destroyed by fire. In Custine's time, Napoleon deemed history so important that he made it subject to the Minister of Police. The powerful "owned" history: they granted permissions to consult the archives, they paid for the printing of books or suppressed, censored, and forbade them.[23]

22. The translation, entitled *L'Histoire de l'empire de Russie* ("par M. Karamsin"), was made by two professors from Saint Petersburg—St. Thomas and Jauffret—and published in nine volumes in Paris, by A. Belin, in the years 1819–1826. Vols. 10 and 11 were subsequently translated by D. G. Divov (or Divoff) and published in Paris by Bossange Père. The history went only to the beginning of the seventeenth century.

23. See G. P. Gooch, *History and Historians in the Nineteenth Century* (Boston: Beacon Press, 1957; first published in 1913), 154–155.

The function of the historiographer of the tsar, then, was borrowed from Western tradition. Karamzin, who was the first to occupy this post, was paid an annual pension by the state and was guaranteed that each of his successive volumes would be printed. The state commissioned the translation into French from which Custine quoted. The writing of the *History of the Russian State* was supervised by Tsar Alexander I, to whom Karamzin read parts of his work. Custine discovered this fact in another Russian source, Wiazemski's *Incendie du palais d'hiver à Saint-Pétersbourg*. Custine's conclusion was that like "every Russian writer," including Wiazemski (whom he had met in Russia), Karamzin was a courtier. As such, he could not be suspected of calumnies against the absolute Russian monarchy, and therefore his credentials as a believable source whenever he described brutal or horrifying events were established. But even though the function of state historiographer may have been modeled on the French, the role of the courtier was for Custine incompatible with that of a historian.

In Russia, history forms a part of the crown domain: it is the moral estate of the prince, as men and lands are the material; it is placed in cabinets with the other imperial treasures, and only such of it is shown as it is wished should be seen. The emperor modifies at his pleasure the annals of the country, and daily dispenses to his people the historic truths that accord with the fiction of the moment. (P. 617)

Custine called Karamzin "the courtier" and "the flattering historian," not only because of his official function as state historiographer but also because Custine strongly disagreed with Karamzin's apologetics for the Russian autocracy. Custine did not study Karamzin thoroughly and was unable to see the evolution and nuance in Karamzin's opinions. As if in despair, he quoted Karamzin's "blood-soaked pages" without restraint. Yet the more he quoted, the more reconciled he became, it seemed, with the historian himself—feeling for him, at the end, "an admiration mixed with pity."[24] And indeed, Karamzin was a courageous, incorruptible man. His independence led to his estrangement from the tsar, whose ideas (initially, at least) were less conservative than Karamzin's.[25] Alexander I did not want his history to prevent his attempts at reform, whereas Karamzin wanted to prove that autocracy was the traditional form of

24. Vol. 3: 225. The entire letter 26 and its appendix are devoted to quotations from Karamzin (3: 175–238). But he is quoted all throughout the book's four volumes.
25. See I. M. Lotman, "The Decembrist in Daily Life (Everyday Behavior as a Historical-Psychological Category)," in *The Semiotics of Russian Cultural History*, 95–149; see pp. 115–119.

government in Russia, and, as such, not to be tampered with. He understood autocracy as a system in which the political power of the monarch was undivided but limited to matters of high politics. (In despotism, by contrast, the monarch's power reached into every sphere of life.) The governing of the "manor," he believed, belonged to the rights and obligations of the gentry. Autocracy, as the traditional Russian system of government and as the result of long historical development was best suited for Russian society and should not, Karamzin felt, be changed according to legalistic, and therefore abstract, Western ways of dealing with the individual's relationship to the state. Karamzin lauded the specific character of Russian society and saw Peter the Great's reforms as the imposition of Western elements on the native body of an authentic culture. Such was generally also the opinion of Custine, who was respectful of tradition and opposed to the imposition of abstract political ideas on a different civilization but who in the particular case of Russian society felt repugnance toward the native culture and toward its political system—despotism. Karamzin and Custine differed in their attitudes to freedom but less radically than Custine thought. Yes, Karamzin did "defend the power that limited freedom, but he defended it as a free man."[26]

According to the oft-quoted passage from Hegel's *Lectures on the Philosophy of History,*

the term *History* unites the objective with the subjective side, and denotes quite as much the *historia rerum gestarum,* as the *res gestae* themselves; on the other hand it comprehends not less what has *happened,* than the *narration* of what has happened.

This quotation is used to prove the point that history is in the writing—in the books—and that the facts cannot be apprehended as such before they are organized in verbal form.[27] For Karamzin, the action of writing history was truly a deed of historic proportions. He opened his "Foreword" to the *History of the Russian State* with a sentence full of biblical overtones:

In a certain sense, history is the sacred book of a nation, the main, the indispensable book, the mirror of its existence and activity, the table of revelations and

26. I. M. Lotman, *Sotworenije Karamzina* (Moscow: Kniga, 1987), 279. For the extraordinary role Karamzin played in Russian culture see pp. 280–320 of Lotman's book and N. Eidelman, *Poslednij Letopisec* (Moscow: Kniga, 1983).

27. It can be found, for example, in Hayden White's *The Content of the Form: Narrative Discourse and Historical Representation* (Baltimore: Johns Hopkins University Press, 1987), 12.

rules, the ancestors' bequest to posterity, the supplement and explanation of the present, and the example for the future.[28]

Custine, although critical of Karamzin's apology, was no less convinced of the outstanding role of the historian.

Karamzin, even though a timid historian, is nevertheless instructive, because he has an underlying loyalty which cuts through his habit of prudence, and which fights against his Russian origin and the prejudices of his education. God called him to avenge humanity, perhaps in spite of himself, and in spite of humanity's wish as well. (3: 224)

In fact, Karamzin's history became a source of enormous national pride: he seemed to have given Russia its past.[29] Also, he may (as one of several factors) have influenced the tsar's retreat from his liberalizing bent. In his "Foreword," Karamzin writes about the necessity for the historian to submit to the factual truth. He describes the glory of strong and undivided power but also the deplorable violence and cruelty perpetrated by some Russian tsars. The pages devoted to the description of the violence were the ones Custine paraphrased, reported, quoted— often in their entirety. Even the "obsequiously partial" Karamzin found it necessary, in Custine's opinion, to write damagingly about Russian history, because Russian history itself was "anti-Russian" in what it revealed about the Russian state. Only "a darkness [is] equally favorable to the repose of the despot and the felicity of his subjects" (p. 94). Thus, the activity of this "most widely read Russian of his time" (Pipes 1959, 89), while strengthening Russian identity, was also *malgré lui* ("in spite of himself") critical of Russia.

In *La Russie en 1839*, Custine made extensive use of Karamzin's history to show not the wisdom but the senseless brutality of the Russian autocracy. He read Russian history as a catalogue of cruelties. "Quoting from a certain author usually provides proof of a specific authority, proof of the aesthetic or conceptual validity of the cited words within a new work of art."[30] But "the same word changes its meaning depending on the force that takes hold of it," wrote Antoine

28. In *Russian Intellectual History: An Anthology,* ed. Marc Raeff, Introduction by Isaiah Berlin (New York: Harcourt, Brace, and World, 1966), 117–124, esp. 117 (in the translation of Jaroslav Pelenski). Karamzin dated his Foreword December 7, 1815.

29. In Stalinist times Karamzin's *History* was not published. Only now, with glasnost, is it being printed (in installments!) in a Moscow publication.

30. Nina Perlina, *Varieties of Poetic Utterance: Quotation in "The Brothers Karamazov"* (Lanham, Md.: University Press of America, 1985), 10.

Compagnon.[31] The example of Custine's use of long quotations from Karamzin proves that point. In Custine's version, Karamzin's history is one long criticism of his country. Even the historian's intention to praise his nation's past is turned into an accusation. Is this illegitimate? Is Custine's version of Russian history truthful? Certainly his description of Russia was truthful to the extent of being faithful in his use of the sources. In historical works, quoted material is verified by checking it against its source and other related texts; Custine found Karamzin's facts true but disputed his opinions. The referentiality of historical quotations is indirect: it cannot simply reside in their relationship to the past (which cannot be visited) but is to be found in written texts and other testimonies. In that sense, travel writing is concerned as much with traveling through books as with traveling through countries.

There is, then, a certain inevitability in a tradition—a necessary course things must run. Karamzin wanted to write a laudatory work, yet he had to adopt the heritage he wanted to become part of: the Western (that is, the only one then available) way of writing history. He used, for example, the French definition of civilization: arts but also laws.[32] He compared Ivan the Terrible to Caligula, to Nero, and to Louis XI, and Custine scoffed at him for this (Custine, 3: 226). The central problems of his work—the questions of authority and responsibility, of the relationship between the people and their princes, between tradition and political institutions—these are the questions of Western historiography. Karamzin belonged to the same tradition as Custine (and Herberstein and Contarini), and he "appropriated" the same quotations.

Yet the texts he quoted from were overwhelmingly hostile to Russia, so Custine was able to build his case against Russia on the work of the native historian. It was in Russian history—history written in Russian, by a Russian, and about Russia—that Custine found and revived Herberstein's Catholic critique of Russia. Of course, Custine was not a historian, as Karamzin was, hence his frank dependence on quotations.

---

31. Antoine Compagnon, *De la Seconde main ou le travail de la citation* (Paris: Seuil, 1979), 38. ("Le même mot change de sens selon la force qui se l'approprie.")

32. "In the happy respite of peace, the monarch feasted with the lords and the people like the father of a large family. Cities populated with chosen inhabitants began to adorn the deserts; Christianity was softening the fierceness of wild customs; Byzantine arts made their appearance on the shores of the Dnieper and Volkhov. Iaroslav gave the people a scroll of simple and sagacious civil laws, which conformed to the laws of the ancient Germans. In one word, Russia became not only the most spacious of all states, but also, compared to others, the most civilized." Karamzin, "Memoir on Ancient and Modern Russia," in Pipes, 104–105.

But his quotations are incomparably longer than is common in travel narratives; there are more of them; and their sources are indicated with more emphasis. The history of Russia, as shown in the quotes from Karamzin, is unacceptably cruel and bloody. Custine does not assimilate the quoted sentences, does not take them out of quotation marks. These quotation marks indicate not authority, as when Custine quotes Herberstein, but distance, rejection, the nonassimilative quality of Russian history, which Custine seemed to be unable to translate into his own words.

The complex working of tradition can be seen here within and without Russia. Karamzin's history was built on and against the Western Catholic opinion about Russia; it contained, then, two diametrically opposed evaluations of that country. The negative one, although rejected, is restated in his history, recalled, and therefore reaffirmed for a moment, just before being negated. Custine has no trouble pulling it out, intact, to use it anew. The name of Herberstein led him to a thread that unraveled the work of the Russian historian.

4

The (Double) Nature of Russia

The Western View

The history of Europe, too, could have been written as one long list of crimes—hence Karamzin's comparisons of Russian tsars with Nero or Caligula. But the history of Russia as presented by Custine was aimed at expelling Russia from Europe. It was not a simple operation, nor was Custine without ambivalence while performing it. The history of Russia, he felt, could be understood only if one knew where Russia belonged: to be understood historically, Russia must be placed geographically. The writer had to decide if it was an Oriental or a European civilization, and if its violence was unique to the "East." By expelling Russia from Europe, Custine could hope to expel the violence as well.

The first step was to approach Russia as mysterious. Custine expressed this thought in traditional terms: he needed to "unmask the colossus," "unveil his mystery" (Tarn 1985, 492). The mystery of Russia was a constant motif, a cliché in the descriptive literature. For centuries, each travel book opened with a promise that the reader would finally understand the mystery of this strange entity. Of course, such introductions had a function of legitimizing the writer's effort: I am writing, it meant, because I have something new or unusual to tell. But they expressed as well a persistent frustration that the Western public felt when confronted with Russia and Russians. Not only did the Russians "hide" their country by consistently limiting Westerners' access to it, but the Westerners themselves were unable to "apprehend" the nature of Russia and neatly assign this country to Europe or to Asia. This difficulty in comprehension took the form of an impossibility of classification.

For an example of this predicament we could look at various attempts made by nineteenth- and twentieth-century travelers to describe a building that was unlike others: Moscow's Cathedral of Saint Basil, on which Custine lavished considerable attention. The cathedral was built in the years 1553–1560 (or 1555–1561, depending on sources) to commemorate Ivan the Terrible's 1552 victory over the Tartars. It is composed of a central tower surrounded by eight small churches, each with a dome; all nine towers are raised on a podium. Each of the domes is different from the others, their exterior bright with a variety of colors. Originally the structure was white, and the colors were added a century after the church had been completed. Its architecture represents the most successful attempt at translating into masonry the Russian medieval wooden church structures. It is so different from the buildings traditionally used for Christian worship that no simple analogy can describe it. "This boldest departure from classic or Byzantine architecture violates the academic laws of symmetry and proportion as understood by the Western world, and the structure is uniquely medieval Russian in content, form, technique, decoration, and feeling."[1]

Western travel writers attempted to convey the uniqueness of the building by comparing it to the most unusual objects. August von Haxthausen, author of a treatise on Russia, wrote in 1847 that Saint Basil "reflects all the colors of the rainbow, and from a certain distance or in foggy weather one might think it was a huge dragon ready to pounce on its prey."[2] Italian writer and painter Carlo Levi compared it to "the back of a gigantic animal . . . a bunch of flowers or strange vegetables . . . a natural object, an elaborate plant."[3] Nestor Considérant likened the church to "a gigantic plate loaded with flowers and fruit, on top of which a mass of rainbow-colored melons and pineapples

1. Arthur Voyce, *Moscow and the Roots of Russian Culture* (Norman: University of Oklahoma Press, 1964), 111.

2. He thought Saint Basil "one of the most unusual and magnificent buildings." See his *Studies on the Interior of Russia* (Chicago: University of Chicago Press, 1972), 20.

3. "La schiena di un immenso animale . . . un mazzo di fiori o di strani ortaggi . . . un oggetto naturale, un vegetale elaborato." In *Il futuro ha un cuore antico* (Turin: Einaudi, 1956), 54.

has been mounted."[4] "I counted seventeen cupolas on the roof of Vassili-Blagennoï," wrote Jacques Angelot, "each is different by its form, color, proportions: one resembles a ball, another a pineapple."[5] Colin Simpson described the cupolas as "colossal cloves of garlic centrifuged into twirled shapes in various paintpots; and . . . as colored onions that have been incised by pineapples."[6] And Waldo Frank called it "an intricately petaled giant flower."[7]

There were writers who compared Saint Basil to human artifacts. The crosses atop the domes of the cathedral reminded Walter Benjamin of "gigantic earrings attached to the sky."[8] Italian writer Mario Praz called it "a massive paperweight *liberty* avant la lettre,"[9] while Jozef Lubomirski thought it was like "an eccentric piece of furniture—heavy, fantastic, bizarre—forgotten in an empty drawing room on the day of moving."[10] Usually, however, writers found comparable objects in the realm of nature. It was by no means an obvious way of describing a church, and often frustration was expressed at the elusiveness and bizarre character of the object of description. "This building is always holding something back," complained Walter Benjamin (1986, 25). Nestor Considérant feels unable to give "an acceptably precise idea of this architecture that departs from nowhere and arrives at nothing" (1857, 112).[11] Even the master painter of unusual sights—Théophile Gautier—declared that he "will not seek comparisons in order to give an idea of a thing that has neither prototype nor similarity." He said this, though, after having already compared the building "to a gigantic

---

4. "Un immense plat chargé de fleurs et de fruits, et au sommet duquel on a empilé des melons et des ananas de toutes les nuances de l'arc-en-ciel." See Nestor Considérant, *La Russie en 1856: Souvenirs de voyage*, 2 vols. (Bruxelles and Leipzig: Auguste Schnée, 1857), 1: 112–113.

5. Jacques Angelot, *Six mois en Russie* (Bruxelles: Wahlen, 1827), 249–250.

6. Colin Simpson, *This Is Russia* (Sydney, Australia: Hodder and Stoughton, 1965), 222.

7. Waldo Frank, *Dawn in Russia: The Record of a Journey* (New York: Charles Scribner and Sons, 1932), 201.

8. Walter Benjamin, *Moscow Diary* (Cambridge: Harvard University Press, 1986), 22.

9. "Un massiccio posacarte liberty avanti lettera." Mario Praz, *Il mondo che ho visto* (Milan: Adelphi Edizioni, 1982), 442.

10. "Un meuble excentrique (lourd, fantastique, bizarre) oublié dans un salon vide le jour d'un déménagement." Jozef Lubomirski, *Scènes de la vie militaire en Russie. Le Prince Soldat. Superstitions russes. Impressions de voyage* (Paris: Didier, 1873), 296.

11. "Une idée passablement précise de cette architecture qui ne dérive de nulle part et qui n'aboutit à rien." *La Russie en 1856,* 112.

madrepore, a colossal crystallization, a grotto of stalactites turned upside down."[12]

All the descriptions found here share two elements: bewilderment, expressed by the unusual second term of comparison, and a feeling of the grandeur of the object they face. Whatever Saint Basil is compared to, be it "madrepore," "paperweight," or "a clove of garlic," it is always "gigantic," "massive," and "colossal." It had a *groznyi*—terrible—look, just like that of its founder—a look at the same time terrifying (in the religious meaning of the word), imposing, and intimidating. But the main element of these descriptions is frustration, inability to "ambush" the building (Walter Benjamin's expression), to describe it in a conventional way. Usually, buildings are compared to buildings, people to people, and landscapes to landscapes. The "incomparable" Saint Basil is compared to the objects outside the pool of things buildings are normally likened to. Not only does it not belong to architecture; it does not belong to the man-made realm of culture. Instead, it reminds writers of fruits, flowers, and vegetables and becomes a part of nature rather than civilization.

The encounter with Saint Basil Cathedral was in fact shocking for the writers. The building is placed at the end of the Red Square—a large, empty space, "entirely enclosed yet . . . infinite and open,"[13] not truly flat but not raised either. It borders the square together with other unusual buildings; in description, it was traditionally juxtaposed to the architecturally eclectic but more classical Kremlin. For the last several decades it has formed a pair of opposites with the Lenin Mausoleum— an opposition in which Saint Basil consists predominantly of surface, whereas the mausoleum is "sinking into the ground like a root" (Frank 1932, 207). "It is not only unlike any other building anywhere, it isn't even shaped like a building" (Simpson 1965, 222). Saint Basil stands out as an object that defies description.

Although their journeys were undertaken in search of something new, the writers express surprise and shock at finding an object so *unlike* anything else. The comparisons they reach for seem capricious, outrageous, arbitrary. And yet the pineapple, the onion, the vegetable are repeated from book to book. Each surprise, each description is controlled by previous surprises and descriptions, and by the general framework of culture the writer operates in. The writer is facing an elaborate

12. Théophile Gautier, *Russia*, trans. Florence MacIntyre Tyson, 2 vols. (Philadelphia: John C. Winston Co., 1905), 1: 379.
13. Waldo Frank, 201.

artwork, a magnificent building. The building does not fulfill the expectations of the writer's canon of beauty. The writer goes back to his first impression—that of surprise and, most often, enchantment—and revises it. I thought it was art, he says, but when I looked more closely I saw it was nature. It has beauty, I agree, but it is the beauty of an artichoke: the unself-conscious beauty of a natural object. It is not a product of civilization: it is, like nature, a result of a caprice. Therefore, it does not need to disturb our ideas about culture.

This reasoning did not need to be made anew by each of the writers: it could be found in books that the writer must have read in order to understand what the cathedral represented. In these books the cathedral's very own history placed it outside civilization. The story has it that Ivan the Terrible had the builder of the cathedral blinded so as to prevent him from creating another, similar masterpiece. Most probably untrue, the story stuck to the building, and it is a rare book that does not mention it. The insistence with which it is repeated, even when doubt is expressed as to its truthfulness, is analogical to the flowering of strange comparisons. To the writer, the cathedral looks like a caprice and is a result of caprice, an accident of history, rather than a product of an orderly development of a civilization. The lack of order in its structure corresponds to lack of order in its origin and, instead of being an example of the truly, uniquely Russian culture the writers were in search of, it becomes a strange growth, an accidental protuberance, or "a dream of a sick mind implemented by a crazy architect."[14]

To appreciate how the operation of exclusion works, we turn again to Custine's *La Russie en 1839*. Custine approaches the subject of Moscow and Saint Basil only in the third volume, when the reader is already quite versed in Russian matters and has been given a tour of Saint Petersburg. Custine recounts his arrival in Moscow and describes a magnificent, distant view of the city, hundreds of whose churches were still in existence.

This first view of the capital of the Slavonians, rising brightly in the cold solitudes of the Christian East, produces an impression that cannot easily be forgotten. Before the eye, spreads a landscape wild and gloomy, but grand as the ocean; and to animate the dreary void, there rises a poetical city, whose architecture is without either a designating name or a known model.[15]

14. As Alexandre Dumas (Père) said in his *Voyage en Russie* (Paris: Hermann, 1960), 482.

15. *The Empire of the Czar,* 394. Another part of the description of Moscow is also very convincing: "A fleet, apparently on land—such is the apparition with which my eye

This wonderful image of the city from the distance is soon juxtaposed to the prosaic character of its streets. The contrast between the splendid exterior and the dull interior—between superficial richness and interior poverty—expresses the very nature of what Custine understands as the "East" or the "Orient."

On entering Moscow we feel as if waking from a brilliant dream to a very dull and prosaic reality—a vast city without any real monuments of art, that is to say, without a single object worthy of a discriminative and thoughtful approbation.

The same contrast functions on other levels of the description: Saint Basil's external beauty contrasts with its internal ugliness; the church's Oriental vivaciousness contrasts with the almost-classical restraint of the Kremlin; its happy, life-affirming colorfulness with the terrible fate of its architect. Saint Basil's form stands in opposition to its content.

Although he had declared a moment before that Moscow has not a single object of art worthy of approbation, the Church of Saint Basil is for Custine "the most singular, if not the most beautiful edifice in Russia." The description that follows displays brilliantly, in a crescendo, all the vegetables and mythical animals of other comparisons quoted here.

It appears as an immense cluster of little turrets forming a bush, or rather giving the idea of some kind of tropical fruit all bristling with excrescences,

he says at the beginning, only to move from the realm of nature to that of strange artifacts:

or a crystallization of a thousand rays, the enamelled skin of a serpent, the most highly polished enamel of China.

Then the comparison moves to the sphere of mythical animals:

It is like gilded scales of fish, the skins of serpents stretched on piles of mis-shapen stones, heads of dragons, shells of chameleons,

---

has been sometimes surprised in Holland, and once in England. . . . Exactly similar is the effect that has been produced upon me by the first view of Moscow: a multitude of spires gleamed alone above the dust of the road, the undulations of the soil, and the misty line that nearly always clothes the distance, under the summer sun of these parts" (p. 393). The passages describing the Cathedral of Saint Basil and its history are quoted from *The Empire of the Czar*, 393–397; additional passages, cut out in the American edition, have been translated from the original, 3: 251–253.

and continues into a purely visual series of associations:

altar ornaments, priests' robes, and the whole is topped by spires painted so that they resemble rich materials of reddish brown silk.

The nouns "cluster," "brush," "bouquet," "excrescences" indicate a chaotic, unorganized, organic character of the church, so chaotic as to defy any orderly description. This "masterpiece of caprice" can hardly be imagined as a place of worship and "the men who go to worship God in this box of glazed fruits are not Christians." Soon the splendid outside is sadly contrasted with the inside of the church which is "narrow, mean, without character." The richness of colors and shapes slowly becomes incomprehensible, the traveler's attention wanes for lack of form. It is not art, because it is not harmonious. So, although the church is beautiful, it is not worthy of "thoughtful approbation."

Custine complained bitterly about the unoriginality of architecture in Saint Petersburg. His initial reaction to Moscow and Saint Basil is one of relief—finally something real and original! But the closer look revealed a truly different city and a truly different church; his enthusiasm weakened. Another closer look and he had nothing more than waning patience for this "box of glazed fruits"; the patience disappeared when he remembered the fate of the architect. The church's history is recalled: "this enervating work caused the misfortune of the man who accomplished it." Hence a description that started with the highest praise (the most beautiful building in Russia) deteriorated into a hostile rejection: the cathedral is judged and condemned.

It is, in fact, the history of Saint Basil Cathedral that allows the writer to move one step away from the breathtaking image of the church into the security of cultural certitudes. From the cultural perspective the building can be handled as just one in a series of artifacts, reflecting the nature of Russia. The comments on the story about the architect, then, reflect an overall attitude of the writer toward Russia. Doubtful as to the truthfulness of the anecdote, Custine nevertheless insists on it because he finds it characteristic of the "Oriental" nature of Russian society. Lucky artist, he says; since the work was so successful he was not impaled but only blinded. His irony points to the reversal of the ways in which the success of an artist is treated in the "Oriental" society and serves as the "final word" on the cathedral's beauty.

Other writers interpreted the church's story in different ways. "A master with rather strange and unpleasant moods!" wrote strongly protsarist Haxthausen about Ivan the Terrible blinding the artist; but soon he rushes to redeem the tsar anyhow:

Curiously enough, in the memory and opinion of the Russian people and in extant popular legends he was a pious and good-natured man who could easily be duped and who was occasionally inclined to play practical jokes. . . . Legend always tells a version different from the one history tells, and yet is nevertheless just as true. What we call history presents the truth from one point of view only. (Haxthausen 1972, 20)

In that way Haxthausen is not confronted with the story as an illustration of Russian history but approaches it from the methodological point of view: without denying its truthfulness, he decides it is only half-true.

Théophile Gautier presented still another attitude. When he visited Russia twenty years after Custine, many changes, most of all the reforms of the new tsar, Alexander II, improved the Russian situation. Also, in the years 1839–1845, Saint Basil's interior was partially frescoed (Voyce 1964, 115). When Custine saw it, its walls were simply white, which explains the shock he felt at comparing the church's interior to its exterior. Gautier's interests and situation were also different: he went to Russia to write a book about Russian art, and the project depended heavily on the Russian government's financial backing. His description of Russia was phrased in a "pittoresque," a-political style similar to the style of his celebrated description of Spain. He very much liked—and described with gusto—both the exterior and the interior of the church. "It would be difficult to imagine," runs his comment on the story of the blinding of its architect, "a cruelty more flattering in its jealousy, and this Ivan the Terrible must have been at bottom a true artist, an impassioned *dilettante*. This ferocity in matters of art displeases us less than indifference" (Gautier 1866, 1: 379). It is, of course, Gautier's own indifference—indifference to the sufferings of this faraway tribe—that made him describe the barbaric act as an expression of jealousy and love of art.

Custine was not indifferent. But both he, an anti-Russian writer if there ever was one, and the pro-Russian Haxthausen compare Saint Basil to a dragon. Why, in spite of ideological differences, were there so many similarities in description? Was the building really similar to a dragon? One answer to this question is that Haxthausen took the comparison from Custine, whom he read and commented upon. Moreover, Gautier read and plagiarized Custine. It is, therefore, an indirectly quoted comparison—quotation being a way in which tradition controls description. But what we see here as well is the binary mind at work. The unexpectedness of the way Saint Basil looks is expressed by the unexpectedness of comparison controlled by the ideological and conceptual dimensions of writer's culture. Saint Basil is fitted into a proliferation of binary oppositions: removed from culture, it is placed in nature; included in the Orient, it is excluded from the West; seen as a caprice, it is denied the status of a sustained work of art; acknowledged as a work of art, it is rejected as a building. The Kremlin, although the work of Italian architects, is seen as Russian and therefore contrasted to the French Louvre; but inside the Red Square, the Kremlin becomes Western, a kind of Louvre, and is opposed to Saint Basil's nativeness. There are here two systems, two "languages"; the reader knows only one of them, the traveler both. Comparison, or more generally, parallelism, is a translation and an interpretation—an effort to find synonyms, correspondences, similar meanings. That effort is performed before our eyes by the narrator-traveler. He is attracted by the unusual, which he is unable to render without using known and accepted notions, the "déjà vu." The dragon of Haxthausen's description and the bouquets and crystallizations of Gautier's are related to Custine's description, which in turn is indebted to many prior descriptions. Hence the comparisons, as original as they seem, are an outgrowth of a collaborative effort modified by the talent each writer brings to the task.

But the uses the image is put to vary a great deal. All three examples, taken as they are from representative nineteenth-century descriptions of Russia, show the ideological use of the image of Saint Basil, or, to phrase it differently, the role of the image in the integrated vision of Russia. An unusual building, it is treated by Custine as typical, capriciousness being the characteristic of Russian culture; by Haxthausen as not so unusual after all; and by Gautier as one work of art in the long series of other works of art he has described, thus turning it into a matter of taste only. In all cases, however, it is strange and therefore typical of Russia.

The Russian View

But what was Russia? Was Russia part of Europe or of Asia? The continuous reemergence of these questions lay at the basis of the West's attitude toward Russia. The answer was never final, and the effort of definition had to be repeated with every description. There were many reasons for that state of affairs. First of all, "Asia" and "Europe" were by no means stable terms. Whatever they meant, however, it was never possible either to entirely include Russia in or entirely expel Russia from either of them. Russia was never simply "Europe" or "Asia" but was always defined in terms of both. Moreover, Russia herself used these two concepts as the limits against which to measure herself. The uncertainty and confusion were shared by the describer and the described.

When Karamzin described the origin of Russia, he presented her as a blend of many traditions.

Situated in the depths of the north, rearing her head between Asiatic and European kingdoms, Russian society contained elements derived from both these parts of the world. It was a compound of ancient customs of the east, carried to Europe by the Slavs and reactivated, so to speak, by our long connection with the Mongols; of Byzantine customs which we had adopted together with Christianity; and of certain German customs, imparted to us by the Normans. . . . The Russians considered such an amalgam of customs brought about by accidents and circumstances as indigenous, and they loved it as their own national heritage.[16]

This balance, however, was upset by Peter the Great. According to Karamzin, the monarch, great as he was, committed unpardonable violence toward his people by tampering with long-established customs. He wrote:

Peter was unable to realize that the national spirit constitutes the moral strength of states, which is as indispensable to their stability as is physical might. . . . It is nothing else than respect for our national dignity. By uprooting ancient customs, by exposing them to ridicule, by causing them to appear stupid, by praising and introducing foreign elements, the sovereign of the Russians humbled Russian hearts. . . . The Russian dress, food, and beards did not interfere with the founding of schools. Two states may stand on the same level of civil enlightenment although their customs differ. One state may borrow from another useful knowledge without borrowing its manners. These manners may change naturally, but to prescribe statutes for them is an act of violence, which is illegal also for an autocratic monarch. The people, in their original covenant with the kings, had told them: "Guard our safety abroad and at home, punish criminals, sacrifice a part to save the whole." They had not said: "Fight the innocent inclinations and tastes of our domestic life." In this realm, the sovereign may equitably act only by example, not by decree. . . . Imitation became for Russians a matter of honor and pride. (Karamzin in Pipes, 1959, 121–123)

16. See Karamzin's *Memoir on Ancient and Modern Russia*, 110–111.

This long quotation contains all the basic elements of Karamzin's thought. In trying to prevent the Tsar Alexander's westernizing reforms, he criticized Peter the Great more severely than he did the cruel rages of Ivan the Terrible. The terms in which this criticism is expressed were a summary of Russian anti-Western conservatism. And yet they were an elaboration of a passage from Montesquieu, whom Karamzin emulated and admired!

Thus, when a prince wants to make great changes in his nation, [wrote Montesquieu,] he must reform by laws what is established by laws, and change by manners what is established by manners and it is a very bad policy to change by laws what should be changed by manners. The law that obliged the Muscovites to cut off their beards, and to shorten their clothes, and the violence of Peter I in trimming up to the knees the long robes of those who entered the towns were instances of tyranny. The means for preventing crimes are penalties; the means for changing manners are examples.[17]

Western arguments were used by the anti-Western writer to criticize the Russian monarch for his Westernizing efforts.

In his Foreword to the *History of the Russian State* (a title reminiscent of Montesquieu's vision of history as a history of institutions) Karamzin frequently used the pronoun *us*. But the meaning of *us* is not always the same. "Contrary to the opinion of Abbé Mably, *we* cannot wax oratorical in history. New achievements of reason have given *us* a clear notion about history's characteristics . . ." ("Foreword," p. 121), he wrote in clear agreement with the West-European intellectuals. A few pages before he had declared, "Besides the special value which Russia's chronicles have for *us*, her sons, they have also a general value" (p. 118; all italics are mine). It is interesting to note that although the text was written in Russian Karamzin felt obliged to specify the Russianness of "us" ("her sons") but not "our" Western character. This was because for him the category of Europeans was larger than that of Russians and included them.

The "wandering" *we* implicitly expressed itself in the use of Western arguments and Western genres and was very characteristic of Russian culture. The mapping of the borders within which the *we* was enclosed could prove a very difficult operation. Until the twentieth century, the Russian *we* never included Asia. Russia's identity was first created in a constant fight for survival *against* nomadic tribes of Asia. "For perhaps

17. Charles Louis Sécondat de la Brède, Baron de Montesquieu, *The Spirit of the Laws*, trans. and ed. A. M. Cohler, B. C. Miller, and H. S. Stone (Cambridge: Cambridge University Press, 1989), bk. 19, ch. 3, p. 309.

a thousand years, if one is to include speculation about prehistory, the basic Russian attitude toward the peoples of the steppe, toward Asia, was that of total apartness and extreme hostility."[18] The Westernization introduced by Peter the Great was, from that point of view, a process of modernization whose aim was to secure final superiority of Russia over her Asiatic neighbors. At the same time the Russian intellectual outlook became part of the Western-centered world-view, in which Asia was relegated to the category of the inferior and incompetent (Riasanovsky 1972, 9). On the eastern front, then, Russian self-identity was created against Asia. But what about Europe?

In a fascinating study,[19] Iurii Lotman and Boris Uspenskii constructed a model of Russian culture built on binary opposition. Whereas in Western culture there is a three-way division of life into the sacred, the profane, and a neutral sphere in-between, in medieval Russia "the basic cultural values (ideological, political, and religious) . . . were distributed in a bipolar field and divided by a sharp boundary without an axiologically neutral zone." Secular power, for example, could be perceived either as diabolical or divine but never as neutral. This accentuated duality was not removed by the reforms of Peter the Great: in fact, in Russian culture "change occurs as a radical negation of the preceding state," not as a creation of neutral zones; the new state incorporates the previous one with a changed, negative sign. Because of this internal mechanism, culture in Russia has always been organized by oppositions in which terms were defined and existed in relation to each other—Christianity versus paganism, knowledge versus ignorance, lower classes versus nobility. The duality of the sacred/profane language changed from Church Slavonic versus Russian to Western (Dutch, then German, then French) versus Russian (Lotman and Uspenskii, 32–33).[20] The very model proposed by Lotman and Uspenskii continues that duality (Russian versus

18. See Nicholas V. Riasanovsky, "Asia Through Russian Eyes," in Wayne S. Vucinich, ed., *Russia and Asia: Essays on the Influence of Russia on the Asian Peoples* (Stanford, Calif.: Hoover Institution Press, 1972), 3–29; the quoted sentence can be found on pp. 6–7.

19. Iurii Lotman and Boris Uspenskii, "Binary Models in the Dynamics of Russian Culture (to the End of the Eighteenth Century)" in *The Semiotics of Russian Cultural History* (Ithaca, N.Y.: Cornell University Press, 1985), 30–66.

20. West European culture also knows the phenomenon of bilingualism, and the entire Catholic tradition of writing about Russia was possible precisely because of the unifying role Latin played in its imposition. (Russia, it is worth remembering, was outside of the Latin family.) Latin was not only the language of power but also the language of religion. No such community was offered by French and German, and these languages played an ambiguous role, perhaps best called colonizing.

Western culture) and "spontaneously reflects the deep structure of Russian consciousness."[21]

One of the main axes of that culture is the opposition between Russia and the West. Whatever the attitude of the Russians, the West was always seen as an inversion, as a bearer of qualities that might be good or bad but that were always diametrically opposed to those to which the Russians either had to aspire or to defend themselves against (p. 65). Starting with the reforms of Peter the Great, this opposition was, so to speak, "internalized," translated into the coexistence of two different groups of people: the Russian people and the Westernized nobility. In other articles in his book, Lotman shows persuasively that this division became an internal one not only in the society but also within each nobleman.[22] It was a very unstable situation, in which the *we* of the Russian nobility was in constant need of definition.

This duality may be accepted as a constant in the Russian culture after Peter the Great—as a source of continuous conflict but also as a dynamic, creative force, and an inspiration for many social phenomena. This duality, however, can also help explain the problems the West had in describing and classifying Russia. The object of description did not fit the categories applied to it. And since the passion for describing and classifying became Russian as well, the problems with description became problems of self-identity. This may be an explanation for Karamzin's wandering *we*.

Grattez le Russe . . .

This is not to say that it was Russia's nature—however it may be conceived—that was responsible for the difficulties the West had in describing her. It was the very concept that countries had "natures" that led to difficulties. Eighteenth- and nineteenth-century travel literature claimed that the concept of national character was purely descriptive.

21. Boris Gasparov, Introduction, *The Semiotics of Russian Cultural History*, 28.

22. "The Russian nobleman was like a foreigner in his own country. As an adult he had to learn through unnatural methods what is usually acquired through direct experience in early childhood . . . [this Europeanization] accentuated rather than obliterated the non-European aspects of daily life. In order to perceive one's behavior as consistently foreign it is essential *not to be* a foreigner. . . . A Russian was not supposed to become a foreigner; he was merely supposed to act like one" (p. 70 in "The Poetics of Behavior in Eighteenth-Century Russian Culture," in *The Semiotics of Russian Cultural History*, 67–94).

Montesquieu, who was credited with the creation of that notion, employed it in a complicated way: the character, or rather *a general spirit* of a nation, was composed of and influenced by the climate, religion, laws, "the maxims of government," history ("examples of past things"), "mores" and "manners." Some of these factors were more important in one society than in others. "Nature and climate almost alone dominate savages; manners govern the Chinese; laws tyrannize Japan; in former times mores set the tone in Lacedaemonia; in Rome it was set by the maxims of government and the ancient mores."[23] All of these factors were interrelated and had to be analyzed carefully.

Travel writers, however, treated the notion of national character as a descriptive, self-evident category not unlike the landscape or the mineral composition of the soil. Every observation could become a permanent feature of a nation's psychological portrait. Some passing scenes and glimpses of social and religious life—a cheating shopkeeper or *vetturino*—were promptly generalized into statements such as "Americans lack probity," "Italians cheat," "Russians are imitators." The cultural facts were assumed to be meaningful in the same way that character traits were, and the movement between the two domains—of facts and of psychological generalizations—was free and unproblematic. Writers often personalized the national character so as to present it more easily. Dealing with a character, with one type, a traveler felt able to find and represent the essence of the visited nation. Once the general idea of a national character, racial type, or climate-related behavior is accepted, each cheating shopkeeper is a particularization of that idea, a source of generalization and its proof. But in reality it was a normative term formulated in a generalized psychological vocabulary. Nations were thought of as people or, rather, as men (though visually they were depicted as women). Further, they were implicitly compared to the standard of a white, mature man, in full possession of his mental and physical capacities, which were seen as active, resourceful, and expanding. The man was either French or English. Of necessity, all other nations had to be found wanting. They were either too young (Americans), or too old (Italians), too feminine (Egyptians), too childish even when old (Chinese). (Not one nation was pro-

---

23. Montesquieu, *De l'esprit des loix*, ed. Jean Brethe de la Gressaye (Paris: Société Les Belles Lettres, 1958), 3: 7–8. English version: *The Spirit of the Laws*, trans. and ed. Anne M. Cohler, Basia Carolyn Miller, and Harold Samuel Stone (Cambridge: Cambridge University Press, 1989), 308–310. The documentation for this monumental work, written in 1749, was largely based on travelers's reports.

nounced to be too masculine.) Russians belonged to the strange in-between category of being too young but already decadent.

In fact, while it was difficult to fit neatly these nations into a single category, Russia seemed to fall directly in between. Diderot was perhaps right, said Madame de Staël, when he remarked that "The Russians rotted before they grew ripe." This remark is sometimes attributed to somebody else, commented her editor.[24] In fact, it was a popular cliché, used with only slight variations and almost mechanically not only about Russia. People kept wondering about the age of the United States. Baudelaire thought America old and young at once, while D. H. Lawrence said it had rotted before it was ripe.[25]

Young but old; civilized but barbaric. "Scratch the Russian and you will find a Tartar," Napoleon was said to be fond of saying; "Open the vest, you will feel the fur," wrote Ségur.[26] In 1872, while advocating the French-Russian anti-German alliance, a writer by the name of Luis exclaimed: "Finally, dear Sirs, you journalists could stop repeating that when one scratches a Russian one discovers a Cossack or a bear" (Corbet 1967, 354). Corbet finds the source of this saying in the words of an Englishman quoted by Count Rostopchin. But the origin of such pieces of wisdom, like that of proverbs, is hard to discover. They were just one way of expressing the in-between nature of Russia. Historians and writers (Michelet, Cyprien Robert, Schnitzler) generalized the idea into the theory of *métissage:* Russians were not pure Slavs, for there is an addition of Mongol blood in them.[27]

Custine's treatment of the problem is very typical. He complains about the double nature of Russia using the current stereotypes.

The alliance of the East and the West, the results of which are discoverable at every step, is the grand characteristic of the Russian empire. . . . The Russians

24. Morroe Berger, in the Preface to Madame de Staël, *Madame de Staël on Politics, Literature, and National Character,* trans., ed., and with an Introduction by Morroe Berger (New York: Doubleday and Co., 1964), 365.
25. See Harry Levin, *"France-Amérique:* The Transatlantic Refraction," in *Refractions: Essays in Comparative Literature* (Oxford: Oxford University Press, 1966), 212–220, esp. 215.
26. In *La Vie de Rostoptchine.* See Corbet, 83.
27. "Semblables à leurs édifices de brique que le moindre accident dépouille du mastic blanc et poli que les couvre, les Russes laissent bientôt apercevoir le Tartare sous cette enveloppe luisante dont une civilisation précoce les a revêtus," wrote Ancelot in 1827 (Corbet, 141). And Balzac saw children behind the adult façade: "Il y a chez les Slaves un côté enfant, comme chez tous les peuples primitivement sauvages, et qui ont plutôt fait irruption chez les nations civilisées, qu'ils ne sont réellment civilisés" (Balzac, *Cousine Bette* [Paris: Garnier, 1962], 211). These are only two of many examples. In fact, these opinions were totally commonplace.

have not yet become polished men, but they are already spoiled savages. (P. 307)

He elaborated the point in another passage:

The customs of the people are the product of the slow and reciprocal action of the laws upon practice, and of practice upon the laws; they do not change as by the stroke of a wand. [A point made by Montesquieu and Karamzin.] The customs of the Russians, notwithstanding all the pretensions of these semi-savages, are and will long remain cruel. Hardly a century passed since they were actual Tartars: it was Peter the Great who first compelled the men to admit women into their social meetings; and underneath their modern elegance, many of these parvenus of civilization retain the hide of the bear; they just turned it inside out, but if one scratches a little, the bristly fur reappears.

An explanatory footnote follows:

These words were spoken by the archbishop of Tarente, of whom Mr. Valéry has just completed a very interesting and thorough portrait in his book *Anecdotes et Curiosités italiennes*. The same thought, I believe, has been expressed even more forcefully by the Emperor Napoleon.

Having quoted these authorities, Custine added as a witness:

Besides, it comes to mind to anyone who has an occasion to observe the Russians.[28]

The predicament Custine finds himself in, and the reason he had to quote others to show that he is not alone, is that none of the definitions turns out to be sufficient. The action of "scratching the Russians" does not produce satisfactory results. One of the most important endeavors of his book is his continuous effort at pinpointing what he thinks is the nature of the Russians, but he never feels satisfied that he has done so. He calls them "semi-savages, Tartars, outwardly elegant parvenus, civilized bears." "According to their notions, discipline is civilization . . . the Russians are not yet civilized. They are enrolled and drilled Tartars, nothing more" (p. 139). "[They] are the Romans of the North. Both people have drawn their arts and sciences from foreign lands" (p. 223). "[They] are disguised Chinese. . . . If they dared to brave the reproach of barbarism as the true Chinese do, access to Petersburg would be as difficult to us as is the access to Peking" (pp. 307–308). "[They] are blond Arabs" (vol. 1: 10), "Oriental people" (p. 18), people, but with

28. These passages, again, had to be translated from the original. See vol. 2, pp. 207–208.

"the hide of bear." "There is between France and Russia a Chinese wall—the Slavonic language and character" (p. 155). It is not Asia, neither is it Europe; it is a "Muscovite civilization" in the land of Siberia, for "Siberia commences on the Vistula" (pp. 346, 155). The difficulty in classifying creates new continents.

Custine is not alone in using comparative labeling to describe Russia. Haxthausen, for example, also compared Russia to Rome—not to emphasize her imitative character but to say that, like Rome, Russia was a young empire with a future. For Napoleon, the Russians were like Teutons—the barbarians from the North who destroyed Rome (Corbet 1967, 44). Such historical comparisons formed the essence of historical and political analysis of the times. Why, one could ask, was there such an insistence on finding the proper comparison? Why not say "the Russians are hiding," "the Russians are lying," without calling them Romans or Tartars? What's in a name? All is in it, or at least may be. In his little travelogue *A Journey to Arzarum*, Alexandr Pushkin described the importance of a name in the following way:

I went out of the tent into the fresh morning air. The sun was rising. Against the clear sky one could see a white-snowcapped, twin-peaked mountain. "What mountain is that?" I asked, stretching myself, and heard the answer: "That's Ararat." What a powerful effect a few syllables can have! Avidly I looked at the Biblical mountain, saw the ark moored to its peak with the hope of regeneration and life, saw both the raven and dove, flying forth, the symbols of punishment and reconciliation. . . .[29]

A translator's note (pitiless little note!) specifies, however, that the mountain Pushkin could see from the place he was in was not Ararat but Aragats! (p. 105.) Similar, and yet what a difference!

Custine himself was well aware of the power of names: ". . . *the steppes! this Oriental word* makes me foresee by itself the unknown and marvelous nature; it wakes up in me a desire that revives my youthfulness, my courage, and reminds me that I was born to travel: such is my fate" (1: 106). How different it would have been if the same flatness were called the prairie. Naming and classifying are serious matters. Traveling—facing a new, incomprehensible reality—is very unsettling. In order to comprehend that new reality, the traveler has to define it, categorize it. The new reality can be, so to speak, pinned down, subdued, domesticated. In this way, even if the traveler's categories are not

29. Alexandr Pushkin, *A Journey to Arzrum*, trans. Birgitta Ingemanson (Ann Arbor, Mich.: Ardis, 1974), 50.

totally applicable, he at least maintains his own identity: in the face of chaos, he says who he is.

The doubts about the nature of Russia have one certain effect: they show to Custine how European he was. Wasn't it obvious? Wasn't Custine as European as could be? There must have been a nagging doubt in his mind, and in the mind of all Europeans. While facing an in-between place such as Russia, one had to ask oneself what it meant to be European. Europe and the West were, after all, composed of many countries, many diverse phenomena. To be European was an ideal state, a *forma mentis;*[30] it meant being rational, logical, controlled, well-educated, profound, chivalrous. But wasn't *that* Europe a thing of the past, destroyed by the Revolution, democracy, and mercantilism? Didn't Custine look for the *real* Europe in Spain, where time has stopped? The borders between Europe and non-Europe were extended in time as well as in space, they passed within each of the Europeans. Hence, in looking at the others, they had to constantly reassess their own positions.

Custine was propelled to Russia by an anxiety that came to him from the French Revolution, which undermined the self-assurance of Europeans such as himself. The boundaries between "us" and "barbarians" became problematic, and one went abroad to reassure oneself that the West was superior to the "others." The questions of identity, although unacknowledged, were at the basis of Custine's effort of comprehending Russia. He wanted to see the difference between himself and those who were not quite civilized, not quite cultured, not quite men. To capture this difference, he planned to use logic. Yet the logical categories, although presented as scientific, were vague and imprecise. Proud of being a dilettante, he strived nevertheless for a description that would be systematic, that would explain the Russians once and for all. And yet he had to take each of their characteristics separately and compare each of them to a different civilization. He believed that a fragment, a segment of the whole, explained that whole in its entirety. Thus his effort was to catch a feature of the national character of the Russians and then on the basis of it to build an adequate, exhaustive description. The difficulty that he—and many others—had in defining the nature of Russia was due to the fact that the terms of the definition, although

30. As said by Federico Chabod; quoted in Reinhard Wittram, *Russia and Europe,* trans. Patrick and Hanneluise Doran (New York: Harcourt, Brace, Jovanovich, 1973), 8.

vague, were nevertheless rigid. There was a mental map of the world with a deep East-West cleavage in its center, and each side governed a definite set of characteristics. What was understood as the nature of Russia did not fit neatly into that division. This is why it was so difficult, and so exhilarating, to write about her. And so irritating. Russia both was and was not Asiatic, was and was not European; "Arab but blond"; young but already old; civilized but primitive; similar to the Romans, the Chinese, the Tartars, yet different from all of them. In the end, after all the specifications and fine points, it still remained unfathomable. This was the moment in which the exhausted writers regularly collapsed into the clichés about the mystery of Russia.

To think means to establish relations. These relations can be of identity, similarity, or dissimilarity. Custine explained the mystery of Russia by establishing for her a set of similarities to other civilizations. The establishment of parallels expressed a belief in an order, in a repeatability of relations, in a continuity of history, in an unchangeable, timeless nature of things. Just as the Romans borrowed from the Greeks, the Russians were borrowing from the French; always, there were, and always there would be, civilizations that were creative and civilizations that were merely imitative. The greatest eighteenth-century French treatise about the nature of history—Montesquieu's *The Spirit of the Laws*—was an expression of this belief in continuity. It was the main source of political ideas for both Custine and Tocqueville. But both of them wrote after the great divide of the Revolution, when things had become uncertain. Although Karamzin is reported to have said that "the Revolution clarified our ideas,"[31] it may have done just the opposite. The categories that for Montesquieu meant order, for Custine and, differently, for Tocqueville, were a constant source of tension. Historical continuity became problematic, and therefore the very nature of the most basic human institutions—the state, the family, war—was liable to change. The categories Montesquieu used did not encapsulate anymore (if they ever did) the things they described in an elegant structure; they just pointed to some of their characteristics. The analogies were partial; a further analogy was needed, and then still another one. For Custine, Tocqueville, and for the Russians themselves, this indeterminacy—the need for another description—was a source of creative energy but also a reason for great anxiety.

31. Quoted in Andrzej Walicki, *A History of Russian Thought*, 54.

A Postscript: The East-West Divide

The discussion is not over yet. Quite the opposite—it is as alive today as ever. The Russians themselves made an attempt at overcoming the duality by creating, in the intellectually fertile period around the time of the Revolution of 1917, the concept of Eurasia.[32] But the East-West divide was not healed. In 1985, the Czech novelist Milan Kundera penned a strong indictment of Russian culture:

In his celebrated Harvard speech, Solzhenitsyn places the starting point of the current crisis of the West squarely in the Renaissance. It is Russia—Russia as a separate civilization—that is explained and revealed by his assessment . . . the Russian mentality maintains a different balance [from the European] between rationality and sentiment; in this other balance (or imbalance) we find the famous mystery of the Russian soul (its profundity as well as its brutality). . . . When feelings supplant rational thought, they become the basis for an absence of understanding, for intolerance. . . . The noblest of national sentiments stand ready to justify the greatest of horrors, and man, his breast swelling with lyric fervor, commits atrocities in the sacred name of love.

Although the supremacy of feeling is a phenomenon that, in Kundera's view, came about with the birth of Christianity, the Renaissance introduced into Europe this other, rational tradition, which Kundera claims as his own. This leads him to be repelled by Dostoevsky but attracted to Diderot, and it underlies his combination of rationality and irony. The supremacy of feeling is not considered by Kundera to be an alien, non-European tradition, and therefore he does not "expel" Russia to Asia. He nevertheless summons the tradition of anti-Russian writings ("the *famous* mystery of Russian soul") and asks, to use Lotman's terms, that Europe be left in peace, in the neutral sphere of ironic rationality, neither sacred nor profane.[33]

Kundera's entire novelistic work has as its main protagonist a man who tries, against the pressures of the extreme politicization of every-day life, to live according to the principles of an ironic (and hedonistic), rational, secular mind. This man even claims a territory for himself—the land of Central Europe—a mythical Middle Europe that denotes "a culture or a fate" rather than geography and, therefore, is

32. See Riasanovsky, 19–29.
33. Milan Kundera, "An Introduction to a Variation," *The New York Times Book Review*, January 6, 1985.

above traditional divisions. In an article about this spiritual entity, Barbara Torunczyk includes as its citizens intellectuals and writers Milan Kundera, Tomas Venclova, Czeslaw Milosz, Joseph Brodsky, Adam Zagajewski, Mircea Eliade, and Witold Gombrowicz. All but Brodsky, who was born in Leningrad and grew up there, are or were exiles in the Western world from what is called Eastern Europe. Brodsky, too, tries to liberate art from the tyranny of politics. However, in an answer to Kundera's article, he emphatically rejects the East-West divide and a concept of culture in which there was no place for Dostoevsky.[34] And he eloquently attacks Kundera on his own territory, that is, Europe.

Mr. Kundera is a Continental, a European man. These people are seldom capable of seeing themselves from the outside. It they do, it's invariably within the context of Europe, for Europe offers them a scale against which their importance is detectable. The advantage of stratified society lies precisely in the ease with which the individual may appreciate his advancement. The reverse side of the coin, however, is that one senses limits, and beyond them, expanses where this individual's life appears irrelevant. That's why a sedentary people always resents nomads: apart from the physical threat, a nomad compromises the concept of border. The people of the Continent are very much a people whose existence is defined by borders, be it that of a nation, community, class, tradition, hierarchy—or of reason. Add to this the mesmerizing bureaucratic structure of the state, and you get a man with no sense of contingencies, either for himself or for his race. Never having heard of multiple options, he can at best only contemplate a wholesale special alternative, one like what he already has— East or West.

Brodsky refers back to Diderot when he points to the Western origin of Marxist ideology, and he reproaches Kundera's "sense of geography . . . conditioned by his sense of history." But Brodsky's sense of geography is mystifying: he writes that Kundera is from "Eastern Europe (Western Asia to some)" but also calls him "Continental" and calls Europe "The Continent," as if Brodsky were an Englishman, or an islander of some sort, or perhaps American. And he himself operates within the binary oppositions, the terms of which define each other. Although he refuses to accept Kundera's divisions as binding—if he did he would find himself in Asia—he uses these divisions nevertheless. As much as a nomad compromises the idea of border, he is necessary for the existence of the very concept of sedentary people. So is the East for the existence

34. Joseph Brodsky, "Why Milan Kundera Is Wrong About Dostoyevsky," *The New York Times Book Review,* February 17, 1985. Barbara Torunczyk's article is entitled "Kings and Spirits in the Eastern European Tales," in *Cross Currents* 7 (1988): 183–206.

of the West. Brodsky attempts to transcend this division by proposing a community of free people to which both "the laughter of Diderot" and "the sorrows of Dostoevsky" belong.

But it turns out that for Brodsky too the West of free people exists in opposition to the East of enslaved masses. In a complicated travel essay, *Flight from Byzantium,* Brodsky establishes the border between these two communities.

Dreading a repetition, [he writes self-consciously and with irony] I will nevertheless state again that if Byzantine soil turned out to be so favorable for Islam it was most likely because of its ethnic texture—a mixture of races and nationalities that had neither local nor, moreover, over-all memory of any kind of coherent tradition of individualism. Dreading generalizations, I will add that the East means, first of all, a tradition of obedience, of hierarchy, of profit, of trade, of adaptability: a tradition, that is drastically alien to the principles of a moral absolute, whose role—I mean the intensity of the sentiment—is fulfilled here by the idea of kinship, of family. I foresee objections, and am even willing to accept them, in whole or in part. But no matter what extreme of idealization of the East we may entertain we'll never be able to ascribe to it the least semblance of democracy.

A historical illustration follows, of a castration, somewhere around the year 1000, of an emperor's uncle so as "to eliminate any possible claim to the throne."[35]

Isn't Brodsky's flight from Byzantium a flight into the old categories? Certainly, he does point out where *we* are, and *ubi leones*. Although geographic divisions became fuzzy, the need to know who we are, it seems, makes us search out the others. And, it seems, there are always plenty of them.

35. Joseph Brodsky, "Flight from Byzantium," *Less Than One: Selected Essays* (New York: Farrar, Straus, Giroux, 1986), 393–446; the quotation is on p. 417.

5

Self-Assertion and the Nature of Others

"Any movement along a plane surface which is not dictated by physical necessity is a spatial form of self-assertion, be it empire building or tourism," writes Brodsky in the previously mentioned essay (p. 389). In fact, Custine's *La Russie en 1839* is as interesting as it is— and, as a work of art, as successful as it is—because, along with being a tenacious attempt to understand the complex phenomenon of Russia, it is an effort at self-assertion and self-description. And, as was already mentioned, Custine had as many problems with his identity—or rather with his place in postrevolutionary society—as he did with the nature of Russia.

In the introduction to the shortened 1975 edition of *La Russie,* Pierre Nora called Custine a *"man of all exiles,"* and he specified:

. . . *historical exile* of this great decapitated family of the Old Régime, excluded from participation in social life by the Revolution and the new order. *Moral exile* of the man condemned to practice customs he himself considered as vices. . . . *Social exile* of this aristocrat rejected by his caste. . . . *Literary exile* . . . [of a writer of second or third rank]. (Pp. 10–11, emphasis added)

Custine was a man of all exiles, and it is not surprising that he understood Russia first of all as a place of exile—a gigantic Siberia—and then, vaguely, as an exiled place, as an outside. It may be that the need to locate Russia on a map returned obsessively because it accompanied this other, personal need to find a place for himself.

Olivier Gassouin, the author of *Le Marquis de Custine. Le courage d'être soi-même,* considers Custine's attachment to the idea of personal freedom—an idea expressed in his acceptance of his homosexuality—as the basis of his understanding of Russia.[1] The most admiring biographer of Custine, Julien-Frédéric Tarn, explains the outstanding range, depth, and perspicacity of *La Russie en 1839* as being due to Custine's character and situation. It is "his long experience of the comedy of salons, of worldly pretenses . . . his schizophrenic hypersensitivity of a homosexual . . . and of a mystic" that allowed his "pitiless clairvoyance." This is the context within which Tarn fits Custine's method "which consists in multiplying points of view [and names!], showing the most different, the most unexpected aspects, choosing the most contrasting lights, so as to create a global vision of the thing he described" (Tarn 1985, 524).

Those who have written about Custine had a clear understanding of the drama of his situation. The titles of books and articles already quoted here talk about "the martyr of Romanticism" (Philippe Sénart) or "les misfortunes of exactitude" (Tarn). Custine was a torn man. He felt acutely the conflictual, fragmentary character of his life. Speaking about his life—always indirectly, as the life of a traveler—he speaks of nothing but contradictions. He declares that there is a difficulty in combining thinking with feeling, and feeling with writing. The very nature of things was contradictory. "As soon as I look into my soul," he confessed in a letter to Rahel Varnhagen, "I find there only doubts, darkness, agitation, scruples. . . ."[2]

To understand the pain and suffering involved in his contradictions and moral conflicts, we must return to Custine's social situation. We can presume—although we do not have any direct evidence (as far as is known, he never wrote about the subject)—that his homosexuality was a source of acute distress. For a while he did lead a married life, even though he was already linked with Edward de Sainte-Barbe—the Englishman whose family came from France and who remained his companion for life. The tragic premature death of his wife and son freed him to live the way he did. He was ardently and traditionally Catholic, and it is difficult to suppose that he could reconcile his faith with his sexuality. His social milieu did not respect him. The writers and artists—his new companions—did not approve of him, either. Sainte-Beuve, certainly

---

1. Custine cohabited with a man and did not hide his male lovers. Olivier Gassouin, *Le Marquis de Custine. Le courage d'être soi-même,* Preface by Hugo Marsan (Paris: Lumière & Justice, 1987), 62.

2. Quoted in Gassouin, 27.

the most influential literary critic of the time, wrote frankly and brutally: "Custine's reputation here is so bad, and this is so notoriously well-justified when it comes to morals . . . that although people read him, and take a liking to him, no one admires him. It has been almost necessary for him to flee."[3] In a letter to an English friend, Stendhal (always in financial trouble) mentioned Custine's homosexuality and then went on to write: "His wealth, more than his behavior, is a stain."[4] He was "held in contempt by some, pitied by others, a problem for everyone," wrote his biographer Pierre de Lacretelle, in 1956.[5] Custine, who wished very much to be admired, demanded comments on his books, carefully read the reviews, and felt rejection very keenly. Many of his letters are a testimony to his bitterness and weariness. He was a frustrated poet, an author of a threatrical flop and of unadmired novels. He was reluctantly received by the aristocracy, yet he was unable to join the artistic élite; his birthrights were partially abrogated, yet he was not recognized on the basis of merit. He was not even respected.

Perhaps his estrangement from his class might have been mended with the passage of time after the scandal that revealed his homosexuality. It seems, however, that in some way he courageously welcomed the freedom to live with the men of his choice. As if to increase his estrangement, these men—or at least the two most important ones—were foreigners. The already-mentioned companion of his life, Edward de Sainte-Barbe, was an Englishman, and the great passion of his later years was a young Pole, Ignacy Gurowski. Neither of these men could be integrated into society, as wives could have been. Most of Custine's other lovers probably belonged to the lower classes. Some of his most important friends—the German Wilhelm Hesse and the German-Jewish Rahel Varnhagen—were foreign as well. Most of his correspondents (and he wrote many letters) were women. He traveled a lot and did his best writing about his travels. His masterpiece—*La Russie en 1839*—was written, elaborated, and corrected abroad. He said many times about himself that he was dislocated, foreign, exiled from his country and from his times.

The dissociation from a natural context—the outsideness—had an importance for Custine's understanding of Russia. We should repeat here the famous declaration from the beginning of his book: "I went to

3. In a private letter. Quoted after Tarn, 535.
4. Quoted in Gassouin, 53.
5. Quoted in George Frost Kennan, *The Marquis de Custine and His "Russia in 1839"* (Princeton, N.J.: Princeton University Press, 1971), 6.

Russia to seek for arguments against representative government. I returned from Russia a partisan of constitutions" (p. 16). This declaration could be easily understood as a literary device: it would make out of a simple journey a discovery *à rebours,* a descent into hell, a gigantic disappointment. It would justify the writing of yet another book about Russia, when so many had been produced already. Could Custine, a quintessential Westerner—a Parisian aristocrat, writer, and esthete—truly expect to find a place for himself in this faraway, "Asiatic," and "barbaric" place? In fact, there is one dimension of Custine's life that made such expectation and the following disappointment possible—his social origin.

During his lifetime, Russia was a place of exile for many of Custine's fellow French aristocrats (as was America). Tsar Nicholas I made a point of welcoming Custine—although he must have known about his objectionable "moeurs"—precisely because of this antirevolutionary class solidarity. Custine was keenly interested in a country in which one could still be an aristocrat. But the same class solidarity dictated to him a sense of social obligation that forced him to criticize the tsar. To fulfill his duty as a nobleman, Custine had to keep his independence.

It was not an easy thing to do. In a letter to Madame Hanska, Balzac, terrified that their acquaintance with Custine might cause the confiscation by the tsar of Madame Hanska's Ukrainian possessions warns her and predicts: ". . . he is writing a book . . . this book will be terrible. . . . There will be storms, even more justified because of his having been well received."[6] He criticized Custine for breaking the code of hospitality, and in this he expressed the opinion of many. Most of his critics dismissed him for his indiscretion and lack of gratitude. In anticipation of such a reaction, the editor's and the author's prefaces to *La Russie* are devoted to a justification of Custine's decision to write about Russia. Several times in the book, Custine returns to this point. And indeed, his situation was difficult. While in Russia, he was most cordially accepted at the court by the emperor himself, who held long (and "frank," as Custine points out) talks with his French visitor. The very amiable empress, the crown prince, and many aristocrats and dignitaries were unusually welcoming to him. He was enlightened about various interesting subjects, permitted to see things and people, invited to the most interesting events. He was provided—and this is an interesting custom—with a guide-driver, who aided him in all his trips inside Russia. Since it was known that he had

6. Quoted after Tarn, 508.

already written some *voyages,* everybody in officialdom went out of his way to impress him as favorably as possible. They were acting as representatives of their culture and state and behaved according to diplomatic protocol. He smiled, talked, listened, observed, and wrote, but his book bitterly disappointed the expectations of his hosts.

The emperor was especially furious. "I am alone to blame; I encouraged and patronized the visit of this scoundrel," he was reported to say. (Later, however, he must have found the book interesting for he read aloud some of its parts to his family.)[7] In fact, it was a serious breach of etiquette. To make such a decision, Custine must have been truly shocked by what he saw and understood in Russia. There are many ways in which he explains his decision. He had to write the truth, he insisted—his conscience was more important than his manners. He could not submit to the pressures of "their political hospitality," which consisted in (as the Russians themselves say in French) *enguirlander* ("engarlanding") the guest with ceremonies, favors, and flattery, to make him blind to social injustice so he will report favorably on Russia (p. 239). "They refuse you nothing, but they accompany you everywhere; politeness becomes a pretext for maintaining a watch over you. In this manner, they tyrannize over us while pretending to do us honor" (p. 306). Besides, there is no real hospitality and politeness among people who are not free; "here, politeness is only the art of reciprocally disguising the double fear that each experiences and inspires" (p. 233). Reticence becomes complicity in Russia, and the traveler who has social position, character, and independence has a duty to record what he had seen (pp. 227–237). The pressure to conform made Custine more tender toward Karamzin: he could see that one needed to be circumspect in Russia. What made Custine understand Karamzin (although perhaps mistakenly, for Karamzin did not write out of fear!) was the gilded chain of being himself, at least for a moment, a courtier. "The chain, though gilded, did not appear to me the less heavy" (p. 252). He did not want to be the tsar's courtier.

To write a travel book is a social act. Although Custine declared that his writing expressed only himself, he represented a tradition, a country, a culture, and even a specific class. And he entered into a relationship with his hosts—a complicated relationship of which one of the aspects was its diplomatic side. Custine belonged to the West, but he was also an aristocrat; therefore he belonged to a social layer that crossed the

7. George F. Kennan, vii.

borders of countries and perhaps even continents. Nicholas I was higher-but-equal in this social dimension, and the relationship between them could take one of two familiar shapes: that of dependency between the ruler and his courtier, or that of an independent nobleman defying the king. Custine opted for the second role, although the traces of the first one remained throughout the text.[8]

The dictates of polite behavior must have been difficult to defy. Custine, however, was not only an aristocrat, he was also a former victim of political persecution. He, who so much needed approval, was flattered by the attention, recognition, and respect accorded him by his Russian hosts. And yet he could not turn away from the signs of unhappiness and misery he detected everywhere—especially in cases in which he could observe the all-powerful state acting against its citizens. In chapter 17 he chillingly described a street-fight that the interference of a gendarme changed into the killing of one of the men involved (pp. 275–276). Once he had noticed the animosity of the state against its own people—its total disregard of the individual—he saw Siberia everywhere. The everyday life of Russia was for him one of continuous persecution.

He knew that the French public, although perhaps fascinated by his behavior, would disapprove of it. But his hesitations had to do as well with the role he had set himself to play. He called on Western civilization to judge Russia. He criticized in Russia a lack of the spirit of chivalry and of a code of honor, but he himself was breaking one of its cardinal rules. Good manners—that is, manners accepted by a social group as binding—have the function of regulating the life of that group and of separating that group from others, and therefore of establishing the group's identity. Unexpectedly, Custine found himself in the same social group with people toward whom he felt no loyalty, and the limitations of protocol became too binding for him. He swiftly proceeded to prove that the code did not apply to this people.

Even as aristocrats, he reasoned, Russians were in a separate category. The nobility in Russia consists of slaves who own other slaves; to be truly polite, as we have seen, one has to be free. But a fundamental Russian characteristic was that of being "something else." Placed "on

---

8. It was visible even 138 years later to Ronald Hingley, who wrote: ". . . Custine was accusing the whole nation of being intoxicated with servility, and commenting on the general atmosphere of sycophancy; of which, incidentally, one seems to detect not a little in that French Marquis's own attitude to the all-powerful Nicholas I." *The Russian Mind* (New York: Charles Scribner's Sons, 1977), 194.

the confines of Asia . . . upon the limits of two continents . . . submitting to the violence and incoherence attendant upon the contact of two civilizations entirely different in character" (p. 229), Russia consists of two nations, "Russia as she is, and Russia as they would have her to appear in the eyes of Europe" (p. 232). "It is not in the nature of that which is European to amalgamate perfectly with that which is Asiatic" (p. 229). Therefore everything is hidden or distorted. "The manners and the policy of the East are here disguised under European urbanity" (p. 208). It is the country of façades, and the duty of the traveler is to look behind them.

He could not expect to learn the truth from the Russians themselves, as they were governed by an overriding duplicity.

They have a dexterity in lying, a natural proneness to deceit, which is revolting. Things that I admire elsewhere, I hate here, because I find them too dearly paid for; order, patience, calmness, elegance, respectfulness, the natural and moral relations which ought to exist between those who think and those who execute—in short, all that gives a worth and a charm to well-organized societies, all that gives a meaning and an object to political institutions, is lost and confounded here in one single sentiment—that of fear . . . it is not order, it is the evil of chaos; where liberty is wanting, there soul and truth must be wanting also. Russia is a body without life, a colossus which subsists only by its head. (P. 233)

The essential duality leads to a reversal, and the world of Russia is the world à rebours. What is politeness in France in Russia becomes a lie. In such a world, to abide by the code of honor is to become the accomplice of the government.

But if only Russia *were* truly the world à *rebours!* Then the situation would have been simple. That would explain everything, it would satisfy the need for clarity and definition. But the world of Russia is far from being simply black by contrast to the white of the West. Custine continuously returns to and insistently reformulates the same points, as if the meaning were always escaping him. Although he *had to* break the rules of hospitality—to deceive the deceivers—he is nevertheless bothered by it. Although he thinks that a country should preserve its own culture, he believes in the superiority of Western civilization; therefore, its partial adoption could be beneficial for Russians. Although he thought of himself as a Westerner, here he found himself conversing in his native language with Russians of his social milieu; although everything in this country was new, there was always something unnervingly familiar as well.

In fact, the problem of language is indicative of a deeper confusion. Russian nobility spoke two languages, belonged to two distinct cultures—one native and one foreign. Many of Custine's interlocutors spoke French the way he did. For Custine this was very upsetting, and he was unable to attend to the content of their words "unproblematically," the way he would if they were French. The meaning of their words was undermined by the co-presence of the other, "real" language. He felt that their French was only a "façade" hiding their mysterious Russianness. When with Russians, these noblemen most often spoke Russian (not always!) and behaved according to a different set of rules.[9] This phenomenon defied Custine's idea of the unity of human person expressed by a unified code of behavior and one language. (Although that person would be torn by internal contradictions.) Only a one-language person could be authentic ("le naturel" was the term he used). A French nobleman's life was "coherent," that is, monocultural, while the Russian's life was, in a manner of speaking, swinging like a pendulum between two poles. The more Frenchified the Russian became, the more inauthentic he seemed to Custine. But if the Russian's French was imperfect, Custine's native ear found it jarring. For him a Slavic accent in French was no less inauthentic than the perfect Parisian spoken by some Russians. Either the purity of language or the purity of culture was offended.

The concept of purity—of a language, of a nation, of a race—is fundamental to the way Custine and his contemporaries thought about their identity. The aspiration toward purity dates in the history of the French language from the sixteenth century and runs parallel to the centralization and strengthening of the French state. The pure language was the language of the political and cultural center—the language continuously defined as pure in opposition to its margins. Purity, then, was a political concept, and as such it was used by Custine. It is interesting to note that he shared that understanding of the purity of language with some moments of the Revolution, when an attempt was made to establish firm control over the language. The decree of the Brumaire 15 of the Second Year opposed regional "vulgar dialects" for maintaining "the infancy of the mind and the old age of the prejudices."[10] This

9. See I. Lotman, "Everyday Behavior," 70–76.

10. Jacques Chaurand, *Histoire de la langue française* (Paris: Presses Universitaires de France, 1969), 92.

prescriptive tendency toward language was shared by pro- and antirevolutionary Frenchmen.[11]

The question of language was always central to French thinking about culture. If the authenticity of a culture was not recognized, its language could be demoted to a status of a dialect. During a discussion in 1840 in the Chambre des Députés regarding a project to found a chair of Slavic languages at the Collège de France, a *député* called Auguis objected: "The Slavic language is not a language proper. . . . Whatever is original among Slavs is a translation from works that belong to France or Germany."[12] In matters of language, Custine shared the attitudes of his contemporaries. He accepted as a matter of course the superiority of French and strived for purity and clarity, in his sentences as well as in his entire work. As a topic, Russia defied this purity and clarity at all levels. It spoke too many languages,[13] literally and figuratively. All of Custine's sources, critical and laudatory alike, declared that the Russians were a racial, cultural, and spiritual mixture. Russian geography was unclearly delineated, its role in history was not yet truly determined, its future was mysterious. Moreover, it eluded the traveler's powers of observation. Superficially, there were no obstacles: the nobility spoke French, and that, for Custine,

11. There was a difference between the French and Russian attitudes toward language. French was compared to its origin—Latin, the language used for intellectual discourse and exercise of power. The relationship of the French language to Latin was very unlike that between Russian and French. French was just one of the Western languages used by the Russians, and it came late in the development of written Russian. Byzantine Christianity had its own language—Old Church Slavonic. It was based on a language formulated in the ninth century by Cyril and Methodius for (Slavic) Moravian converts and, unlike Latin of Europe in the Middle Ages, Old Church Slavonic cut Russia off from the outside (which in this case meant Greek) tradition. Russia did not have the experience of pervasive bilingualism that France and Western Europe had undergone: all West-European languages were in steady contact with Latin. Although many foreign words have been incorporated into Russian, the contact Russian language had with other languages was external. Neither did the concept of purity of the Russian establish itself as dominant. Many Russian writers wrote in French, Pushkin included. One of the best Russian novels—*War and Peace*—has entire pages of conversations in French.

12. Corbet, 168.

13. "How could the national genius develop in a society where people speak four languages without knowing any one well? Originality of thought has a nearer connection than is imagined with the purity of idiom. This fact has been forgotten in Russia for a century, and in France for some years now. Our children will feel the effects of the rage for English nurses which possessed all 'fashionable' [in English in the original] mothers" (p. 289). This is not the only time Custine alerts his readers to the dangers the excessive use of English brings to the French language. He fears the vulnerability of French, its purity constantly assaulted by foreign influences.

made it a French-speaking country. (There was no question of learning Russian: people "worth" talking to knew French.) Even though talking was easy, the entire "continent" was left linguistically obscure. The same duality of light-and-shadow dwelled inside each of his interlocutors. They were not passive objects of his inquiry. They asserted themselves, as if their relationship with him was one of reciprocity; but when they were showing themselves similar to the foreigners, they were hiding their gigantic other self. If they denied this difference they made him angry and confused.

This situation made Custine suspect deceit and duplicity everywhere. He recognized a spy when he met one—Nikolai Ivanovich Grech, who was a fellow-passenger on the boat on which Custine went to Russia, was a spy for the Russian government, and Custine identified him as such. His distrust of certain of his noble interlocutors—especially of Alexander Ivanovich Turgenev—turned out to be justified; the archives show that while in the West Turgenev did report to the Russian government on his compatriots. But to find people who were spying on him, Custine did not, in fact, have to look so far afield. He, like most privileged travelers, was given a guide—a driver he called "feldjäger"—who arranged for all his needs and controlled his every step. Custine was very afraid of him, but he was helpless to do anything about it in a country where a foreigner could not pass unnoticed. When he arrived, driven by his feldjäger, at a destination—be it a museum, a palace, a park, a fortress—there he always found another guide waiting for him, to lead him around and explain everything. In this way—Custine bitterly complained—everything, while shown, is concealed and obscured. "Nothing can be seen here alone. A native of the country is always with you to do the honors of the public establishments. . . . Russia [is] scarcely better seen in Petersburg than in France" (p. 187).

The spy-guide played in Custine's visit a role similar to that of the French language: he made everything accessible while at the same time falsifying it hopelessly. Everything seemed clearer but was in reality skewed. Virtually all visitors to Russia, starting with Herberstein (or even earlier), were forbidden to travel by themselves. The problem of language was specific to French visitors and limited to certain periods; the spying guide is present in all Russian travelogues. A constant companion, a guide (in recent times an Intourist agent) is present sometimes as a character in the book; sometimes only his shadow remains. Nevertheless it has to be kept in mind that almost all the visits we have read about have been made in the company of a state-appointed controller. In tsarist Russia, the guides limited the visitor's access to places deemed unrepresentative of Russian reality or too important militarily. (All the public buildings were in any case guarded—the suspiciousness being directed toward natives and foreigners equally.) In the Soviet Union, particularly at the height of Stalinism, two other ways of controlling visitors were practiced: one obligatory itinerary for all was provided (always the same steel mill, maternity ward, day-care center, kolkhoz, or model prison), and group visits were required. Whatever the variation, the guests became (pampered) children for the time of the visit. Some guests rejected the game (Gide); some accepted it, especially since a lot of flattery was added (G. B. Shaw). In every case, the country was difficult to see. As Custine wrote, "Most assuredly it is not sufficient to visit this country in order to know it" (p. 187).

Like most modern travelers, he left home because he was looking for something new.

We travel to escape the world in which we have passed our lives, [but] we find it is impossible to leave it behind.

It is the new uniformity of customs, the lack of difference that he mourns in "modern Europe," where

one is at a loss where to go to find original manners, and habits which may be taken as the true expression of characters. The customs recently adopted by each people are the results of a crowd of borrowed notions. There arises from this digest of all characters in the crucible of universal civilization, a monotony that is any thing but conductive to the enjoyment of the traveller. (P. 417)

This complaint, so common (and only partially true) as to become one of the most frequent travel clichés, has a certain built-in ambiguity: the familiar may be reassuring in an alien environment. Moreover, this yearning for difference was in conflict with Custine's dream, expressed in his preface and repeated in the book itself, of unity of all nations in spiritual Catholicism—unity that could be realized only by overcoming differences. Today, he said,

the human race is reuniting, languages are being lost, nations are disappearing, philosophy is reducing creeds to a matter of private belief. . . . The malediction of Babel approaches its prescribed term, and the nations are going to be one, notwithstanding all that has tended to disunite them. (P. 418)

But in Russia he disliked the similarities he could see. Equally, he disliked the differences.

The problem of language was one of the reasons for his ambivalence. It was good that French, the language of civilization, was spreading. But its use brought along imitation of things French. Russian literature was not national; all its writers, including the best, were imitators.[14] As was well known, the Slavic race was imitative by nature. (Custine read this in many of his sources, including the most laudatory. It was usually thought to be a result of the mixing of races.)[15] The visit to Russia, where many of his interlocutors spoke French, confirmed this opinion. The question of language must have been crucial in this matter.

Similar accusations have been leveled against another "new" nation using an "old" language: the United States. The derivative character of America was felt most keenly by the British. Many elements of the American political system, customs, and language were modeled after and similar to the English: similar but different. The difference implied an imperfection, a failing; English language was a standard and its American version a distortion. In fact, the entire country—as described in books by Captain Basil Hall, Mrs. Frances Trollope, or Charles Dickens, for example—seemed a distortion. And since Americans were imitators by nature, no national literature was expected to arise.

The imitative nature of the Slavic race was a cliché in the literature of the period. Custine's attraction to this notion might have come from his own struggle with imitation: the derivative character of his writings. But—what was very important—the concepts of distortion and imitation provided a powerful interpretative and organizing tool. Double in their nature, they implied a model and an imperfect copy. In Custine's descriptive practice, this duality was expressed by a pair, of which the second term contradicted the very essence of the first. The Russians had "a natural dexterity in lying" ("natural" is a positive word for Custine) and a natural talent for imitation; their order was in reality disguised chaos, their hospitality Oriental (therefore false), their politeness superficial (pp. 233, 239). They did not have the death penalty in their legal code—it was abolished—and yet they executed people by sentencing them to beating with the knout (the rod), not naming what they were doing. Truly, a confessed tyranny would have been better than this

14. Custine's most famous mistake was to dismiss Pushkin (and Mickiewicz) as able imitators of foreign literary fashions. See pp. 288–289; in the original this discussion of the relationship between national language and foreign models is much longer.

15. See J.-H. Schnitzler, *La Russie, la Pologne et la Finlande: Tableau statistique, géographique et historique* (Saint Petersburg and Paris: Jules Renouard, 1835), 13, 524. Schnitzler was one of the sources quoted by Custine.

masked one. The entire country, although it seemed to be nothing but a huge, open expanse, was in reality a prison, with the Tsar Nicholas as its warden. The description has always two opposite terms—expanse versus prison—but the second term does not dispose of the first one, and the description does not arrive at the opposite of the first term. Order in Russian society may hide a profound chaos, but it is also an evident military order—a rigid organization of life—which Custine complained about several times. Emerging in description, the new, third term is elusive, incomplete. Tension is not resolved. Russia falls between categories. The blond Arabs, the Romans of the North, the chaotic order evade again the attempts at definition. The essence of the country is still mysterious. The search has to continue.

In the detailed summaries that precede each of his chapters, Custine gives us an idea of what problems and mysteries he attempts to solve; " . . . What truth there is in the popularity of the tsar . . . Russia as it is shown to foreigners and Russia as it is . . . The essence of things . . . Dissimulation as a point of order."[16] But he also has an entire system of titles which dissect his narrative into mini-genres and show his models. There are, for example, *anecdotes* and longer *histoires;* a quotation from an author is indicated in the summary as *un mot de* . . . (Madame de Staël about Russians being like Tartars, for example). There are also *tableaux,* both of *moeurs* and of nature; there are *portraits* and *caractères,* the first stressing the physical presence of the persons described, the second their moral characteristics. There are long *réflexions* and *définitions, souvenirs* and *paysages.* All of these genres are repeatedly named in the summaries and abundantly used in the text. Custine's narration is composed of well-structured, closed units, which by themselves are independent genres learned by Custine in his French lessons.[17] These genres were used because Custine was writing a work of literature: just as "poetic" words were essential to a poetic style, so were literary mini-units essential for a literary work. It was an important point, because *les*

16. From the summary preceding letter 15 (2: 107). Edited out of the American edition.

17. A manual for French composition, published when Custine was learning how to write, combined in its title the idea of the beauty of language with morality. Written by a Monsieur Noel, *Leçons françaises de littérature et de morale* (Paris, 1812) offered various models for different types of compositions: Madame de Sévigné's letter on the death of Vatel was to be imitated when writing *narrations,* Chateaubriand's description of the Niagara Falls when attempting a *tableau;* "L'Amour propre" by La Rochefoucauld was to be followed when writing a *définition,* and so forth. Besides the models, the manuals offer mostly interdictions, and the students were constantly warned of mistakes against the purity of the language. See Chaurand, 96.

voyages were not literature. Each single traveler had to decide whether he would try to follow in Chateaubriand's footsteps (to Jerusalem) and aspire to high literature, even to poetry, or whether he would be content to be prosaic, informative, and useful. *La Russie en 1839* could not but follow Chateaubriand.

But what is more important, by using classical literary genres Custine expressed a certain attitude toward the reality he tried to describe. All of these forms speak of a belief in essence that can be apprehended in description. A well-taken portrait or a convincing tableau were to reflect a person one had encountered, or a thing. The travel memoir—a loose structure—could then accommodate these assimilable segments of reality. Unfortunately, Russia's reality (and perhaps any reality) was unmasterable with this method. Russia proved elusive, incompatible with beautiful style. It was best suited for endless, inelegantly long quotations from her historian. Though described in many volumes, and summarized with many an aphorism, it remained mysterious.

The mystery of Russia is the key concept in this entire effort of definition. It explains, or at least in a way unifies, an entire set of phenomena that otherwise would have remained random. The duality of Russian culture, the lying to foreigners, the sentimentality combined with brutality, all of this is "hidden [and revealed] in the mist of the Slavonic soul."[18] Combined with other notions—of race, linguistic purity, and social behavior—it creates a system for the description of Russian civilization.

In the opposition culture-versus-nature, Russia, although covered by a "European veneer" of culture, finds herself on the side of nature. The notion of the mystery of Russia is also inherent in the relation the West had to Russia. It is related to the "impurity"—the mixed character—of Russian culture and to the ensuing resistance of this culture to the categories applied to it. The West, complicated as it was, was referred to only as the West, whereas Russia was Rome, and Greece, Byzantium, the Orient, the North. None of these names were accepted as final, none exhausted her nature. The West did not and could not understand Russia, therefore Russia was in its essence mysterious. What Simone de Beauvoir wrote about the "eternal mystery of femininity" describes the West's relationship to Russia as well: "The categories in which men think of the world are established from their point of view as absolute:

18. As Eric Newby wrote in 1978(!) in his *Big Train Ride: Ride on the Trans-Siberian Railway* (Middlesex, Eng.: Penguin Books, 1978), 55.

they misconceive reciprocity, here as elsewhere. A mystery for man, woman is considered to be mysterious in essence."[19] The mystery of Russia contained all that was incomprehensible and created a contrast with the clarity and transparence of the West. This is one of the meanings of Custine's feeling of discovery. A traveler is a "speaking mirror" (*L'Espagne,* 1: 86); his own face could be clear and understandable only if reflected in the mysteriousness of Russia.

19. Simone de Beauvoir, *The Second Sex* (New York: Knopf, 1953), 257.

6

Mental Geography

Siberia

"How many reasons for not going to Siberia!" wrote Custine at the beginning of his journey. He did not plan to go literally to Siberia: for him Russia and Siberia were synonymous. "And yet I go there."[1] From a country that for Herberstein was too distant even to know if it had cities, Siberia was now a place that was everywhere. Siberia was, in fact, not only a place but also a state of mind.

As we have already said, geography may become a way of thinking about identity. The division between "our" world and the world where "lions dwell" may "help the mind to intensify its own sense of itself by dramatizing the distance and difference between what is close to it and what is far away." This is how Edward Said describes the function of what he calls "imaginative geography and history."[2] The way Custine used the name of Siberia is an example of imaginative geography at work.

Custine's opinions were based on what he saw, what he read, and what he imagined. Certainly, the place he knew best was the center of Russian political life—the court—as far away from Siberia as one could get in Russia. At court he saw unmatched splendors, but also a servility

1. Custine, 1: 127.
2. As opposed to "positive" geography and history; see Edward Said, *Orientalism,* 55.

and submission he did not see anywhere else. He accused Russians of using civilization to increase their importance and power and not to improve the life of their society: it was only their image they were worrying about (*La Russie en 1839*, vol. 1: 97). The enslavement of the peasants and of the nobility; the brutality of persecution; the forced uniformity of behavior, dress, and thinking; the military organization of everyday life accompanied by extreme poverty and dirt all made him call Russia "a desert." A desert was a place of solitude, where no civilization could be found. Romantic writers applied that term to many countries, including the United States. For Custine, the Russia of Nicholas I was such a desert, and there was even a name for it—Siberia.

Siberia commenced on the Vistula,[3] that is, in the partitioned Poland, wrote Custine in one of his attempts to delineate Siberia's borders. Wherever fear governed, there he saw Siberia. The many beginnings of his voyage, the very slowness of his approach to Russia (we have to wait for at least two hundred pages before he crosses the border) are an expression of this geographical indeterminacy.[4] Once he was in Russia, Siberia was what he saw behind every façade.

At each step I here take, I see rising before me the phantom of Siberia, and I think of all that is implied in the name of that political desert, that abyss of misery, this tomb of living men,—a world of fabulous griefs, a land peopled with infamous criminals and sublime heroes, a colony without which this Empire would be as incomplete as a palace without cellars. (P. 239)

Custine was not an explorer, and he never ventured very far toward the northeast. Interested mainly in the political system and in high society, he stayed mostly in the salons. Once, though, he traveled on a road that turned out to be the great exile route to Siberia. The psychological proximity (he was not any closer to Siberia) did not make his description any more concrete.

Siberia! This word made my blood run cold . . . that Russian hell is incessantly before me with all its phantoms. It has upon me the effect that the eye of the basilisk has upon the fascinated bird. (P. 504)

3. Warsaw was then one of Russia's provincial cities. See *The Empire of the Czar*, 155.
4. There is a special topic that should be addressed here: transportation. Every travel book starts with a boat or train. Going to Russia at that time was truly an adventure. Custine's list of means of transportation is awesome: droshka, taranta, telega, kibitka. And the distances seemed endless. His description of travel reminds one of readings about kinds of torture, torture by transportation. With the introduction of railroad, traveling in Russia became easier and travelers' moods improved.

These exclamations, interpolated by the author, written as if he were fighting for his breath, are followed by a description of the plain the great exile route crosses. The description is totally negative:

[It is] a plain without limit, without colors, without lines, but for the line, always the same, traced by the leaden circle of the sky on the iron surface of the land![5]

Too much space makes him feel claustrophobic:

Winter and death are felt to be hovering over these scenes: the Northern light and climate give to all objects a funereal hue; at the end of a few weeks, the terrified traveller feels himself buried alive; he would like to destroy his funeral shroud and escape this cemetery, which has no closure and no limits but for those of how far he can see; and, stifling, he struggles to burst his coffin-lid, that leaden veil that separates him from the living. (P. 504)

Custine describes Siberia by using two powerful images that had been imposed by Chateaubriand: the desert and the tomb. Chateaubriand's America is presented in his famous short novels *René, Atala,* and *Les Natchez* (1902) as a social desert that in the end becomes a tomb. Like America, Russia, and especially Siberia, have no historical ruins, no visible tombs of their past. It was therefore the boundless spaces that became their tomb. Like everything in Russia—indeed, like Russia herself—Siberia is not what is seems to be. Space serves to enclose, to enslave, to kill, not to set free.

The population of this desert are "the colonists of Siberia"; because of that, "there is, in that distant exile, a vague poetry which adds to the severity of the sentence all the influence of the imagination" (p. 505). Custine looked at Siberia through the eyes of the political convict and saw it in all its horror. While traveling on the grand exile route, he saw a group of convicts and convinced himself that they were Poles, "heroes of unhappiness and devotion." The fear of his *feldjäger* makes him pass the convoy without speaking to the unfortunates, and he feels profoundly humilitated. "I would wish to be far away from a country where the miserable creature who acts as my courier can become formidable enough to compel me by his presence to dissimulate the most natural feelings of my heart" (p. 505).

This entire episode of the great exile route to Siberia is added almost as an afterthought toward the end of the last volume. It is of particular interest because it shows Custine's style: Chateaubriandesque imagery,

5. ". . . with immense, colorless rivers, dull as the heavens they reflect!" (p. 504).

extreme sensitivity, very strong involvement, and frank confession of fear. A passing convoy—if indeed it was a passing convoy and not a shadow—evokes in him a psychological chain-reaction in which all his thoughts and images of Siberia are combined and reiterated. He shows, with himself as example, the working of the Russian "despotism." He does not tell a story of attempts at heroism: in silence the prisoners pass, and he remains confused, ashamed, humiliated—that is, touched and stained by fear. It is an antiheroic description and, as such, extremely modern.

One needs to have an iron body (de fer) and an infernal imagination (d'enfer) to travel in Russia, he said. His imagination certainly is infernal. He is truly hypnotized by fear, like a bird by the glance of a basilisk. This obsession reflected the reality. The atmosphere of paranoia was not in the head of the traveler but all around him, although a privileged traveler like himself had to make an effort to see it. His critics accused him of inventing the meeting with the prisoners and, in general, of having too much imagination. It is not clear whether he did actually see the prisoners, but, as Isaiah Berlin has said, "Victims make acute observers."[6] Custine made a political convict a presence in his travels because it was his way of talking about the most important phenomenon of Russian everyday reality—fear.

There were many travel descriptions of Russia in which no mention was made of political deportees. Théophile Gautier, in his *Voyage dans Russie,* treats Siberia as "pittoresque,"[7] while George Kennan, the American nineteenth-century writer (and no relation of George Frost Kennan) wrote a book about *The Tent Life in Siberia* which did not mention the penal colonies. Only later did he "discover" the archipelago of prisons and camps, to which he devoted a separate book. Siberia was like a continent—spacious enough to accommodate many descriptions. But hers was not a dry, regular geographic name. "The very mention of Siberia conjures up a foreboding image," wrote August von Haxt-

---

6. Quoted in George F. Kennan, 26.

7. See the already quoted *Russia*. The original edition was intitled *Voyage en Russie,* 2 vols. (Paris: Chapentier, 1866, 1867). This was a collection of essays, some of them published in magazines. Gautier concentrated on Russian art and the beauty of the landscape. He plagiarized heavily Custine's *La Russie,* mentioning its author only once, in passing. Tarn made an amusing comparison of various plagiarized fragments. When *Voyage* was published, Custine was already dead. In his famous Spanish travels, *Tra los Montes* (1843), Gautier also plagiarized Custine's book on Spain, although Custine was still alive. Tarn considered this fact a victory for Custine, whose unjustly forgotten Spanish book reappeared, in a "digested" form, in Gautier's bestseller (Tarn, 465–468).

hausen, a great admirer of Russia.[8] There were other untranslatable Russian words that were incorporated into Western culture in quotation marks. These were words like *knout*, a lash used to kill; or *bunt*, a violent revolt of peasants; *muzhik*, a peasant slave (later metamorphosed into *kulak*); *ukaz*, the tsar's "fiat"; and, by the end of the nineteenth century, the word *pogrom*. In this little dictionary, Siberia meant the place, a punishment, and the political system that stood behind it. For Custine, it replaced the very word Russia.

The Russians themselves talked about Siberia in similarly vague and terrified terms. Lotman quotes a letter written in 1821 by a Russian nobleman called Katenin who said that he was in exile "not far from Siberia."

This is a geographical absurdity: Kostromskii province, where Katenin was exiled, is closer not only to Moscow but also to St. Petersburg than it is to Siberia, and both men knew this. But by the time of their correspondence, Siberia had already become the place of exile in literary plots and the oral mythology of Russian culture . . . real space was interpreted through literary space.[9]

Literary but also real. Siberia stood for punishment, cruel and merciless, because such was her history. It is difficult to think of an equivalent place in all of geography. None of the other places that were used for prisons and confinement—Australia, various islands—became so firmly associated with this function as did Siberia.

According to George Kennan's *Siberia and the Exile System*, Russian convicts and exiles began to be sent to Siberia as soon as it was conquered. The first mention of exile in Russian law was in 1648.[10] The horror surrounding the name of Siberia was due to the harshness of its climate and to the extreme cruelty with which the entire prison and exile system was organized. Throughout the centuries, the Russian state used not only force but also climate, distance, and neglect as means of punishment. The prisoners' own bodies were turned into instruments of torture. In heat or cold, people were marched for months, with fetters on their feet, disfigured by mutilation or head-shaving, with insufficient food or water. Those who survived found themselves in mines or prisons, or settlements in places not fit for human habitation. This punishment was meted out arbitrarily and irrevocably. At least half of the

8. August von Haxthausen, *Studies on the Interior of Russia*, 185.
9. I. Lotman, "The Decembrist in Daily Life," 110–111.
10. George Kennan, *Siberia and the Exile System* (Chicago: University of Chicago Press, 1958), 74. This is an abridged version of the first edition of 1891.

convicts were sent there through extralegal measures—for example, because of a landlord's dislike or a rural commune's decision. In order to colonize the land and provide labor for the mines, the slightest offense was punished by exile.[11] In the nineteenth century, the loss of a document was often enough to dispatch a peasant to Siberia. And only a few ever came back. While passing the boundary post of Siberia, George Kennan, not at all given to exclamations or exaggerations, declared that "no other boundary post in the world has witnessed so much human suffering, or been passed by such multitudes of heart-broken people" (*Siberia*, 52). Many have offered a similar opinion.

Yet there was another attitude to Siberia, exemplified, among others, by Haxthausen. He saw a great future awaiting Siberia. "It is one part of the globe whose destiny is boundless and wholly uncertain," he wrote with admiration, comparing the promise of Siberia to that of North America (p. 186). Many people, including Chateaubriand,[12] defended exile as a form of social control superior to prison. France made ample use of her colonies for that purpose. Custine often quotes *Coup d'oeil sur la législation russe*, written in 1839 by Anatol N. Demidov, an ardent defender of the exile system in Russia. The idea of populating Siberia could certainly be convincing. There were even people—though few believed them—who thought Siberia beautiful and its climate healthy.[13] Throughout Russian history, many religious dissenters and fleeing serfs had gone to Siberia, which meant for them escape from central authority and, therefore, freedom. Several proponents of Russian uniqueness saw in Siberia a place where an authentic peasant communal life could thrive and develop. For Haxthausen, Siberia was the land of the future but one in which old traditions could survive. His undoubtedly very influential book[14] was written at the instigation of (and with the finan-

11. "This is called in Petersburg *peopling* Asia," ironized Custine who was always attentive to the insincere use of language (p. 126).

12. In his *Voyage en Amérique*, published by C. A. Sainte-Beuve (Paris: Calmann-Lévy, n.d.), 268.

13. In her memoir from Soviet camps, Erica Wallach wrote that the prisoners were often struck by the beauty of the landscape around them. But they "did not dare admit it openly to each other—how could we possibly enjoy anything in the inferno?" They thought, however, that they would admire the place if they had come as tourists (Erica Wallach, *Light at Midnight* [New York: Doubleday, 1967], 285). That enjoyment would have been impossible, the image of prisoners being by then an integral part of the landscape.

14. Especially inside Russia; see Introduction to his *Studies*, xxii–xlii. He formulated the problem of the peasant commune in a way that made it appealing for both the Westernized Russians like Alexandr Herzen, and the conservative Slavophiles.

cial support of) the Russian government, eager for a rebuttal to Custine's book. Haxthausen enthusiastically endorsed a Russian autocracy as based on unity and obedience, which were precisely what Custine abhorred.

For Custine, Siberia was a symbol (and reality) of everything that was wrong in Russia. The arbitrariness of the Russian system of justice made nonsense of any discussion of the social usefulness of the exile system. It was a place where the individual was crushed, thrown away by the arbitrary will of the state. And nobody objected! If he compared Siberia to a desert and tomb, it was because no public, no testimony remained to watch the endless sacrifice. The arbitrariness and irrevocability of the sentence made Siberia a true inferno. To be sent there was to be buried alive.

Custine was very afraid in Russia. Fear, usually, clouds vision, but in this case, with so many obstacles in the way of clear vision, only the acuity that comes from fear could pierce them. He saw very clearly that the Russian state was serving only itself—concerned with its own glory and expansion at the expense of everything else. He saw that obedience to the state was thought to be the people's most sacred duty, and he considered this a sacrilege. He thought each individual unhappy and saw no possibility of happiness in Russia. He understood what was later called "the critical attitude" that those in power had toward the people—always trying to change them, always violently unhappy with the way they were. Custine rose to the defense of the people by writing his book. To interpret the silence, to unmask the tyranny, was to punish it (*Empire of the Czar*, 234–235; *La Russie en 1839*, vol. 2: 122). It was the only means of punishment he had.

Siberia symbolized Russia for Custine because of its greatness—the greatness of its possible future, the greatness of its space, but, most of all, the greatness of its inexpressible suffering—suffering as limitless as its space. He found no justification for its existence in culture: no true, human law was observed or realized there, and the social function of punishment was simply reduced to cruelty. Nor was history on Siberia's side: there was none, since the names of the victims went unrecorded. From the point of view of the individual, it was the most horrible, lonely place to die. Neither faith nor freedom could be found there, neither salvation nor glory. In this way of dying Custine saw the denial of individuality—the pulverization of the victim. He rebelled against it with all his might.

Siberia—this "political desert"—was a huge, silent presence in Custine's book, a place on which everything converged. In this geographic name we can observe three realities intersecting: the traveler, the place, and a tradition. The traveler's sensibilities and experiences are, to use Hippolyte Taine's metaphor, a filter, a lens coloring what is being perceived.[15] In Custine's case, his experience as a victim of political violence and as a social outcast—an experience not only undergone but remembered and understood—provided the dark glass through which he looked at everything. But, we can ask, what had he looked at? Would his opinion be different had he actually seen a Siberian city or prison? Most probably he would have been even more horrified. In his mind the place was a political phenomenon, and it is doubtful that any amount of physical experience could change it. And why should it? Although there were other aspects to Siberian reality, the suffering of the exiles and the prisoners could not have been overshadowed in Custine's mind by a nice city, a pleasant landscape, or evidence of happiness—had there been any. It was a land populated by "the phantoms," which no amount of physical experience could dispel.

The "phantoms" came from the knowledge of Siberia that Custine brought with him to Russia. This knowledge was contained in books he read, theatrical performances he saw, stories he heard from his Polish friends. It filled the very name of Siberia with dread. Although it was a tradition that could be ignored (as Gautier proved), it was also one that had a long history and a receptive public. In his one look at Siberia—a look from far away—Custine found proof of all he had read and heard about it.

One could object that "the place" does not participate in this transaction, that Custine spins out of his tradition a vision of Siberia not only without having seen it but also without the necessity of coming to Russia at all. But the way we *know* and *see* things is very complex indeed. Our description and our understanding of a place is never totally dependent on our physical experience of it. Siberia was not some neutral, geographical entity that Custine wanted to describe. It had earned its name in history and, even unseen, felt oppressive to the increasingly anxious Europeans. The history of the place—in this case the history-less, nameless continuity of suffering—is more important than its physical characteristics. The past defines the place. In itself the landscape is incomprehensible, inchoate: it needs words to be explained. Siberia was

15. Hippolyte Taine, *Italy, Rome and Naples,* trans. J. Durand (New York: Henry Holt, 1889), p. v.

understood by Custine as an expression of the entire system of govern-
ment: it represented Russia politically, geographically, and symbolically.
The road *leading* to Siberia was enough of a geographical experience.
The rest was on the map in the traveler's head.

The Cities

In addition to describing what he did not see—Siberia—
Custine presented the reader with places he did visit. His descriptions
were vivid, dramatic, and often unusually imaginative. Almost all of
them reproduced in miniature the author's point of view and the drama
of his discovery of the real nature of Russia. The description of the city
of Moscow is an example. The first, positive impression of the city from
afar turns, at closer scrutiny, into profound rejection. Every sentence,
every detail of the description fits into a larger, ideological category.
Everything is infused with judgment.

Through his descriptions, however, one could see the shape of Moscow's churches and feel its dust. His descriptions are lively and convincing and have been pirated by the master-describer himself: Théophile
Gautier. Gautier was perhaps the most accomplished of an entire tradition of writers called "tourists" by Michel Cadot—writers who set aside
political problems, deliberately untreated, and concentrated on "the
purely picturesque."[16] As was already mentioned, Théophile Gautier
wrote his account when the tsar, Alexander II, was introducing some of
the most important reforms in Russian history (i.e., the abolition, in
1861, of serfdom). Despite such programs, there was still much that
might have been criticized. The "tourist" writers Cadot mentions—
Xavier Marmier, Louis Viardot, Henri Merimée, Charles de Saint-Julien,
and Horace Vernet—traveled to Russia in the years 1839–1848, that is,
at the height of the rigid and uncompromising régime of Nicholas I.
Nevertheless, they were favorably impressed by what they saw. Indeed,
one's opinion of a country seems to depend to an astonishingly high
degree on matters outside the political reality of that country. Nowhere
can this be observed more clearly than in the case of Russia, both in tsarist
and in Soviet times. The attitude expressed by the writers depended directly on their feeling about their own country rather than about the one

16. Michel Cadot, 103.

visited. The most favorable accounts of visits to the Soviet Union, clothed as they were in the all-obscuring language of statistics, were produced when the Stalinist terror and purges were at their highest intensity. But the writers wanted to strike out against the corruption, unemployment, and hypocrisy of their homelands; they therefore accepted the proffered image not only unquestioningly but with enthusiasm.

Russia's autocratic system of government presented an irresistible temptation to various kinds of reformers. The friendship between Catherine the Great and "les philosophes"—especially Denis Diderot—is an illustration of this. The *philosophes* were enthusiastically pro-Russian because they believed in the possibility of convincing the monarch to improve social conditions; once the monarch was enlightened, nothing stood in the way of social experiments. For the same reason Leibnitz wanted to offer his advice to Peter the Great, and innumerable other writers and intellectuals planned to implement their ideas in that distant place, which was always in need of improvement. And Leibnitz, Voltaire, and Diderot were only the early ones in a long list of "fellow travellers."[17]

It did help that the advice was rewarded by income and that the Russian government was always very attentive to the needs of its apologists—and very eager in punishing those who criticized it. Russians were always intensely, painfully interested in the opinion of foreigners. The intensity of this interest was perhaps the reason the foreigners felt free to give their advice abundantly. But it was also the country's duality, the oscillation between its Western and non-Western character, that liberated in the visitors the energies of classification, comparison, and judgment. In no other place did the French philosophes, the German landowners, and the English merchants feel so compelled to give advice and express their opinions. And, although there were many "tourist" descriptions of Russia, the typical reactions were extreme: strong approval or disapproval. To the Westerners, the country was a challenge, an irritation to be classified away. In that sense, Custine's approach was not unique, it was just unusually thorough.

Indeed, to him, everything in Russia spoke of sadness and suffering. Every detail expressed a lack of harmony of the whole. The description of another city he visited in Russia—Saint Petersburg—may serve as an illustration of this. While approaching the city, Custine presented the

17. See Albert Lortholary, *Le Mirage russe en France au XVIIIe siècle* (Paris: B. Boivin, 1951).

view-from-afar, a traditional way of introducing a city in the travel narrative. Such view is usually organized in terms identical to those of travel lithographs and, later, photographs: the city is reduced in size, miniaturized, but with an effort to show it in its completeness. There is a traditional spot from which the city is presented. The next step is "the telling detail." Custine approached Saint Petersburg from the sea, anxious at the thought of entering a city whose existence was due to one man's—Peter the Great's—single-handed decision:

I have never seen, in the approaches to any other great city, a landscape so melancholy as the banks of the Neva. The *campagna* of Rome is a desert, but what picturesque objects, what past associations, what light, what fire, what poetry, if I might be allowed the expression, I would say, what passion animates this biblical land! To reach St. Petersburg, you must pass a desert of water framed in a desert of peat earth: sea, shore, and sky, everything mingles; it is like a mirror, but so muddy, so dull you would say that the glass has been tarnished, for it reflects nothing. (P. 78)

This description is reminiscent of the description of Siberia. In both cases, there is endless space that is not a symbol of freedom. The desert, there called "political," here could be called "historical": the essence of the space around Saint Petersburg is that it has no memory. The "muddy mirror" of the waters of the Neva is juxtaposed to the other desert, made famous by Chateaubriand (and before him, by Goethe), of the Roman countryside. Called here, in the imaginative geography of Custine's creation, "the biblical land" (perhaps in association with Chateaubriand's pilgrimages?), the countryside outside of Rome evoked Chateaubriand's melancholy musings on the passing of time and on the decline of civilizations. This pose became obligatory in the literature about Italy—so obligatory that even such a sober and witty traveler as Dickens felt compelled forty years later to strike a similarly romantic note. The ruins of aqueducts—signs of human industry defeated by time—were what arrested Chateaubriand's attention. Indeed, it is a most common sight in travel photography: the segment of the Roman aqueduct in a desolate, austere landscape. It says: *tempus fugit, memento mori*. In Custine's description the Roman countryside is evoked to show the double, triple desert of Russia—a desert not only physical but historical and psychological as well.

Russia did not have history—that is, Russia did not have a history that Custine (and his contemporaries) knew from school or casual readings. Roman, Greek, or medieval Italian history belonged to the vocabulary of an educated Frenchman at the time; Russian history was not a part of the common European heritage. Custine learned Russian history later, and learned it not as his own history. While approaching cities in the West of Europe, Custine felt a gradual awakening of memory. Arriving in Saint Petersburg, he was reminded of nothing: it was his memory that was the muddy, dull mirror, and nothing was awakened in it. Here everything was not only new but also unsettling. Like the Tuilleries, Saint Petersburg was a city-court, but it had no Paris in the vicinity; it was a capital of the Empire but built in a place that was unfit for human habitation.

> There is here no harmony between the inventions of man and the gifts of nature. . . . Contradiction seems to me the outstanding characteristic in the architecture of this huge city. (P. 89)

The city is so confusing that Custine ends one of his attempts at description with a self-justifying exclamation:

> Let me not be reproached for my contradictions . . . they lie in the things which I contemplate . . . in physical as in moral order, truth is only an assemblage of crying contrasts—contrasts so glaring, that it might be said nature and society have been created only in order to hold together elements which would otherwise oppose and repel each other. (P. 220)

Custine's contradictions were caused by a feeling of displacement coming from something more than just his traveling. The things he came in contact with had the unsettling quality of being somewhat unlike what they were supposed to be. Saint Petersburg—so different from other Russian cities—shared with them the strange characteristic of being very countrylike. The West-European city Custine knew was sharply divided from the countryside by walls and gates or other fortifications, and its internal space was organized in a dense way that was recognized as urban. That division was not clearly visible in Russia. The contrast between city and country was muted or even absent. Unlike Paris, Saint Petersburg was very empty and spacious. Inside Russian cities, spaces were very large and used for agriculture. The roads were unpaved, the houses built of wood with no fortifications around them. Such cities burned easily and often, and therefore contained no antiquities. With a few exceptions, they were founded by a governmental decree of the Building Commission established by Catherine the Great in an effort to produce a Russian middle class. The places chosen for them were at a distance of three or four days on horseback from each other, in order to be convenient for state communication. The local population or conditions were not a major concern.[18] Because of the distances, the cities had to be self-sufficient and therefore identically unspecific in their crafts and crops. Also, the wooden houses were identical in most of the places, and some of them were even prefabricated. The feeling of monotony was reinforced by the fact that the decree that founded the cities also prescribed their design, of which only four possible configurations, or some combination of them, were allowed.

All these factors [, wrote Patricia Herlihy,] dampened the contrasts between city and countryside, and diluted the nature of urbanism itself. The Russian town, aesthetically and . . . socially, was more an extension of the countryside than an exit from it; it was not really an entrance into a radically different society and culture.[19]

And Custine complains:

At every twenty or thirty leagues on all the roads a single town greets your eyes; this is everywhere the same. (P. 597)

For Western travelers, such cities were very confusing. Like many other things in Russia, the actual city did not neatly correspond to the image evoked by the word "city" in Western experience. The cities in Russia were an extension of the countryside, not its opposite. As a consequence, Russia had neither burghers nor a Western-type urban culture. High culture was limited to the court and had no roots in urban society. Peasant life was also different: in Russia peasants were serfs, organized in rural communes and not bound by local patriotism.[20] Some visitors found this difference—the communal life of the peasants—worth emulating (Haxthausen). Although Custine approved of traditions, he believed freedom to be the most important characteristic of social life, and this opinion precluded any appreciation of *mir* or *obshchina*—the institutions of peasant life based on compulsory cooperation. Serfdom made Russian peasant life a nightmare.

The profound unease felt by Custine in Russia was due in part to this inapplicability of his vocabulary to what he saw before his eyes. "The word 'prison' signifies something more here than it does elsewhere"

18. See J. Michael Hittle, "The Service City in the Eighteenth Century," in Michael F. Hamm, ed., *The City in Russian History* (Lexington: University Press of Kentucky, 1976), 53–68.

19. Patricia Herlihy, "Visitors' Perceptions of Urbanization: Travel Literature in Tsarist Russia," in *The Pursuit of Urban History*, ed. Derek Fraser and Anthony Sutcliffe (London: Edward Arnold Pub., 1983), 125–137, esp. 137.

20. Herlihy, 127.

(*Empire of the Czar,* 238). "In appearances everything happens as it does everywhere else. There is no difference except in the very foundation of things" (*La Russie en 1839,* vol. 1: 288). For him, culture and civilization in Russia were just images of Western culture and civilization, not things themselves; the Russians themselves oscillated between nature and culture. For Custine, the very basis of the Russian political system made slaves of everybody, including the aristocrats. This lack of freedom, by preventing any spontaneous expression of national needs and talents, disfigured everything and made Russia a social, political, historical, and moral desert.

Conclusions: In-between

Custine's critique of Russia, although very much his own, was, as I have mentioned, based on many sources. His Russian interlocutors were Westernized noblemen torn between love of their country and disrespect for its autocratic ruler. Custine was indebted mostly to (or, one may say, found most in common with) two of them: Prince Pyotr Borisovich Kozlovski and Pyotr Yakovlevich Chaadayev. Both men were Catholics and believed in the superiority of the universal Catholic Church over the national Greek-Orthodox Church of their country. Fragments of Chaadayev's famous *Philosophic Letter,* written in French and published in 1836, three years before Custine's journey, sound extremely familiar to the reader of Custine.[21] He described Russia as a land of wasted opportunity, its people as immature, neither European nor Asiatic—belonging, as he put it, to geography rather than to history. This binary negative framework of Chaadayev's *Letter* is identical to Custine's way of thinking. It is difficult to say if these were the Russian sources of Custine's opinions or opinions that originated in the West and then filtered back to Custine through Russia. Perhaps in this case, the distinction loses its meaning.

Custine did read the *Philosophic Letter* and probably met with its author. In the book, he summarized it as a plea for the introduction of Catholicism into Russia (*La Russie en 1839,* vol. 4: app.). Second only to liberty, Catholicism was the other prism through which Custine looked at Russia. Both were intermingled, the religion being for Cus-

21. This striking similarity has been noticed, among others, by G. F. Kennan (p. 40) and Pierre Nora (p. 403).

tine the warranty and highest expression of individual freedom. Not only Chaadayev's words but his very life served to convince Custine of the unacceptability of Russian despotism. Chaadayev was a thinker who wrote a critique of his country—and this was considered the gravest of crimes. To punish him, the tsar declared him mentally sick and confined him to his house and to the care of doctors. This use of psychiatric treatment for political dissent profoundly horrified Custine.

Today, *at the end of three years* [Custine's emphasis], of a treatment rigorously observed, a treatment as degrading as it was cruel, the unfortunate theologian of broad horizons . . . doubts his own sanity and, on the faith of the imperial word, he declares himself insane.[22]

The attempt of the regime to get inside the minds of its victims, to alter their thinking and perceptions, evoked Custine's strongest protest.

This case of human rights abuse (as we would say today) prompted him to pose a question: "Has the traveller, fortunate or unfortunate enough to have collected such data, the right to allow it to remain unknown?" And he answered this question himself: "In this kind of thing what you know positively throws light on what you suppose; and out of all this comes a conviction which you are obligated to share with the world if you can" (p. 373). In defense of the victims of political persecution or arbitrary power, he wrote a book that was an effort to build the memory he found lacking in Russia. That memory would record, expose, and ultimately limit injustice.

He spoke as a witness and reported, in an autobiographical account, on an encounter with social evil. Bearing testimony was only one of his ambitions. He tried to explain and analyze the foundations of the unjust system and to write a treatise about Russian politics. He succeeded admirably. His image of Russia became part of the West-European and American political landscape. In quoting him, various writers have emphasized different aspects of his description, but its astonishing vitality has remained intact. His book was deeply appreciated by some of his contemporaries, including such important Russian thinkers as Aleksandr Herzen. As late as the 1950s, Moscow's American Embassy personnel read and translated Custine, marveling at the correspondence between tsarist and Stalinist Russia. George F. Kennan admired Custine, and it is legitimate to suppose that his influential theory of containment, based, as it was, on a special understanding of the workings of

22. The appendix from the last volume of *La Russie en 1839* is cut from the American edition. Here I use the translation from the *Journey for Our Time*, 372–373.

Russian and Soviet systems, was related to this reading. Although he found *La Russie en 1839* to be an imperfect critique of the Russia of Nicholas I (too partial!), he was struck by its clairvoyant understanding of the country as it existed in the 1950s. The aspect of Custine's critique that impressed Kennan most was the stress on Russia's plans for the future. Unable to explain the grandiose scale of the government's undertakings by reference either to past tradition or to contemporary needs, Custine saw in them a secret preparation for future world conquest. Without this "arrière-pensée," he wrote, "the history of Russia would appear to me an inexplicable enigma" (2: 313). Kennan found this explanation fully justified. Moreover, in Custine, he discovered a comprehensive political program of peace and disarmament: "he rejected materialism, imperialism, and war, in all their forms. How it was possible," Kennan continued, "for a man to arrive at ideas so wholly contrary to the entire developing atmosphere of his own century and culture remains one of the mysteries with which Custine's person and cast of mind seem always to have been surrounded" (Kennan 1971, 93).

The explanation of this mystery may lie in the tendency of Kennan's to think anachronistically: no program of peace and disarmament is to be found in Custine. What is interesting here is that both Custine and Kennan, in the face of an incomprehensible phenomenon, resort to the already-described method of "explanation by mystery." Custine did indeed hide some particulars of his visit to Russia; it was a reasonable precaution to protect people with whom he came in contact. He also had to conceal what Kennan called his "lurid behavior." Otherwise, rather than mysterious, he was a complex man who defied our categories.

Astolphe de Custine is perhaps best characterized as a man in-between. The most successful—for us—of his writings are his travel books. They belong to neither the low nor the high culture; they combine reportage with fiction; their ambitions are literary but also journalistic and political; they are devoted to the description of a foreign country, but they are strongly personal and autobiographical; they are contemporary yet strongly historical; they are about "them," but most of all they are about "us." His politics were also in flux. He left for Russia a professed monarchist and conservative; he returned accepting "the representative system [as] the most moral form of government" (p. 499), because it was able to defend the individual against the abuses of both autocracy and excessive democracy. He felt distaste for the imperial expansion of Russia or of any other country—he thought that each nation had enough territory to be happy—yet he had an unshakable certainty of the superiority of French civilization, which, therefore, should influence the world. He disliked religious proselytizing but believed strongly in, and incessantly proclaimed, the superiority of the Catholic Church; the universal Catholic Church was for him the only hope of escaping the ills of the modern world. He did not fit into a conservative or monarchist tradition, nor did he look for a place in the democratic camp. His dominant concern—a concern for personal freedom—was joined with an American kind of requirement that the people be happy; yet these coexisted with a conservative nostalgia, respect for tradition, and abhorrence of change. But he found change inevitable and linked happiness to freedom rather than to tradition. Attached as he was to his class, he found aristocracy, in France as well as elsewhere, unable to perform its social functions and therefore superfluous. He held very strong political ideas but did not make of them a coherent system: he felt compelled to measure them against each new experience. All of this made him very difficult to classify.

And yet, as a writer, he felt a strong need to systematize and simplify. He could have said, with Auden, that "the Truth is one and incapable of self-contradiction; / All knowledge that conflicts with itself is Poetic Fiction" (*Shorts*). All of his efforts at clear, intellectual definition were, however, undermined by his poetic sensitivity to detail, to reality. Never happy with his verbal definition, he returns again and again to the same point, building an anthill of facts, definitions, reformulations. His topics are marginal, his chosen genre is in-between, his method of writing combines different styles and modes. He looks for complexities and, when they do not fall into a system, he follows them along their many uneven paths.

In *La Russie en 1839*, a complex writer used an intricate tradition to describe a tremendously complicated country. The result is puzzling and compelling and full of life today, a century and a half later. Custine's appeal for modern readers resides not only in his amazing perspicacity about Russia but also in his guarded, ambivalent attitude toward the world around him. His analysis (and rejection) of an all-powerful state is modern, as are his complaints against modernity. He does not find easy solutions, and the only example of action he gives us to follow is that of his own (imperfect) personal *engagement*. Today, we share his fears—of violence, of revolutions; and we share his in-between state. We see in him a man who fulfilled his obligation to warn us against evils that still live. He is our contemporary.

PART TWO

Tocqueville in America

7

Democracy in America

When Alexis de Tocqueville went to America—in 1831—
he was twenty-five years old. A disenchanted jurist, he embarked on a
journey to study the characteristics of the American penitentiary system.
In reality, however, he was interested in the functioning of democracy.
Later, he wrote about many other things—about the French prison
system, the political dangers of equality, the French Revolution, colonial
expansion, and the revolution of 1848—but he is known today mostly
for his first book, *Democracy in America*. Read and reread by countless
students of the American system, *Democracy* is a model of political writing and makes part of a canon. Tocqueville's intellectual alertness, as if in
imitation of the American "free circulation of things and ideas" (1: 167),
makes his analysis active, mobile, and undogmatic, always following new
openings and probing the limits of the visible. There is nothing capricious about it, however: he operates through "pairs in tension" (to use
James Schleifer's formulation), and his analysis is held within the boundaries of binary divisions leading to further division, comparisons, and
definitions.[1] The aristocratic system of government is opposed to the
democratic; within the latter, the possibilities of freedom are measured
against the dangers of tyranny; the relationship of equality to freedom is
then debated; an appraisal of the workings of American democracy

---

1. "It was the idea of right that enabled men to define anarchy and tyranny," he writes
in one typical instance. See Alexis de Tocqueville, *Democracy in America*, the Henry Reeve
text rev. by Francis Bowen (New York: Knopf, 1945), 1: 244. Translations are sometimes
made more literal.

shows the working of the safeguards against the tyranny of the majority. Each of the divisions is pursued as long as is necessary to exhaust its ramifications; all lead back to the New World. This movement reflects the major image that Tocqueville sees before his eyes: that of the unstoppable march of equality. His thought attempts to follow that march with matching energy and determination.

In describing Tocqueville's method, I use the words "visible" and "sees" very deliberately: to see, to look, and to perceive are Tocqueville's three most common verbs in describing his cognitive attitude to America. He uses them extremely frequently both in their literal and metaphorical sense. "Among the novel objects that attracted my attention during my stay in the United States, nothing struck me more forcibly [frappé mes regards] than the general equality of the condition of the people," he wrote in the first sentence of the introduction.[2] "However sudden and momentous the events which have just been accomplished before our very eyes [viennent de s'accomplir sous nos yeux], the author of this book has a right to say that they have not taken him by surprise," he writes in the famous 1848 introduction to the twelfth edition (1: cx). And the text proper opens with a sweeping first sentence also alluding to eyes and to visual perception: "North America presents in its external form certain general features which it is easy to distinguish at the first glance [au premier coup d'oeil]" (1: 17). These first sentences are not casual: verbs denoting seeing are Tocqueville's way of writing about his intellectual discovery of the American system of government.

What he sees in *Democracy in America*—"homme de tête" that he was—he sees with "les yeux de la tête" (to use Stendhal's phrase).[3] America presents herself to him as a "spectacle" that attracts his attention ("attire, frappe ses regards"). In his description of the exterior form of North America, he sees her beauty in symmetry, in "a sort of methodical order [that] seems to have regulated the separation of land and water, mountains and valleys" (1: 17). Symmetry, then, is not only a characteristic of his thinking, it also characterizes the beauty to which he aspires. The beautiful objects he sees in America are of the ideal order, and the most beautiful among them is the Constitution—that "fine creation of human industry" (1: 167). The consistent use of "voir" and of its many synonyms in *Democracy in America* ("percevoir," "aperce-

2. Alexis de Tocqueville, *Democracy in America*, 1: 3.
3. He wrote the first two volumes sustaining, as he said in a letter, an "existence toute de tête" for very long periods of time. See James Schleifer, *The Making of Tocqueville's "Democracy in America"* (Chapel Hill: University of North Carolina Press, 1980), 17.

voir," "reconnaître," "jetter un coup d'oeil") expresses the empirical nature of his thinking—the fact that it is a reaction and response to reality rather than a purely intellectual enterprise. Yet, his intense and open reaction to America was singularly predetermined, and he looked for answers to the questions he brought with himself from France.

Tocqueville displayed extraordinary energy during his American trip: he was working intensely, thinking, talking, and writing about what he saw. His notebooks show that many of the ideas in *Democracy in America* were conceived en route there, and some of them may have been brought to America ready-made. "Tocqueville is an extreme example of an intellectual who never 'learned' anything outside of the conceptual framework that he had developed beforehand."[4] It was his "feeling of the irreversible march of history," shared with the generations marked by the French Revolution, that made his encounter with the "New World" so astonishingly fruitful.

For the French historian François Furet, Tocqueville's thought is one long meditation on the nobility. "Tocqueville posited as an axiom, or a self-evident truth, that mankind was moving in great strides toward the age of democracy. This conclusion was not the outcome of a systematic inquiry; it was merely the abstract expression—in keeping with the nature of Tocqueville's genius—of the actual experience of Tocqueville and his milieu" (Furet 1984, 17).[5] In fact, Tocqueville saw the democracy of America as a negation of France—France was the underlying measure for all his comparisons. Although equality was marching forward in both countries, in France it was hampered by old and degenerate institutions, whereas America faced no such obstacles. America was first described—and this is particularly noticeable in his travel notes—in terms of absence. There was no bureaucratic government there, no capital like Paris; power was not embodied in a king or in a "prefect"; the class structure was different: there was no aristocracy and no peasantry, and therefore no violent resentments that characterized France during the late "Old Régime." Politics as understood in France was absent in America: there were no parties, no ideologues, no revolutionary spirit. America's positive aspects were also a negation of France: unlike diversified France, America was a country of uniformity, of the

4. François Furet, "The Conceptual System of *Democracy in America*," in *In the Workshop of History* (Chicago: Chicago University Press, 1984), 167–196; 169.

5. See also the chapter "Tocqueville's Aristocratic Heritage" in Roger Boesche, *The Strange Liberalism of Alexis de Tocqueville* (Ithaca: Cornell University Press, 1987), 169–172.

widespread education so necessary for democracy, of widespread participation in social life. France was an aristocratic society, and America was not.

Tocqueville circumvented the rigidity of the binary system by continuously introducing third elements. England was also an aristocratic society, but very much unlike France; Tocqueville often compared America to England and other societies. The comparisons were never final, and the "destabilization" of the "pairs" saved *Democracy in America* from becoming a system, which Tocqueville would have abhorred. Unlike many of his contemporaries—Marx, Proudhon, Fourier, Saint-Simon— he escaped the temptation to encapsulate human history in a formula.[6] The march of equality is irresistible, but the shape it takes in practice depends on human effort. He was deeply pessimistic and thought that the human mind and understanding are limited; but there was always a margin for the inexplicable in human life and activity, and human free will permitted history to rebel against systems. This is why he insisted that what he wrote was the result of observation, and the verb "to see" allowed him to express this particularity of his position. He was "essentially practical in all his intellectual meditations," Beaumont wrote about him (as always, very perceptively), "he thought of the past only from the perspective of the present, and of foreign peoples only with his own country in mind" (Beaumont 1897, 13). Being capable of sight, he was also capable of foresight.

Democracy in America, as its title indicates, is a book about the workings of democracy in general and about the democratic system of government in the United States of America in particular. The first two volumes (1835) stay close to the American experience. In these, Tocqueville discusses various aspects of the social condition of the Americans, including the Constitution, associations, newspapers, geography, government, and the parties. He pays attention to the role of religion and the family, to "manners," and to the relationship between the races. (These last subjects were also treated by Beaumont in his companion text to *Democracy in America,* the novel *Marie or Slavery in the United States,* published also in 1835.) In the following two volumes, finished eight years after the American voyage, he felt free to detach himself

6. "I am aware that many of my contemporaries maintain that nations are never their own masters here below, and that they necessarily obey some insurmountable and unintelligent power, arising from anterior events, from their race, or from the soil and climate of their country. Such principles are false and cowardly; such principles can never produce aught but feeble men and pusillanimous nations" (*Democracy,* 2: 334).

more from the particularities of American society. Democracy was not a uniquely American system, and its shape had to be different in other countries; in the second part, therefore, the comparison of various countries and systems is wider and more general, with long reflections on democracy in France and the aristocratic system in England. This volume is "more about democracy, and less about America," Tocqueville wrote in a letter. It ends, as it began, with Tocqueville *seeing* a great panorama, but this time it is not a panorama of America but of humanity itself:

For myself, who now look back from this extreme limit of my task and discover from afar, but at once, the various objects which have attracted my more attentive investigation upon my way, I am full of apprehensions and of hopes. I perceive mighty dangers which it is possible to ward off, mighty evils which may be avoided or alleviated; and I cling with a firmer hold to the belief that for democratic nations to be virtuous and prosperous, they require but to will it. . . . Providence has not created mankind entirely independent or entirely free. It is true that around every man a fatal circle is traced beyond which he cannot pass; but within the wide verge of that circle he is powerful and free; as it is with man, so with communities. The nations of our time cannot prevent the conditions of men from becoming equal, but it depends upon themselves whether the principle of equality is to lead them to servitude or freedom, to knowledge or barbarism, to prosperity or wretchedness. (2: 334)

This soaring ending does not come unexpectedly. It is the result of a long and strenuous climb, a march or a race (*course*), to use Tocqueville's terms. In the last part of his work, he reiterates many of the images and metaphors that reappear consistently throughout his work and reflect his emotional vision of America. As he attempted to see the general image of the society he described in four volumes, he was "stopped by the difficulty of the task" which caused his "sight" to be "troubled" and his "reason" to "fail." What he sees in front of his eyes is chaos: "The world that is rising into existence is still half encumbered by the remains of the world that is waning into decay" (1: 331). It is striking to find this image at the very end of what for the most part has been a sustained and rigorous analysis. And yet this image of America predated Tocqueville's analysis and, as I will show, even his visit. It was an image that the analysis lacked the power to dispel. It is an America of chaos, of debris, of life-in-death which haunts Tocqueville's book—an America of exile, of forests, America as a forest; prerational, nonrational, and yet present throughout his work. To discover its origins, we must return to Chateaubriand.

8

Journey to Lake Oneida

The Empty Place

Describing the preparations by the young Tocqueville and Beaumont for the American voyage, the contemporary biographer of Tocqueville, André Jardin, devotes a page to Chateaubriand, who had gone to America forty years before. In 1792 the French Revolution was threatening young Chateaubriand's life, and he was prompted to go to America by Tocqueville's great-grandfather Malesherbes. In the Preface to the first edition of *René* (1802), Chateaubriand linked his American journey to the Revolution and described, as Custine did later in his memoir, the massacre of his family during the Terror. The success of this short novel established a certain vision of America—a place of exile for victims of the Revolution. But it was a strangely Romantic and impractical vision.

Chateaubriand wrote about America frequently. "America was to be one of the great themes of his work, a theme that would keep reappearing from *Atala* to the *Mémoires d'outre-tombe* [from his first to his last work]. Combining what he had seen, what he had read, what he had imagined, he recreated an America in unforgettable colors," wrote Jardin. Chateaubriand, too, thought that democracy might flourish in the future of humanity, or at least so he said in his *Travels in America* (1827). "How could the two young travellers," asks Jardin, "close to Chateaubriand as they were, not have been aware of this, the great man's verdict on the future of democracy?" (pp. 104–105).

Chateaubriand declared that democracy was general in nature and not particular to any country. The twenty-year-old Tocqueville rejected this idea with fury,[1] only to embrace it wholeheartedly a few years later. But it was an idea that could be found in many authors of the period.[2] The influence of Chateaubriand's strictly political ideas on Tocqueville's generation was probably only secondary; in Tocqueville's case, Montesquieu was the most important political influence.[3] Chateaubriand was, however, of utmost importance in what Pierre Michel has called the joining of the poetic and the political.[4] The poetic vision of "American desert," the vision of the Indian as a symbol of individual independence, and the vision of the exiled Frenchman are the three key images in which the political problems of the times were expressed. All three were imposed on the imagination of the French by Chateaubriand's early American novels, René, Atala, and Les Natchez.

The truly Chateaubriandesque element in Tocqueville's writings is his vision of America as a symbolic, desolate landscape of the postrevolutionary world. Democracy in America, the work of a lucid mind, is built on and against this landscape, as are other works by Tocqueville. Take, for example, Tocqueville's description in his Recollections (Souvenirs) of his visit, in 1848, to the family château. It is an echo, almost a repetition, of another visit fifty years earlier to a family château—that of young René in Chateaubriand's famous novel. On the way to see his sister, René arrives at the forest where he had spent the only happy years of his life; the château, sold by his older brother, is empty:

Walking across the deserted courtyard, I stopped to gaze at the closed and partly broken windows, the thistle growing at the foot of the walls, the leaves strewn over the threshold of the doors. . . . I entered the dwelling of my ancestors. I paced through the resounding halls where nothing could be heard but the sound of my footsteps. The chambers were barely lit by a faint glimmer filtering

1. In an unpublished article written in 1825 in answer to an article by Chateaubriand from *Journal des Débats*. Quoted by E. Doran after A. Rédier, *Comme disait Monsieur de Tocqueville* (Paris: Perrin, 1925), 92. See Eva Doran, "Two Men and a Forest: Chateaubriand, Tocqueville, and the American Wilderness," *Essays in French Studies*, 13 (Nov. 1976): 44–61; 59.

2. François Furet, "The Conceptual System of *Democracy in America*," 171.

3. James Schleifer called *Democracy in America* "a wonderful dialogue between Tocqueville and Montesquieu. As he composed, Tocqueville repeated, revised, and reversed the observations of his great predecessor." In James T. Schleifer, "Tocqueville as Historian," *Reconsidering Tocqueville's "Democracy in America*," ed. Abraham S. Eisenstadt (New Brunswick, N.J.: Rutgers University Press, 1988), 146–167; 161.

4. Pierre Michel, *Un mythe Romantique: Les Barbares, 1789–1848* (Lyon: Presses Universitaires de Lyon, 1981), 83.

in through the closed shutters. . . . Everywhere the rooms were neglected, and spiders spun their webs in the abandoned beds.

He leaves precipitously, without looking back. How sweet but short are the moments of family happiness, he reflects; God scatters the family's children like smoke. "The oak sees its acorns take root all around it; it is not so with the children of men!"[5]

Tocqueville's description is, if this is possible, even more Chateaubriandesque than that of Chateaubriand. Like René, he came to the château unexpectedly and unexpected.

On entering the house I was flooded with such an intense and peculiar sadness that the memory of it still remains firmly engraved on my mind, although much else happened to remember then.

The empty rooms—only his dog to greet him—

the uncurtained windows, the piles of dusty furniture, fires gone out, clocks run down, the mournful look of the place, the damp walls—all these things seemed witnesses of neglect and prophets of doom. This little isolated corner of the world . . . which had often been the most delightful retreat [la plus charmante solitude] for me, now seemed a deserted wilderness. But through the desolation of the present I could see, as if looking out from the bottom of a tomb, the tenderest and gayest memories of my life.

It was at that moment that, thanks to his imagination,[6] he understood better than ever "the utter bitterness of revolutions."[7] This image has an extraordinary resonance: there can be no doubt that the wanderer, catching a glimpse of the ruined ancestral home—looking from the tomb at his early happiness—is a younger brother of René. The vocabulary is strikingly Romantic: *berceau, trace, vestige, tombeau, ruine*—favorite

5. Françqis-René de Chateaubriand, *René,* in *Atala, René,* trans. Irving Putter (Berkeley: University of California Press, 1952), 104–105.

6. "It is wonderful how much brighter and more vivid than reality are the colours of a man's imagination." Tocqueville, *Recollections,* trans. George Lawrence, ed. J. P. Mayer (New York: Doubleday, 1970), 94.

7. Tocqueville, *Recollections,* 94–95. This is how it sounds in the original: "Je fus saisi, en y entrant, d'une tristesse si grande et si particulière, qu'elle a laissé dans mon souvenir des traces qu'aujourd'hui encore je retrouve marquées et visibles, parmi tous les vestiges des événements de ce temps-là. Ces chambres vides, ces fenêtres détendues, ces meubles entassés et poudreux, ces foyers éteins, ces horloges arrêtées, l'air morne du lieu, l'humidité des murs, tout me parut annoncer l'abandon et présager la ruine. Ce petit coin de terre isolé . . . qui m'avait paru tant de fois la plus charmante solitude, me sembla dans l'état actuel de mes pensées, un désert désolé; mais, à travers la désolation de l'aspect présent, j'apercevais, comme du fond d'un tombeau, les images les plus douces et les plus riantes de ma vie." Tocqueville, *Souvenirs,* in *Oeuvres Complètes* (1964), 12: 112–113.

words of Chateaubriand—suggest the passage of time; *solitude, désert* denote the spiritual space in which René wandered. The family, for Tocqueville one of the two sacred links of society (the other being private property), belongs to the past, scattered like smoke by the winds of history. The description is of a state of mind as well as of a château. The building itself becomes a sign of physical and spiritual destruction, of the end of a certain world seen by a remnant of that world, a ruin seen by walking débris. Le Château de Tocqueville, just like René's château and Chateaubriand's own Combourg, is, par excellence, an *empty place.*[8]

There are in Tocqueville's writings other descriptions of his château. In a letter to his fiancée (later his wife) Mary Mottley, written some eighteen years before, Tocqueville described it as a cumbersome, impractical place "where nothing seems made for comfort and even less for the pleasure of the eye: dark rooms, large chimneys that offer more cold than heat, armchairs in which three would easily fit, humid walls and corridors in which the wind whistles. . . ." The emptiness and humidity are here devoid of any tragic meaning. It is a place of calm, of "profound tranquility," and of recollections.[9] Although devoid of people, it is not an *empty place (le lieu vide),* a metaphorical ruin, a place of past human actions and feelings, the symbol of the unavoidable end of human time. In fact, the feeling of emptiness and ruin was not necessarily linked to the ancestral site and was not limited to a concrete place: Chateaubriand had a similar reaction on the site of Carthage, while looking at the countryside around the city of Rome, facing ruins, a small city, or a forest. And since he travels continuously, and his protagonists travel as well,[10] he looks for and finds empty places everywhere.

In his continuous displacements, Chateaubriand's René always met the same site. In a kind of Grand Tour *manqué,* he first goes to sit on the debris of Rome and Greece, where he can see "power of nature and weakness of man: a blade of grass will pierce through the hardest marble of these tombs, while their weight can never be lifted by all these mighty dead!" (*René,* 90). Seated at the top of Mount Etna, he cried over the fate of "mortal men whose dwellings he could barely distin-

8. For an excellent discussion of the *lieu vide* motif in Chateaubriand's writings, see Michael Riffaterre, "Chateaubriand et le monument imaginaire," in *Chateaubriand Today,* ed. Richard Switzer (Madison: University of Wisconsin Press, 1970), 63–81; 72–76.

9. Quoted in Xavier de la Fournière, *Alexis de Tocqueville: Un monarchiste indépendant* (Paris: Librairie Académique Perrin, 1981), 17.

10. Michael Riffaterre said that Chateaubriand's works of fiction take the form of an itinerary. See his "Chateaubriand et le monument imaginaire," 67.

guish far off below him" (p. 92). "In the schematic recounting of his travels," writes Margaret Waller, ". . . René makes little pretense of 'realistic' exposition. Each stage of his journey serves instead as an occasion for lyrical apostrophes and philosophical speculations on mortality."[11] Instead of integrating him into the culture he was born to continue, his "Grand Tour" showed him his social uselessness and plunged him into even greater isolation. Self-exiled, first to the "desert" at the outskirts of the city and then to a *chaumière* in the countryside, he finally decides to depart for America. There he finds the most deserted of deserts, nature showing fallen trees as monuments of the past and the doomed Indian race as a sort of walking ruin. "They still point out a rock where he would go off and sit in the setting sun" runs the last sentence of *René* (p. 114). Nature was also *le lieu vide* if the hero's life was empty.

There is a text among Tocqueville's papers in which we find a quintessential America-as-an-empty-place and a René contemplating "the force of nature and the weakness of man." It is a short travel account called "Journey to Lake Oneida." Written right after his American trip, it was first published by Beaumont in 1866, together with another travel story, "A Fortnight in the Wilds." Beaumont attached great importance to these two travel accounts: these were the texts, he thought, in which Alexis de Tocqueville "let himself go with the flow of impressions [produced by] the irresistible charm of these great solitudes of America, where everything united to intoxicate the senses and put the mind to sleep" (Beaumont 1897, 25).[12] His mind asleep, Tocqueville did describe the America of his dreams, or of his unconscious—the America of Chateaubriand.

The six-page story describes an episode in the westward travel of Tocqueville and Beaumont, an episode that both writers remembered as particularly moving. On no other journey were their impressions equally "vivid and lasting," wrote Beaumont, quoting Tocqueville's opinion (Beaumont 1897, 24). This was an expedition that brought

11. Margaret Waller, "Cherchez la Femme: Male Malady and Narrative Politics in the French Romantic Novel," *PMLA* 104, 2 (March 1989): 141–151; 145.

12. This quotation is reminiscent of the sentence from Chateaubriand's *Travels in America:* "The traveler's reverie is a sort of plenitude of the heart and emptiness of the mind which allows one to enjoy his existence in repose." This thought is expressed while the traveler is seated on the banks of an island in the middle of a lake in exotic Florida. See Chateaubriand, *Travels in America,* trans. Richard Schwitzer (Lexington: University of Kentucky Press, 1969), 65. As for travelers by the side of lakes, Custine was drawn "Au bord du lac" by Edward de Sainte-Barbe in Scotland, in 1822.

Tocqueville and Beaumont from Syracuse to Fort Brewerton in New York, and then to an island on Lake Oneida where they went to search for traces of a Frenchman who had lived there right after the Revolution. The first three pages of the account show the travelers in the American forest; then we are told the story of the Frenchman. The second half describes the travelers' arrival on the island, their search for traces of their compatriot, and their melancholy retreat. Sadder and wiser, the two young Frenchmen go back to the mainland.[13]

The opening of the story is truly majestic. After the readers are provided with initial information, the story plunges into the forest, to leave it only three pages later. The forest inspires in Tocqueville "a sort of religious terror" and is described as if it were a cathedral. The travelers move under a dome of tree branches, in a majestic half-shadow, with sunrays piercing through the branches—they remain silent for hours, their "souls filled with the grandeur and novelty of the sight." The forest described in these terms becomes sublime, religious, monumental, a moral as well as a natural structure. But this is only half the image. Below the

vast dome of vegetation, below the thick veil . . . the eye perceived immense confusion, a sort of chaos. . . . Trees of all ages, foliage of all colors, plants, fruits and flowers of a thousand species, entangled and intertwined. Generations of trees have succeeded one another there through uninterrupted centuries and the ground is covered with their debris. . . . Sometimes we happened to come on an immense tree that the wind had torn up by the roots, but the ranks are so crowded in the forest that often despite its weight it had not been able to make its way right down to the ground.[14] Its withered branches still balanced in the air. (Pp. 343–344)

In this last image, the travelers again raise their eyes up, the forest becomes again a cathedral, and, out of the chaos, a tree-symbol of Christ emerges.

There was no man in this forest, yet it was not a desert: "On the contrary, everything in nature showed a creative force unknown elsewhere; everything was in movement. . . . It was as if one heard an inner sound that betrayed the work of creation." After several hours of walk-

13. Alexis de Tocqueville, "Journey to Lake Oneida" (Voyage au lac Onéida), in vol. 5 of the *Oeuvres Complètes* (1957), pp. 336–341. English translation (often made more literal by me) in Tocqueville, *Journey to America*, trans. George Lawrence, ed. J. P. Mayer (New York: Doubleday, 1971), 343–349.

14. In the original, a surprising expression attracts the reader's attention here: "il n'avait pu se faire jour jusqu'à la terre" (p. 337). "Se faire jour" indicates movement in the opposite direction, toward the light.

ing through the forest, the two travelers come upon a settler's cabin, surrounded by the signs of his efforts, "some trees cut down, trunks burnt and charred, and a few plants useful to the life of man." This is how "a European" tried to establish his residence in the midst of a "desert."[15] This little scene is a preparation—*a mise-en-abîme*—of what awaited the travelers on the island.

Finally, the travelers arrived at the edge of the lake from which they could admire its calm and isolation, with two little islands completely covered by trees and peacefully floating on its surface. They did not come here by accident. Many years before, Tocqueville had read a book called *Journey to Lake Oneida*, about a French exile who, after the Revolution, came with his wife to live on this island. The book left such a lasting impression on him that the two travelers "often talked about it, and always ended by saying . . . 'the only happiness in the world is on the shores of Lake Oneida.' " It is an important sentence because it reveals the "unofficial" motive for Tocqueville's trip to America. When finally they reached the shores of the lake, the place did not strike them as new; "on the contrary, we seemed to be revisiting a place in which we had passed part of our youth."[16]

The second part of the story opens with the travelers stopping at a fisherman's hut, the only one on the lakeshore. The fisherman's wife tells them that the Frenchman is no longer there: the woman died and the man left the island without anyone knowing where he went. When she settled on the shore, twenty-one years earlier, the Frenchman was already a legend; she has visited the already abandoned but still lovely island. She lends them a boat, expressing her surprise at their going there, and they set off, their "hearts filled with gentle and sad emotions." The island seems totally wild but, once they make their way inside, they perceive "a spectacle" that is the opposite of what they had noticed in the clearing of the European pioneer: "We had often seen man struggling with nature hand to hand. . . . Here, by contrast, we saw the forest regaining its empire, marching out again to conquer the

15. In *Democracy in America* Tocqueville observes that there are no Europeans among the pioneers. Europeans establish themselves in cities after their arrival. One needs to be born an American to have the necessary determination to go into the forest. (Often, though, he said that Americans are Europeans, that he considers them offspring within the European family.)

16. The idea of revisiting is introduced by a sentence that is almost identical to the sentence I quoted in the description of the Château Tocqueville: "Consider how strange is the power of imagination over the human mind." In fact, these sentences come in "clusters": linked to a repeated image or situation, they "belong" together.

desert, defying man and quickly making the traces of his passing victory disappear."

Although the forest covering the island was young, it was impossible to find the "abandoned dwellings." For over an hour the travelers looked for them but were able to find only a half-dead apple tree and a climbing vine. They looked on the ground, under the debris, for "the remains of her who was not afraid to exchange the delights of a civilized life for a tomb on a deserted island in the New World," but they found nothing. It was with "hearts full of emotion" and inspired by some sort of "religious feeling" that they devoted themselves to their search: they could not imagine a more wretched man than that Frenchman. Rejected by society, he flees into the wild with the only being that loves him. He starts his life anew, but his wife dies. "What can become of him? . . . He is no longer adapted either for solitude or for the world; he does not know how to live either with men or without them; he is neither a savage nor a civilized man: he is nothing but a piece of debris, like those trees in the American forest which the wind has had the power to uproot, but not to blow down. He stands erect, but he lives no more." After seeing the island's "every debris," the two travelers set off on their way, leaving behind "this vast rampart of greenery" that could defend the *chaumière* of the exiles from everything but death. It is the words "la mort" that end the story.

Let us reconsider what has happened. Tocqueville, having read a book about the Frenchman's island, sets off with Beaumont to visit it. They go through the forest, meet a settler, talk to a fisherman's wife, go to the island, find an old apple tree, and go off. The island is a perfect, complete *lieu vide*—it is covered with nothing but disappearing traces. Everything in the story is said twice in absolute symmetry. We have two islands, two forests—old and new; two settlers—one establishing his residence in the forest, the other gone already; we have two visits to the island—the fisherman's wife's and our travelers', for whom it feels like a second visit. The excursion is the result of reading, so the story is a repetition of another story; the title of the first book is given in the text—it is *Journey to Lake Oneida*—and repeated as the title of Tocqueville's episode, as if reflecting on the surface its very origin, just as the surface of Lake Oneida reflects the surrounding, ever-present forest. On the island, we have a half-dead apple tree and the vanished Frenchman metaphorically turning into a half-dead tree, still standing but already "deraciné." The same tree was standing over the travelers' heads at the beginning of the story, when they were contemplating the cathedral of the forest. The general organization of the story is also double: the narrator follows the traces of the Frenchman, and the two subplots meet on the island in a climatic nonevent—a vain search for the Frenchman's house. The last page repeats the Frenchman's story rephrased in moral and emotional terms. And at the end, the two travelers return to their voyages.

The parallelism and repetition is also visible on the level of the sentence. A certain number of words—words that we know already: *désert, solitude, trace, vestige, mort*—are repeated over and over; *solitude* and *désert* run through the story together, setting an echo, a resonance between similar but slightly different elements. The nouns are often described by couples of adjectives ("une trace profonde et durable") or are themselves coupled (the island is "le but et le terme" of their voyage); verbs are doubled, sentences introduced by parallel structures, while paragraphs repeat and echo the previous ones. Symmetry, doubling, synonymy are the way the story is organized, showing its style and literary character, since what is worth repeating must be literary. Repetition and parallelism are here fundamental: the apple tree and the vine are signs of Eden, and the island—"the only possibility of happiness"—is the *lieu vide* par excellence, the place from which the couple has been exiled, leaving behind the memory of their happiness. That memory is what is repeated in the story.

A Tangled Story

In fact, this *was* a second visit. Everything was recognizable. The forest was the forest of Chateaubriand, with its architectural grandeur—the scene of God's creation, of death and life in perpetual embrace. The tree symbolized man, as it did in *René*. The Frenchman was a brother of René, and his story was a well-known one. The island was a paradise but also a château, or one's own country—the place from which one was exiled. Even the American continent was by then exotic in a familiar way. The reader, too, had a sense of having been taken there before.

The two forests are not similar, they are identical.

Who can tell the feeling one has on entering these forests as old as the world, which alone give the idea of creation as it left the hands of God? [wrote

Chateaubriand.] The daylight, falling from on high through a veil of foliage, spreads through the depths of the woods a changing and mobile half-light which gives fantastic size to things. Everywhere we must climb over fallen trees, above which rise new generations of trees. In vain I seek some outlet from this solitude. Misled by a brighter light, I advance through the grasses, the nettles, the mosses, the lianas, and the thick humus composed of vegetable debris; but I arrive only at a clearing formed by some fallen pines. Soon the forest becomes somber again; the eye sees only trunks of oaks and walnuts which follow one upon another and seem to come closer together as they recede into distance. I become aware of the idea of infinity.[17]

The sublime dome and the chaos down below, the religious twilight, the hum of creation uniting life to death—all this was revisited by Tocqueville, seen and heard because remembered. Written many years apart, these images should be different.[18] And yet, the forest of the "Journey to Lake Oneida" shares light, sounds, solemnity, and meaning with its model, and there are no differences between them.[19] Indeed, the similarities between the Frenchman and René are no less striking. Young, French, and presumably aristocratic, both men are rejected by society and find themselves in an American exile. They could perhaps continue living but for the terrible loss of the loved one. Without a home, with death in their souls, they wither away, like the tree still standing but already dead.

It is easy to understand why Tocqueville used again Chateaubriand's vision. Although many literary historians have proved *Atala* and *René*'s

17. Chateaubriand, *Travels in America*, 30.

18. In the already-quoted article, Eva Doran notes the striking similarities but also finds various differences between the two forests. (For comparison, though, she uses a quotation from Tocqueville's more down-to-earth "A Fortnight in the Wilds.") She repeats the words of Sainte-Beuve and of Chateaubriand himself (in the previously quoted opposition of Tocqueville's *Amérique civilisée* to his own *Amérique des forêts*), pointing to the cerebral tone of Tocqueville as opposed to the poetic vision of the older writer. Many other critics assumed without hesitation that Tocqueville was a cool observer; Eva Doran quotes J. P. Mayer's praise of Tocqueville's "keenness of observation, reminiscent of Alexander von Humboldt's travel papers," and Christian Bazin's juxtaposition of Chateaubriand's romanticism to Tocqueville's classicism (p. 59, fn.). André Jardin, in agreeing with Eva Doran's opinion, quotes Sainte-Beuve's comment upon reading Tocqueville's "Quinze jours dans le désert" (A Fortnight in the Wilds): Tocqueville "gives us in very nice prose what Chateaubriand has already given us in daring and sublime poetry" (Jardin, 127). It is an opinion that is derived from the general reputation of both writers rather than from comparison of their works.

19. Beaumont called Chateaubriand "the poet of the American forest" and wrote an imitative description that is an homage to the "French Homer." See Gustave de Beaumont, *Marie, or Slavery in the United States*, 116. Tocqueville and Beaumont shared their models.

dependence on previous models,[20] the works captured and expressed in a powerful way the fears and conflicts of the moment. Thirty years later these images were just as timely, and, no longer extraordinary, they circulated freely in the cultural bloodstream: they represented an accepted, obvious way of expressing feelings and thoughts. In America, Tocqueville looked through Chateaubriand's eyes and disputed him quite frequently. In "A Fortnight in the Wilds," Tocqueville starts by denying Chateaubriand's (and James Fenimore Cooper's) descriptions of Indians, another American image that remained firmly in his memory, only to agree with it by the end of the story. But Tocqueville was not aware of following Chateaubriand in any way, nor did he like the man. The forest and the character of the Frenchman were part of Tocqueville's poetic vocabulary, the terms of which were best formulated by Chateaubriand but, in the 1830s, truly belonged to everybody. It was the language of Romanticism.

In "Journey to Lake Oneida" we can see a travel experience that was caused by a Romantic tale and which, in turn, produced one. There are several different testimonies about this episode in Tocqueville's and Beaumont's travels in America, additional information about the Frenchman who lived on the island, and the book, *Voyage d'un Allemand au Lac Onéida,* that young Tocqueville had read. By comparing these materials we can see the process of distilling or selecting information, to create a meaningful—that is, recognizable—synthesis. The juxtaposition of these writings and testimonies serves to reconstruct a particular moment in history, in an effort analogical to the analysis of the Catholic tradition that Custine revived while writing about Russia. We see a reality, we know the books that were read about it, and we have the final text that resulted from the interaction of the writer, his readings, and his experience. We can thus follow the migration of images and ideas and their repetitions; we are looking at a writer enmeshed in tradition, writing about what he felt and saw, and seeing what he had read.

To show the process of filtration and the passage of actual events into literature, one should start from the beginning, that is from the Frenchman himself. (This is how Tocqueville begins his tale about the Frenchman in the letter to his sister-in-law.) The story of the Frenchman's life

20. See for example pp. xiii–xx of the préface by Maurice Regard to the *Oeuvres romanesques et voyages de Chateaubriand* (Paris: Gallimard [Pléiade]), 1: 1969. See also pp. 9–10 and 107 of *Oeuvres* ("Sources").

is based on an extraordinarily well-researched article by Victor Lange.[21] The Frenchman's name was Louis Des Watines, and he came to America to make his fortune. The article makes it possible to follow the transformation of the life of Louis Des Watines into the exemplary Romantic biography of "the Frenchman."

A nobleman who came to the United States before the Revolution, Des Watines seems to have stayed on the westernmost island of Lake Oneida for over a year, in 1792–1793. He was not there alone but with his wife and two children; the third child, a girl called Camille, was born during their Oneida stay—not on the island but in an Indian encampment. Two men, "an old Canadian and a savage," helped him to clear the island. He left the island he thought he had discovered (and called by his name) when he was informed that it already belonged to somebody else. The family then bought one hundred acres on the lake's northern shore. They were not successful in their financial dealings and, around 1799, after having sold their land and their small collection of French and Latin books, "our French Robinson"[22] and his family returned to France. The legend had it that the father of Madame Julie Des Watines made them rich by leaving her his entire fortune. And, as was written some years later by J. V. H. Clark, "Those children, born upon that island (which has ever since been known as 'Frenchman's Island'), are said to be today among the most distinguished personages of France."

Lange starts his article with a portrait of the sentimental German writer Sophie von La Roche (1731–1807) who, in 1798, published the novel *Erscheinungen am See Oneida*. The impulse for writing the novel came from her son and daughter-in-law: the couple had lived for some time in the United States and moved in the circles of exiled French nobility. There they heard about the Des Watines, who had already left the island. How they told the story to Sophie von La Roche can be gathered from her requests to them, in 1795, to tell her again the life of "this Frenchman and Frenchwoman who lived amongst savages" (she wrote to them in French). Her daughter-in-law, Elsina, obliged her. There is no doubt that the story, although using real names and places, had been "improved" before Sophie von La Roche heard it, with the

21. Victor Lange, "Visitors to Lake Oneida: An Account of the Background of Sophie von La Roche's Novel *Erscheinungen am See Oneida*," in *Symposium* 2 (1948): 48–78.

22. As he was referred to in the diary of Desjardins, commissioner of the Castorland Company (Sunday, October 13, 1793). Quoted in Victor Lange, 75.

"low" (economic) reason for Des Watines' emigration turned into a flight from persecution. In her book, she stresses the abyss between the high birth of the couple and the dire need into which they fell. The story ends with the couple moving to a community of settlers, rejoining society. The death of the wife and the disappearance of the Frenchman is Tocqueville's much later contribution to the tale.

But the story was evolving right from the start, and many people had a hand in shaping it. This was not accidental. The fate of exiles whose families suffered during the Revolution was evoking warm interest, and the public was ready to see one of them settle on an island in the New World. Sophie von La Roche's sentimental novel was rather popular, and five years after its appearance a German publisher, Joachim-Heinrich Campe, produced a condensed edition for young readers. He was an author of many instructive books for the young, the most popular of which was his version of *Robinson Crusoe*. And, in fact, in his version, the life of Des Watines came closer to that of Robinson Crusoe. Entitled *Voyage d'un Allemand au Lac Onéida*,[23] the book reproduced, in simplified form, the story of the original, adding instructive and edifying information about America. The narrator disparagingly mentions Madame von La Roche's book, criticizing its length and florid style; he wrote only for unaffected youth, he said, not for important personages. The story is less of a sentimental antirevolutionary tale than an instructive, though still moving, travel book. Lange thought the change an improvement.[24] In its French edition the book was published as one volume in a series subscribed to by Hippolyte de Tocqueville (then five years old), the older brother of Alexis, who would be born two years later.[25] We do not know when Alexis read it, but what he remembered from it was not the "happy ending" with Des Watines settling on the other side of the lake. Tocqueville retained from the story its dark, Romantic side.

The romanticization of the story was not due to the personality of Louis Des Watines. Unlike his wife and children, he did not evoke

23. *Voyage d'un Allemand au Lac Onéida*, Rédigé pour l'instruction et l'amusement de la jeunesse, par Campe. Traduit de l'allemand, avec des notes, par J. B. J. Breton . . . (Paris, Amsterdam: J. E. F. Dufour, 1803), in J. H. Campe, *Bibliothèque géographique et instructive, ou recueil de voyages intéressants,* vol. 10.

24. Sophie von La Roche used many travel sources for her description of American settings. "But she treated her sources with detached amusement," writes Lange, "and the kind of condescension towards tedious factual accuracy that must have endeared her to many of her *female* readers" (p. 63; emphasis added).

25. See Jardin, 123.

sympathy in people who met him. Indeed, Des Watines openly blamed his own character for all his misfortunes.[26] The contrast between the real events and Tocqueville's version is rather striking, and many critics, in a sort of *mise-en-point*, are a bit ironic about the whole story. Victor Lange calls the Des Watines "the enterprising family,"[27] and G. W. Pierson, author of *Tocqueville and Beaumont in America* (1938), calls them "a jolly couple."[28] In the biography of Tocqueville, André Jardin described Louis Des Watines as "shallow and greedy."[29] But the setting itself—an empty island in the middle of a lake lost in the American forest—lent itself very well to being a place of illusion. While working on his *Tocqueville and Beaumont in America*, G. W. Pierson visited the island and succumbed to the same melancholic influence. Remembering Tocqueville's blisters (mentioned in his letter to his sister-in-law), Pierson rowed with gloves on. Upon his arrival on the island, he, like Beaumont and Tocqueville, could hardly step ashore, so dense and wild was the vegetation. After finally penetrating her shores, he found the island abandoned, with traces of an old house and a few illegible names scratched on an old apple tree. He was convinced that the island had witnessed some terrible tragedy, and he was much moved by it. He discovered later, in another *mise-en-point*, that the old house was an abandoned hotel, and the names were probably those of some of its guests. The fisherman's wife was right—the island was too far from the market and unfit for business.[30]

Travel Diary and Letter

It was on the island that Tocqueville wrote the first account of the Frenchman's story. In his notebook,[31] he devoted a separate entry to this episode in his travels. Since the travel notes were destined for himself, they are organized in temporal rather than causal

26. Jardin, 124.
27. Lange, 60.
28. George W. Pierson, *Tocqueville and Beaumont in America* (New York: Oxford University Press, 1938), 203.
29. Jardin, 124.
30. As he told me in a conversation in the fall of 1978.
31. "Cahier portatif nr. 1," pp. 161–162 of vol. 5 of his *Oeuvres Complètes* (1957). "Pocket Notebook Number 1" in Alexis de Tocqueville, *Journey to America*, trans. George Lawrence (New York: Doubleday, 1971), 127–128.

order: he knew the *why*, he just needed a reminder of *what*. (Also, the less important things were written down, being more likely to be forgotten.) Yet even in this case we can see his effort to get rid of secondary facts, to purge his experience from interferences, to relate and structure its various elements—to make it stand on its own as a story. The entry is one-page long and, just like "Journey to Lake Oneida," falls into two parts, the first one dealing with the arrival at the lake and the second with the stay on Frenchman's Island. All the basic elements we encountered in "Journey to Lake Oneida" can be found here. Noted in telegraphic style, there is the traveling on horseback from Syracuse, first to Fort Brewerton and then to the lake itself. Two general remarks about the "immense forest" summarize the images developed in "Journey": "The forest in permanent contest with man" and "America in all her glory"; an entire paragraph (one-fourth of the entry) is devoted to impressions of the forest. The Frenchman is mentioned for the first time in the sentence opening the second part of the entry; Tocqueville jots down some information about him taken from his conversation with the fisherman's wife (here referred to only as "she"). Upon setting foot on the island, he and Beaumont experience deep emotion. The image of a paradise is there: in a clearing, in the center of the island, they find the apple tree and the by-now wild vine.[32] "The house was there." They leave their names on a tree, a trace added to other traces. The last two sentences are the fullest: "We traversed the whole island without finding any trace of the two beings who had made it their universe. This expedition is what has most vividly interested and moved me, not only since I have been in America, but since I have been travelling."

When one compares Tocqueville's American travel notes with the text of *Democracy in America,* one is struck by the frequency with which the first impression, the first idea, is the one that comes up in the final text. Tocqueville was in a state of extreme concentration while in America, and the direct contact with unusual landscapes and people had a profoundly inspiring influence on him. His entire American stay was spent in a state of feverish, excited work.[33] Before writing the "Journey to Lake Oneida," Tocqueville repeated the Frenchman's story in a letter to his sister-in-law. Yet the notebook entry is closer to the version

32. In his summary of "Journey to Lake Oneida," Jardin points out that the vine was already present in the Campe version. The vine plays multiple roles in the story; it is a sign of the Frenchness of the Frenchman, of his unsuccessful attempt at transplanting his civilization; looking like a liana, it is a sign of the exotic; "entrelacée" [twining] right up to the top of the apple tree, it is an image of the serpent, and therefore a symbol of Eden.

33. See Beaumont, *Notice,* 20–21.

related in the "Journey." Although the text is fragmented and sketchy, it contains several elliptic sentences that later will be developed into the core of the Frenchman's story. The structure that will underlie the story is provided already in the notes; "Journey" will rewrite it for the general audience. Words like "forest in permanent contest with man," here separated from other phrases by its different tone, will suffuse the entire text.

The text of the entry starts by being extremely choppy; but the second part acquires a flow and ends with a rather literary finale. The reportorial "we" of the first part also is gradually abandoned, and by the end, the voice of the narrator emerges in its full individuality. This reader had the impression that the writer was sorting out his opinions; he started by being uncertain and, as he wrote, he found out what this experience was all about. His writing becomes more and more focused, smooth, and elaborate. Obviously, the entry was written after the event; the sense of the whole experience, however, does not seem to have been clearly formulated in the writer's mind before being written down. The very process of writing offered an occasion to think things through. The entry is a search, an exploration. The later versions will be but presentations.

In a gesture typical of tourists, Tocqueville and Beaumont leave their names on an old "platane." They were leaving a trace on a site that functioned only as a trace. There are, however, in the "Pocket Notebook" other indications (or traces) of what happened on the island. The entry dated for the day before describes briefly a visit to Mr. Elam Lynds; elsewhere in Tocqueville's papers we find copious notes on Tocqueville's conversation with this man. The entry ends with the following statement: "(This is written on 'the Frenchman's island' in the middle of Lake Oneida)."[34] Not only had Tocqueville looked for traces of the two unhappy beings, but he had also done a bit of work. The report of such diligence had no place in a Romantic story, so he divided the stay on the island into two separate entries. I point this out to indicate that even while tentatively jotting in his notebook, Tocqueville was already creating a story he liked more and more as he went along. He came to the island, he did not find the Frenchman, and out of this "visite manquée," he spun a wonderful tale.

Three weeks later, a very social version of the story appeared in a letter written by Tocqueville. The letters the two travelers wrote from America were not merely personal communications to their relatives

34. See p. 161 of "Cahier portatif nr. 1," in vol. 5 of *Oeuvres*, and, in the same volume, "Cahier non-alphabétique nr.1," pp. 63–67. English edition, pp. 126–127.

and friends. Together with the copious notes both of them were taking, the letters were to serve as a basis for their future book or books on America.[35] Thus their function was to preserve the wealth of information and thoughts inspired by the American journey. They strove also to satisfy their friends' and families' justifiable curiosity: they gathered to read them aloud and share them with other people.[36] The substantial length of the letters was also due to the high price of postage.[37]

The Oneida episode was not the only subject of the letter written by Tocqueville to his sister-in-law on July 25, 1831. Tocqueville did not use his notes while writing it and displayed a sort of disdain for detail, not unlike Sophie von La Roche (perhaps because it was addressed to a lady?). In fact, the letter has a very different tone than both the notes and the final version. It is light, conversational, nonpedantic; Tocqueville puts himself forward here and teases his "little sister" a bit. The letter is personal but not intimate: both Tocqueville and Beaumont conform in their correspondence to the literary standards of "familiar" letter-writing. (The model for such letters was established by Charles de Brosses's *Letters from Italy*.) The letters were full of literary allusions, quoted conversations (in the convention of "perfect memory"), with people described as if they were literary characters. The literariness and the ornamental style were not related to the factual or fictional nature of the letter.[38] Yet there were other characteristics of the letter that are linked to the transformation of the story. "The epistolary form," writes Bakhtin, "is most favorable . . . for the reflected word of another person," and it is characterized by "the writer's acute awareness of his interlocutor."[39] Tocqueville shaped his story so that it would interest his readers.

The letter opens with a presentation of the Frenchman, and the narra-

---

35. This is why Beaumont's letters were later copied by himself or by his brother Jules. His notes have been lost, but Tocqueville's were kept by his family and have been published.

36. In the nineteenth century, correspondence did not have the private character we grant it today. See J.-F. Tarn, *Marquis de Custine*, 121.

37. Beaumont's letter mentioning (in one paragraph) the episode of Lake Oneida occupies eleven pages of print in the volume of his letters. It is one of the longest letters written by Beaumont in America, but not unusually so. See Gustave de Beaumont, *Lettres d'Amérique (1831–1832)*, ed. André Jardin and G. W. Pierson (Paris: Presses Universitaires de France, 1973).

38. Analysis of letters of Pushkin, Tocqueville's contemporary, shows more figures of speech and tropes than are found in Pushkin's strictly literary prose. A. Z. Lezhnev, *Proza Pushkina* (1937). Quoted in William M. Todd, *The Familiar Letter as a Literary Genre in the Age of Pushkin* (Princeton, N.J.: Princeton University Press, 1976), 13.

39. Mikhail Bakhtin, *Problems of Dostoevsky's Poetics* (Ann Arbor, Mich.: Ardis, 1973), 170.

tion, again similarly to that of Sophie von La Roche, stresses the contrast between his birthright and the lowly conditions of his exile. Many details are furnished about his station and excellent health. The forest part is abandoned, to be described, perhaps, "one day" for the "dear sister." A short description of Lake Oneida follows, presented in the paradisiacal terms of "a tranquillity as complete as it must have been at the beginnings of the world." He started to worry, Tocqueville writes, that the traveler who preceded him invented the story, but the conversation with the fisherman's wife dissipated his doubts. The fisherman's wife here had little eyes ("little watering [chassieux] eyes," in the copy of the letter held in the Beinecke Library of Yale University), but in the final version she will be limping instead. From her we learn that the wife had died and her husband "disappeared and nobody knows how he crossed the lake and where he went." She is presented as a very prosaic character, so that the reader will not suspect her of Romantic invention—she being the source of the most important part of the story. Tocqueville remembered correctly that in the book he had read the couple was still alive. (He did forget, though, that they had left the island for the mainland.) She then describes her only visit to the island, apple tree and vine included, and lends them a little boat. The narrator and his fellow-traveler begin to "row madly" (and they end up with callouses); they have difficulty in penetrating the dense bushes that cover the island; once arrived, they see "an interesting but sad spectacle." Nature had covered the traces of human work, and it took them two hours to find the apple tree, the wild vine, and some vestiges of the house. The travelers are very moved, and when they leave the island, they discuss the fate of this man "equally incapable of living the life of a savage and the one of a civilized man." Alas, one needs to have an iron constitution to live in the forest.

Twice, Tocqueville mentions his ignorance of the Frenchman's name. He seems to be asking to be excused for being unable to "introduce" the Frenchman, whom, otherwise, both he and the "sister" could perhaps have met in their social circle. His place of exile is of obvious interest to them: it is evident in the letter that "the Frenchman" is, for Tocqueville, an occasion to talk, with self-ironic reserve, about the possibility or danger of exile. The tone of conversation "socializes" the Frenchman and lowers the pitch of the story. The expression of the writer's emotion is toned down to the exigencies of "drawing room" behavior, and the story remains within the limits of social conversation: it is interesting, sentimental, and rather moving. And it entertains.

The same can be said about Beaumont's version of the story. In his letter to his sister Eugénie, written just six days after the visit (on July 14, 1831), he described the entire adventure in one paragraph. Local tradition (no mention of a book) had it that a Frenchman came to the island at the time of the Revolution. They were curious to see "the solitary retreat of our countryman; who knows, perhaps one day we will be happy to find there a place of exile. We went, then, to inspect the house." Unfortunately, no trace of habitation remains. They find an apple tree and the vine; "it is impossible to imagine a more joyous place which would appeal more to imagination. We have spent there two hours in a state of true ecstasies." Although the story remains the same, the tone is ironic, because it is about himself that Beaumont is writing. The Frenchman of the letters of Tocqueville and Beaumont is the same one we met in "Journey to Lake Oneida," but without his resonance and tragic depth.

However, there are in Beaumont's work other versions of the story that are more pathetic. One can even argue that the entire novel Beaumont wrote about his American stay is an echo of the Frenchman's story. The Frenchman was an expression of existential anguish, and he "traveled" with them wherever they went.

9

A Seated Man

Beaumont's Frenchman

I have often quoted here opinions expressed by Beaumont
on Tocqueville's character, on his way of working, and on their American
journey. Beaumont was a very close friend of Tocqueville's, his collabora-
tor and, finally, after Tocqueville's death, the editor of his collected
works. Unlike Tocqueville, Beaumont was warm and outgoing—Heine
described them as "oil and ice." He was also a talented writer, although
perhaps not as talented as he wished to be. Beaumont came from an
aristocratic family (and married Lafayette's granddaughter), and his education and background were similar to his friend's. He agreed with
Tocqueville on most subjects, and in Beaumont's writings many of the
same opinions and images can be found, often pushed one step further
toward explicitness. The influence was not one-sided; the two friends
prepared together for their journey, discussed everything while visiting
America, and, later, often worked together on various projects. Beaumont offered Tocqueville an intellectual friendship that lasted all their
lives. Together they wrote *On the Penitentiary System in the United States*
(Beaumont doing most of the work), but another book they planned to
write together about America was never written. Instead, Tocqueville
wrote his *Democracy,* and Beaumont wrote a much less well-known novel
called *Marie, or Slavery in the United States.* Although not the title character, the "Frenchman" is the real protagonist of the novel.

121

Marie appeared in 1835, the same year as the first volume of *Democracy in America*. It was a two-volume novel devoted to a description of American manners and meant to complement *Democracy*'s presentation of American political institutions. *Marie*'s central problem was that of racism in the United States: it spoke not only about slavery but also about the plight of liberated blacks and the persecution of Indians. Both Tocqueville and Beaumont rightly predicted that the abolition of slavery would not stop the persecution of blacks and that the consequences of this terrible original sin of the American republic would last into the far future. Beaumont was so shocked by what he saw in America that he decided to devote his entire book to the problem.

But the author had broader ambitions for *Marie*. Beaumont wanted his work to be an encyclopedia of knowledge about the United States and, at the same time, an appealing and moving Romantic tale of—as its first-name title indicates—the same kind as *René, Aloys, Armance, Ourika,* and many others. In his introduction, Beaumont explained that he wanted to lighten the seriousness of his observations by using a more entertaining form, in order to attract the reader who "seeks in a book ideas for the intellect and emotions for the heart."[1] Although the book went through seven printings and received a prestigious literary prize, it was soon forgotten. Its first American translation appeared only in 1958 as an offshoot of the still-growing popularity of Tocqueville's *Democracy*.

One reason for the demise of the book was that it was a mixture of unintegrated elements. Short essays, notes, footnotes, and appendices burst open the narrative frame of the story. The characters would pause to discuss numerous topics, ranging from slavery to the beauty of American women; the story was interrupted by full descriptions and explanations, supplemented by bibliographic references. The main protagonists travel across the United States and, although in a terrible plight, stop to inform the readers about the places they go through. Their itinerary repeats that of Tocqueville and Beaumont; and twice there is mention of Frenchman's Island. This is not the only thing recognizable to the reader of Tocqueville's work. As Pierson has rightly said, *Marie* seems "strangely and wonderfully familiar . . . [it is] a book of echoes."[2] Everything here, too, is a repetition.

Beaumont attempted to reconcile the two aspects of the attitude he

1. *Marie* (1835), 1: ii; American edition, p. 3.
2. Pierson, *Tocqueville and Beaumont in America,* 523.

and his companion had toward America: the rational and the emotional. Whereas Tocqueville exiled the Frenchman from his masterwork to a short and secondary story, Beaumont placed him at the center of his novel but without relinquishing his other urge: to understand the New World. The knowledge he transmitted obscured the plight of the Frenchman, and the Frenchman's suffering rendered the knowledge superfluous. For the Frenchman's story is fundamentally antisocial and irreconcilable with an encyclopedic interest in manners and institutions.

The book is introduced to the reader by the narrator who interferes in the story through footnotes and appendices. The story itself is told as the confession of "un solitaire" to a traveler, both of them Frenchmen. We are, of course, in America, the traveler having left France frustrated in his effort to live a dignified life. Now he wants to settle on the border between the forest and civilization to enjoy solitude but, at the same time, to participate in the American politics of self-government. The traveler, whose first name, Gaston, is revealed only in the last pages of the book (as if to keep the reader wondering if it was not Gustave, Beaumont's first name), is twenty-five years old, just like Beaumont and Tocqueville. The year is 1831, the year of their visit. Ludovic, because such is the name of the hermit, is ten years older than Tocqueville and Beaumont, and five years younger than Custine's Aloys; he therefore fills the generational gap between René and Gaston: as in the forest, where there were the trees of all ages, we have "Renés" of all generations. The traveler meets Ludovic in the place where he would like to settle: the place, wonderfully familiar, is a repetition of the scenery of Lake Oneida. A peaceful surface of water, reflecting, like a mirror, the surrounding trees, emanates sweet tranquility. As we learn later, the lake is the place of the suicide of an Indian woman called, in a sort of echo, Onéda. The two Frenchmen, the hermit, and the traveler, sit down under an old tree at the bottom of a rock. Contemplating the lake, one tells his story, the other listens.

This familiar scene—René told his story in exactly the same position at a similar spot—is the frame of the entire book. Throughout the narrative the men sit, telling and listening to the tale. Ludovic is seated because he is at the end of his life, surviving only to tell his story.[3] He decides to tell his past so that it does not become Gaston's future. His life, and the one that may await Gaston, is the Frenchman's, René's life.

3. This is another of the characteristics of the "mal du siècle" novel. See Margaret Waller, 148.

The details are an amplification of the life of René: restless, he travels, comes to America, falls in love with a girl who, Atala-like, has a terrible secret; they escape into the forest, where their happiness is cut short by her death. They were chased to death by racial prejudice: Marie looks white, she even *is* white, but one of her ancestors had a drop of colored blood—this is the secret, and, according to implacable local custom, she is considered black. In their escape, the pair pass close to Frenchman's Island (which is described in the text and in the footnote) but cannot settle there because the lake's shores are already "invaded" by people. The island is (now) in the middle of this wonderfully peaceful lake that, like a mirror, reflects the surrounding trees and the sky. In itself, the island does not interest the narrator, but "a man lived there, and this man was French, unhappy and banished." This is another mise-en-abîme, an echo of the main story. The details are not mentioned, yet they constitute, nevertheless, the content of the main plot. It is still another lake, the same privileged place, reflecting the previous lakes and, in them, the face of the writer. As the couple travels in search of "asylum," the plot takes some of the obligatory steps. The love is unconsummated, the woman dies—all the women in René-like stories do—and the last word belongs to the priest, whose consolation leaves Ludovic still unhappy but no longer impious. He survives, *un mort-vivant*, to guard the grave of his beloved and to tell his tale.

Marie falls between the genres; it is a hybrid book. One part travel story, it has an itinerary, descriptions of the sites, and a typical ending: Gaston, having learned that there is no better place than France (as Custine learned in Russia), returns to his homeland, never to leave it again. The encyclopedic content, with its thoroughness and detail, is part of the travel description. The second aspect consists of the Frenchman's story, but here, in contrast to travel descriptions, the detail is blurred and unimportant. The two facets intertwine but are easily separable. Curious and observant when relating American realities, Ludovic becomes singularly vague when talking about himself. What he remembers best are his feelings. The reasons for his emigration to America are stated in general terms: it was his restlessness that pushed him away from a place that was recuperating from great social upheavals. He would have liked to participate in social life there, but he was repelled by people; love was the only way for him, but now it is not possible anymore; once he was alive, now he is sitting motionless, remembering his past happiness.

The contrast between his state of mind and the practical, busy reporting about America is what undermined *Marie*. Beaumont was unsuccessful in reconciling the two sides of America, both equally attractive: "advanced civilization" on the one hand, with "virgin nature" on the other. His alter ego, in fact, wanted to settle in-between. But, as was pointed out to him by the already-defeated Ludovic, these two visions of America were unreconcilable. The division into two Americas was also an idea of Chateaubriand: as was already mentioned, the America of the forests is opposed to the civilized America when he talks about the young Tocqueville. Beaumont believed in this duality and could not decide which America was the one he was truly interested in. The entire novel reflects this ambiguity. The title protagnoist, Marie, is not the novel's main character; she is born between the races—white but considered black, therefore white but black. As a result, she belongs to no group and is placed outside society. Almost married, she remains a virgin; a beautiful woman, she is, like Atala, an angel, a child. In her long, slightly operatic death scene, her saintliness reminds the reader of the other Marie—Virgin Mary. Although persecuted by an unjust society, her drama is presented as one of internal suffering: she is doomed, the short blissful love notwithstanding. As she dies, Ludovic withdraws into this other America, not the country of democracy, not even a society at all, but a shelter that devours its occupants, only to immortalize them in traces and debris to be deciphered from the peaceful face of her lakes by future travelers.

Although Beaumont was a very intelligent and very gifted man, his imagination was limited, and in his attempt at glory (*Marie* was supposed to be "the great work that should immortalize me")[4] he reached for ready-made artistic forms. These forms reflected so well his divided state of mind that he felt no need to modify them. *Marie* followed the tradition of the French anticolonial novel: a protagonist of mixed blood was the perfect device for unmasking the absurdity of racial prejudice. In these novels, the Frenchmen were always the real protagonists— generous rescuers doomed to failure.[5] The travel narrative and explanatory treatise were also well-known forms of writing and needed no apologies: *Corinne,* the famous novel by Madame de Staël, had united these elements in 1805. Each of these genres had its own logic and pulled the text in its own direction. But the overriding form and the

4. He wrote this in a letter to his brother Achille; cf. Beaumont, *Lettres d'Amérique,* 176.

5. See Léon-François Hoffman, *Le nègre romantique; personnage littéraire et obsession collective* (Paris: Payot, 1973).

central image of the book did not belong to any single genre: it was that of Ludovic telling his story to Gaston—the image of the seated man. In fact, the real protagonist of *Marie* is Gaston—the seated man, who tells his story to the other seated man—the traveler. They were both literary descendants of René. Although few Renés went to America, the New World made a good setting for their suffering. America, as "discovered" by Chateaubriand, was a country of duality and nostalgia. As René looked at it, the country was a lost opportunity: it might have been a French colony. He recalled the colonial competition between France and England that ended in 1763, with the Paris Treaty, in which France left Canada to Britain and Louisiana to Spain. In the war with the English, the French were allied with the Indian nations (except the Iroquois). It is this memory that Chateaubriand and Tocqueville invoke in their nostalgia for the Empire. This is also the basis for what Lafitau, then Chateaubriand, and then Tocqueville perceived as the natural affinity between the French and the Indians. Hence the search for the traces of the Frenchman concentrated not only on his sorrowful individual fate or one's own possible future exile but on nostalgia for past or potential French imperial greatness.

As Chateaubriand (and later Tocqueville) looked at Protestant America, they saw a possible Catholic "New France." It was not only this matter that made the writer see one thing and envision another. He suffered an interior discontinuity that made him reject what he saw: he was "here" but, as he looked around, he thought only about "there"— the homeland he had left, the château of his childhood. His present consisted of contemplating the traces of his past. Life reminded him of death, and death was a sign of the life that passed. The freedom of today was a result of yesterday's prisons, but it was an aimless, useless freedom, unlike the freedom one used to dream about. Everything was in a state of change: the forest still stood erect but was being destroyed by the encroachment of "civilization"; civilization, though, was fragile and easily covered by the forest. Nature set the model for life—creation was identical with destruction, and death coexisted with life. Nature's immensity, its infinity, reduced man to the dimension of a tree in the forest but simultaneously made him part of an endless life cycle. The fallen trees were monuments, then ruins, only to continue nature's cycle and regrow as new offspring. The tree, just like the Frenchman, was taken out of time's frame; neither alive nor dead, they keep recurring in a continuous cycle, their existence both general and individual. Nostalgia is explained: time is used here as if it were space—it can be revisited. The half-dead tree stands, Christ-like, over the forest.

The many people who populated that landscape had similarly in-between natures. Of mixed race or racially mixed upbringing, civilized savages and savage Frenchmen—"faux Indiens," travelers, exiles, they were, together with the landscapes, expressions of a malaise, of a "mal du siècle." Chactas was a half-civilized Indian chief—he had even met Louis XIV in Paris; René tried to become "savage"; Atala was of Span-ish lineage and Christian but of Indian upbringing; Beaumont's Ludo-vic is called a "civilized savage"; and the Frenchman is characterized as "no longer adapted either for solitude or for the world . . . neither a savage nor a civilized man: nothing but a piece of debris" (p. 349). All these characters belong to two social orders at the same time and are the embodiment of contradictions. America was for them not a place of social integration but an empty space to wander in. They came there not because they wanted to but because they were dissatisfied with the place they had been in before. Even those who were born there, like Chactas or Atala, were displaced and homeless. In this empty, asocial space, they sit, looking not at landscapes but within themselves. What they see is ruin.

Beaumont wrote about the seated man and also drew him. During his American travel Beaumont carried with him two sketching albums, one for his rough on-the-spot sketches, the second for final and more ambitious drawings. Both albums survived and, although the authentic-ity of the second one may be doubted, it at least contains "extraordi-narily careful copies" of the supposed originals.[6] The chapter on the excursion to Lake Oneida in Pierson's book is illustrated with a repro-duction of *The View of Lake Oneida from Frenchman's Island* from the second album. In the foreground, in the left corner of the sketch, we see a fragment of a rocky island. Under a tall tree, full of leaves but with a withered top, there are two small male figures: one standing with a gun in his hand, turned toward the second, who is sitting and looking sadly into the surrounding water. The horizon is delineated by the forest on the opposite shore. There are some boats on the water. The date July 8, 1831, is written in the right lower corner, and it coincides with the date of the excursion.

This drawing is the second version of the original, which contained

6. Pierson, *Tocqueville and Beaumont in America*, xi.

only one figure and no boats. It is very likely that this was the figure of the sitting man. A second figure and boats were added later in the process of transferring, "rewriting" the first rough sketch into the final pen-and-ink version. The difference of meaning between the two sketches is analogical to the difference between *Marie* as a travel story and *Marie* as a "mal du siècle" novel. The boats and the second man (holding a gun, the very symbol of action) suggest some sort of story; the boats tell how the two figures arrived on the island, also the way they may depart. The second male figure gives the scene a social dimension; it is a travel scene, a moment of rest during a journey, the travelers or the explorers sadly contemplating the place. The title, *The View of Lake Oneida from Frenchman's Island,* is very appropriate for this scene; it is one view among many from a journey.

Nothing of that sort in the first sketch. No boats; a lonely European male figure in a deserted setting, seated, with sad, melancholy resignation, under a half-dead tree. No movement, no past or future, no life; the figure is still another version of the *mort-vivant.* Perhaps it was to be Tocqueville's silhouette; Beaumont often drew him in his American sketches. The fact that the sketch featured only one person might be a sign of its realism. But would Tocqueville not have looked from the lake to the island, not vice-versa? He was, after all, a traveler, an explorer. Also, access to the island was, in reality, very difficult: Tocqueville complained in his letter and in the "Journey" how difficult it had been to set foot on it. So the lonely figure seated under a half-dead tree is not a realistic rendering of a scene, it is the projection of a mood. To convey this mood, Beaumont cleared the shore, placed on it a withered tree, and sat under it a young man. In this way, he instantly entered a convention, a cliché, without altogether abandoning representation.

This drawing and its metamorphosis is an excellent illustration of the double function of Beaumont's American writings and drawings. With a couple of boats, or two travelers, it was an exploration. With one man, it was a Romantic reverie. The young seated man is not different from the Frenchman and is similar to many other young men: to the one gazing at the moon in the Le Barbier illustration to the first edition of *Génie du Christianisme* (*René* and *Atala* were parts of this work by Chateaubriand); to the grieving figure of Chactas sitting in a Christ Man of Sorrows posture in the 1836 sculpture by François-Joseph Duret; to Caius Marius looking at the ruins of Carthage in John Vanderlyn's 1807 painting; to the bitterly sad Napoleon sitting on a rock in the Delaroche painting and in many popular lithographs; to young Lamartine in the first "Méditation"; to Giacomo Leopardi in his "idyll" *L'infinito;* and to Ugo Foscolo's Jacopo Ortis writing his *Ultime lettere* on the mountainous border of Northern Italy. They are brothers, members of the same family, sharing the same biography: they survived defeat. The surroundings were changeable—sea, mountain, lake, forest, or ruins; the young man was always the same, meditating on the debris of a civilization, of a life, of a love.

A Seated Man

The Romantic sitting man was a traveler contemplating the terrifying grandeur of nature. "The sight of unlimited distances," wrote Friedrich von Schiller in his *On the Sublime,*

and heights lost to view, the vast ocean at his feet and the vaster ocean above him, pluck his spirit out of the narrow sphere of the actual and out of the oppressive bondage of physical life. A mightier measure of esteem is exemplified for him by the simple majesty of nature, and surrounded by her massive forms he can no longer tolerate pettiness in his mode of thought. Who knows how many illumined thoughts or heroic decisions that could never have been born in a cell-like study or a society salon have been produced out of this bold struggle of the mind with the great spirit of nature while wandering abroad . . . the mind of the nomad remains as open and free as the firmament beneath which he camps.[7]

The trajectory of this wandering nomad is well known to us from later Romantic literature: in the plains of Sicily he would (writes Schiller) "marvel at the wonderful battle between fecundity and destruction," on the "treacherous crater of Vesuvius . . . and in the ruins of Syracuse and Carthage," he will observe "the terrifying and magnificent spectacle of change which destroys everything and creates it anew, and destroys again. . . ." (pp. 205, 210).

It was this young wanderer that was waiting for Beaumont and Tocqueville in the depths of the American forest. Their reactions to the forest—finding there the spectacle of death and life, the Frenchman's death, religious awe—were the product of the literary, visual, and emotional vocabulary that was current in their milieu. The appeal of the

7. Friedrich von Schiller, *Naïve and Sentimental Poetry, and On the Sublime: Two Essays,* trans. with Introduction and Notes by Julius A. Elias (New York: Ungar, 1966), 204.

sublime was strong because it promised to set them free, to "transform actual suffering [which they were right to expect] into sublime emotion."[8] The story of the Frenchman allowed them to live through, master, and finally overcome fear of their own exile, abandonment, and death. This is why this unusual landscape was so easy for them to understand.

In the iconography of the end of the eighteenth century, only kings and the bourgeoisie could remain seated. When Revolution arrived, its attributes—Equality, Liberty, and Fraternity—were presented as women.[9] And then the seated man appeared. In literature he could be traced to Goethe's *Werther* (1774); also in the visual realm, one of the precursors of the seated man may have been the famous painting by Wilhelm Tischbein, *Goethe in the Campagna* (1787). Here Goethe, wearing his hat, is reclining on a stone with the ruins and hills of the Roman countryside behind him. The seated man was also preceded by the Melancholy figures, because he is certainly an artist. Neither a statesman on horseback nor a bourgeois in his royal-looking armchair, he was a young man in nature, sitting on a volcano, on a rock, or under a tree, outside of his social environment, away from human artifacts, except for those in ruin before his eyes. He was delicate, uncomfortable, unhappy, and often wept (although only in literature, never in pictures). Young, he was at the end of something; he had nowhere to go, no will to survive. But he was a man of genius, or at least of talent, and of enormous sensitivity. His immobility belied the intensity of his suffering.

This image had a certain repetitive style: it was very scrupulously realistic but not very concrete. It reflected perfectly a certain state of mind without concerning itself with the accuracy of surrounding detail. In the famous 1809 portrait of Chateaubriand by A.-L. Girodet de Roucy-Trioson, the French Homer is standing leaning on a rock with the ruins of Rome behind him, looking very sad. (His hair was "windswept," which provoked Napoleon to say that he looked "like a conspirator who had come down the chimney.")[10] In another painting of Chateaubriand, entitled "Chateaubriand and Madame de Staël among the

8. Schiller, 209.

9. In the European allegories, America was presented as a seated young woman. See Hugh Honour, *The New Golden Land: European Images of America from the Discoveries to the Present Time* (New York: Pantheon, 1975), 85–90. (The bronze sculpture of Chactas in the same volume, p. 223.)

10. Hugh Honour, *Romanticism* (New York: Harper and Row, 1979), 249.

Greeks," the artist, H.L.V.J.B. Aubry-Lecomte, showed the two Romantic writers as muses of the Greek war of liberation. Although Madame
de Staël was already dead (she died in 1817, and the painting is dated
1827, which is when the war was going on), she is nevertheless shown
as vividly alive. Both protagonists are seated mournfully, almost lan-
guidly, Chateaubriand looking at the horizon, and Madame de Staël,
with a lyre in her hand, to the sky. Although she is sitting in a contorted
position and in antique clothes, he is dressed in a dark cape, his distress
expressed only in his eyes. Their faces are full of sorrow—not a very
belligerent attitude. In the background there are mountains and the sea;
behind Chateaubriand, there is a group of men at the left (none of them
looking ready to fight), and, on his right, a group of women looking up
at the sky; both groups, one supposes, inspired by the two writers.

It is not common to find a man seated in company; he is usually all by
himself. Also, the context of the fight for national liberation is too active
for a seated man. There is a substantial difference between a standing and
a sitting man. (Napoleon is said never to have sat down when he planned
to refuse a request.) The standing man is ready for action—not so the
sitting man. His "sitting down" is an attempt at reformulating the terms
of his participation in social life. The war of liberation was not so much
an action as a "just cause," and the young man (or the poet) would share
its griefs and defeats. Helping the weak was his way of participating in
the world, and the Greek cause became a commonplace of Romantic art.
The seated man of Beaumont's *Marie*, Ludovic, lists the Greek war together with his other mournful wanderings:

An unexpected event suddenly reanimated my languishing energy and smiled
on my imagination. It was the year 1825; liberty was astir in enslaved Greece—
here was the cause of civilization against barbarism! Filled with pious enthusiasm, I rushed to the fatherland of Homer. Poetic stirrings of a young soul! How
noble and impetuous! Alas! why is it that these sublime aspirations meet only
deception and lies? I shed my blood in the cause of liberty. I saw the Greeks
triumphant, and to this day I know not which is baser, the victors or the
vanquished. The Greeks are no longer slaves to the Moslems, but, still doomed
to servitude, they have gained only the sad privilege of choosing their own
masters and tyrants.

"What could I do in that land of memories and tombs?" he asks, revert-
ing again to his role of traveler. ". . . Indifferent, without thought or
aim, I directed my steps at random" (pp. 28–29).

This episode expresses well, as all of *Marie* does, the central problem
of the seated man: withdrawal is his form of action. The popularity, the

explosive multiplication of this image in French culture at the beginning of the nineteenth century, was due to the fact that it embodied an anxiety that was common to many. In contemporary sociopsychological language it can be said to express a profound identity crisis.

Many critics have pointed out the feminization of the Romantic protagonist, his sensitivity, his refusal to act.[11] René was seated because he did not want to submerge himself in the bustle of bureaucracy or commerce, or even in "the oppressive bondage of physical life." Yet he had to do something, not only because he needed money but also in order to know who he was. His château was empty; there was nothing about his father he was proud of; or, if he was, there was nothing he could do as a son of his father. His identity used to come from a hierarchical order attached to a geographic place; this order did not exist anymore, and the place was empty. He had no last name, nothing to live on, nothing to do. He therefore goes to America where he is forcibly socialized by marrying (against his will!) into an Indian tribe. This traditionally feminine way of gaining name, income, and social identity does not work in René's case. He refuses, or is unable, to consummate his marriage. In order to fulfill it social role, marriage requires more than passive consent. René sadly withdraws.[12]

There is no doubt that René was an aristocrat, but the appeal of his story went far beyond his class. Chateaubriand did not insist on details of René's lineage or finances and even went so far in his blurring of the historical details as to move the action into the prerevolutionary world. The old France that stirs René's nostalgia is the France of Louis XIV. Barbéris interpreted this choice as Chateaubriand's political attempt at obscuring, for "complex [political] reasons," his antirevolutionary stance; but it also serves as a very effective introduction of the sense of historical crisis into the novel as a genre (pp. 157–161). This act of generalizing, "spreading" of the crisis into other historical areas, was a result of the conviction Chateaubriand shared with many of his aristocratic contemporaries that the Revolution was only the end of a long process of change and decline. The aristocracy did not resist the Revolution at the start and was unable and unwilling to defend its own rights. The state, to use Tocqueville's interpretation from *The Old Régime and the Revolution*, through centralization took

11. See especially the analysis of *René* by Pierre Barbéris ("*René*" *de Chateaubriand* [Paris: Larousse, 1973]), and the already-quoted article by Margaret Waller.

12. Only partially, since we learn elsewhere in *Génie du Christianisme* that he had a daughter of mixed blood.

away the aristocracy's social functions. They were left with only external marks of distinction that had no political significance. These
empty signs of former usefulness could be obtained for money by
nonaristocrats, breeding a fierce internal hierarchy of imagined supe-
riorities. Arrogance was joined to powerlessness, and this combination
caused violent social resentment against the aristocracy. It was the Old
Régime itself, then, that destroyed the aristocracy and provoked the
Revolution.[13]

Before the Revolution, the French aristocracy counted approximately 200,000 people; of these, 40,000 were men capable of holding a
job. Only a small percentage of them were landowners; most were in
the professions, the army, and the bureaucracy. They shared with the
other classes the belief that a useful life is a life of work, and their
identity was more and more linked to what they did.[14] "The true aim of
existence," wrote Custine, "appears to a man only within social life. It is
in participating in public endeavors that he becomes something for
everybody and his right to exist is recognized" (*Aloys*, 29). Even before
the Revolution, René could be integrated into society only through the
bureaucracy, army, or the professions, and his château had already been
empty for quite some time. All of this, however, was hidden from him.
The Revolution abolished the ranks of nobility and therefore made clear
and irrevocable what before could have remained unsaid—the Revolution made René's situation clear. (In this respect Karamzin was right,
the Revolution did clarify "our ideas.")

The knowledge that the decline had started long before the Revolution brought no relief and did not dispel the feeling of radical change.
"Chateaubriand tries to reconcile the old royalty with the new democracy," wrote François Furet, "but he nourishes his books with the irre-
pressible sentiment of the end of a world and the beginning of a new
age."[15] René's main characteristic was that he was a survivor of a catastrophe. The attractiveness of his image was due in large part to its
vagueness and generality. Later incarnations were often more concrete.
Beaumont presents his alter ego Gaston in a clear way: there were
political reasons for his maladjustment and emigration: "[after the revo-

13. Alexis de Tocqueville, *The Old Régime and the Revolution,* trans. Stuart Gilbert
(New York: Doubleday, 1955). See especially pt. 2.
14. See David D. Bien, "Aristocratie," in *Dictionnaire Critique de la Révolution Française,* ed. François Furet and Mona Ozouf (Paris: Flammarion, 1988), 647–651.
15. François Furet, "L'Ancient Régime," *Dictionnaire Critique de la Révolution Française,* 627–637; 627.

lution of 1830] his sympathies and convictions drew him to one party; his family ties held him in another." Then, there were financial reasons. "Hoping to escape from the vexations of political life, he tried to go into business, but fortune was against him. At the age of twenty-five, he found himself without a career, having nothing to look forward to but a share in a modest patrimony" (Beaumont, 9–10). Nothing of the sort in René. He has a secret—his incestuous desire for his sister—and the rest is more or less vague. But on reading the text attentively, as Pierre Barbéris did, one can discover that money was a problem. René did not have enough money, did not want to "prendre un état" (as his sister advised him to do), that is, to work in order to earn his living. His refusal to work is not perceived as a sign of laziness (which is a character-istic of colonial populations, children, and women) but of purity.[16] He is withdrawing, refusing to participate in a situation in which his uniqueness is negated and his identity derived from outside criteria—decreed by the state or drawn from his profession. René sat in defense of his unique self, of his irreducible difference that he believed indepen-dent of his social situation. He was the first in a long line of poor young men who in this way *stood up* against society.

René (and the Frenchman, and Gaston, and Ludovic, and, let us not forget, Aloys) were the characters who translated a social aristocracy into a spiritual aristocracy. This is why their ranks are not limited to the aristocracy of blood, and their most accomplished brothers—for exam-ple Julien Sorel—are commoners. Withdrawal had the positive function of reintegrating what Stendhal called "la classe pensante" into society. Refusal to compromise and the figure of the individual in conflict with society are the legacy of this transformation. That individual became today's intellectual. Chateaubriand, Tocqueville, Beaumont, Custine (and many others) were trying to find a place of usefulness for the elite—to create and become part of the aristocracy of spirit. Today the image is only slightly modified: the man still sits but in a prison cell.

The Seated Man and His Politics

But one does not need to pity the seated man. Chateaubri-and, Tocqueville, Beaumont, Custine, and other authors who wrote

16. P. Barbéris, 163–165.

about him were energetic and even inflexible when they felt his existence endangered. This determination was encoded in their language and is quite clearly visible in Tocqueville's writings. The image of the seated man is emphatically present in Tocqueville's works, especially in the early ones. In his *Voyage en Sicile*, written when he was twenty-two years old,[17] he described himself sitting in a boat cabin during a terrible storm, "[his] head resting against his hand, [his] eyes searching the horizon" (p. 38). A little later, he goes to see Etna—volcanoes being the privileged place for the seated man[18]—to sit down and contemplate the historical sublime, the change that destroys everything (p. 46). Next, he sits down "in the sand, [his] head pressing against [his] hands, [his] eyes turned towards open sea, thinking and rethinking at leisure about the saddest things" (p. 48). But his worries and sad contemplations were only one aspect of the text; his political interests were asserting themselves very strongly already. As he looks at Sicily at his feet, he contemplates the sublime, but he also tries to observe the workings of human society. "If I were a king of England," he writes after having seen and interpreted the size of land property in Sicily, "and had to make a decision, I would favor big property; if I were master of Sicily, I would encourage small ones."[19] He did feel called on to think about and influence the world, and the sense of political responsibility coincided in him with the pensive withdrawal of the seated man.

The Sicilian journey, which he made with his brother Edouard, remained memorable because of its emphasis on the historical sublime, and even in his American writings Tocqueville returns to it. In "A Fortnight in the Wilds" he recalls, in a typically Chateaubriandesque pose, how

one evening in Sicily we happened to get lost in a vast marsh that now occupies the place where once was the city of Himera; the sight of that once famous city turned back to savage wilds made a great and deep impression on us. Never had we seen beneath our feet more magnificent witness to the instability of human things and the wretchedness of our nature.[20]

17. But published posthumously, and in excerpts only, by Beaumont. The original manuscript was lost and the excerpts are all that remain. See vol. 5 of his *Oeuvres Complètes* (1957), 33–54.
18. Chateaubriand was called, among other names, "le Solitaire de Vésuve."
19. "But being neither one nor the other, I return to my diary," he concludes (p. 45).
20. In *Journey to America*, 350–403, esp. 399. Beamont, in an attempt to unite the sublime of history with the sublime of nature, had his Ludovic imagine Rome's Saint Peter's Cathedral on top of Mont Blanc. "Oh, what a magnificent altar to Divinity it would make!" he exclaimed. This passage has been cut out in the only American edition

But Italy was not the only place where contemplation was possible, or its only subject. In his biography of Tocqueville, André Jardin quotes one of his letters to Mary Mottley, written from England while Tocqueville was preparing to start working on *Democracy*. He visited by night the ruins of Kenilworth Castle—an empty château—and found it

truly a great and solemn spectacle: in the middle of this solitary place there reigned a silence and an air of inexpressible desolation. I went into the halls of this magnificent manor; the upper stories were destroyed, I could see the sky above my head, but the walls still stood, and the moon, penetrating every part through the Gothic windows, cast a sepulchral light that was in harmony with all these things. Was I not truly in the realm of the dead there? After exploring the ruins in every direction and with my footsteps awakening echoes that had probably been mute for many years, I came back to the center. Here, I sat down on a rock and fell in to a sort of somnambulism during which it seemed to me that my soul was pulled into the past with an inexpressible force. (P. 198)

As the letter continues, we can clearly see that the rock he is sitting on is within the walls of the castle. The empty château became part of nature. The letter shows Tocqueville's literary taste, and his attachment, if one may call it so, to the seated man. The old castle, a ruin, moonlight, echoes, spirits of the dead, and a seated man—there could be nothing more Romantic.

This visit is analogical to the visit to Lake Oneida: an empty place, an exploration "in every direction," return to the center, sitting down to dream, to think, and . . . to write. Here, in the castle, Tocqueville does not look for the Frenchman, he himself is the Frenchman. The image of the man seated on a rock inside a ruined château is a (slightly funny) vision of withdrawal that expressed a deeply felt dissatisfaction with the present times. Tocqueville shared the convictions and feelings of his contemporaries, who saw the individual as powerless, isolated, and rejected. The past was thought to have contained all greatness, and there was no possibility of glory in the present time. In *Democracy in America*, Tocqueville invoked the names of René, Childe Harold, and Lamartine's Jocelyn as symbols of the age (2: 81). These convictions

---

of *Marie* (p. 30). In general, almost all of the books that are discussed here have been republished with cuts. Their integrity is obviously not recognized any longer. It makes one think of Tocqueville and Beaumont's complaints about the commercialization of life. Books, these industrial products par excellence (reproduced, identical, in large quantities), can also be trimmed to more comfortable size or enlarged with commentaries and footnotes. See L. Febvre and H.-J. Martin, *L'Apparition du livre* (Paris: Albin Michel, 1958).

accompanied depressions and despondence that pursued him through most of his life.[21]

And yet while he was in England Tocqueville was also much occupied with inquiries into British political life. His working habits were very similar to those he had in America, and he came back with copious notes from meetings, conversations, parliamentary sessions, and other political events. He understood England very well and was able to predict the course of events accurately. But throughout his life his Romantic side was just beneath the analytical surface of his writings, as the example of the empty château from his *Recollections* shows. Tocqueville was a Romantic with a very lucid mind.

There was a certain contradiction in this combination: the Romantic's contemplation of the sublime should have rendered him averse to analyzing what in the words of Schiller was the "spiritless regularity" of everyday life. "Man has a need beyond living and securing his welfare," Schiller thought, "and quite another destiny than to comprehend the phenomena that surround him."[22] Schiller's man was a traveler: he rejected human company, looked at cities only when they were in ruins, and found the sublime in nature. This was also one of the ways in which Tocqueville—especially young Tocqueville—"traveled."[23]

Sublime in nature was associated with certain well-known places: volcanoes, the Alps, and the Niagara Falls. These were the gigantic spectacles that showed man the real scale of things and his own insignificance. Tocqueville, however, denied that the sublime was to be found in the United States. He associated it only with Europe.

I have been through terrifying solitudes in the Alps where nature rejects the work of man, and where even in its very horror the sheer grandeur of the scene has something that transports one's soul with excitement.[24] Here [in America] the solitude is as profound but does not bring the same sensations to birth. All that one feels in passing through these flowery wildernesses where everything,

21. See Roger Boesche, *The Strange Liberalism of Alexis de Tocqueville*. Pt. 1 of this book analyzes the cultural context of some of the ideas of Tocqueville's theories. Boesche shows very convincingly "the ways and extent to which Tocqueville's ideas emerged from the aspirations and anxieties of his generation" (p. 23). It is also Boesche who points out Tocqueville's depressions.

22. Schiller, 204–205.

23. Tocqueville did not have to read Schiller's essay to use his categories, which were later repeated in many other works. He certainly knew and admired Schiller's dramas. See Reino Virtanen, "Tocqueville and the Romantics," *Symposium* 13 (1959): 167–185, esp. 170. Custine, too, admired Schiller very much. See Tarn, 59.

24. Custine has an analogical description of Alpes. See *Aloys*, 31. Many such descriptions could be found in the literature of the epoch.

as in Milton's *Paradise*,[25] is ready to receive man, is a quiet admiration, a gentle melancholy sense, and a vague distaste for civilized life; a sort of primitive instinct that makes one think with sadness that soon this delightful solitude will have changed its looks.

And he continues with a little reversal of the image of Lake Oneida:

In fact already the white race is advancing across the forest that surrounds it, and in but few years the European will have cut the trees that are now reflected in the limpid waters of the lake."[26]

Yet, his denials notwithstanding, he does find in the American forest the sublime in both its forms: as a moment of supreme insight (when he enters the American forest-cathedral at the beginning of "Journey to Lake Oneida") and as a sustained tension toward the spiritual. The deepest sense of awe and religious terror comes to him in the United States not from nature but from history. The very essence of America illustrated for him the working of Providence, and the existence of *Democracy in America* was due to his feeling of the sublime:

The whole book that is here offered to the public has been written under the influence of a kind of religious awe produced in the author's mind by the view of that irresistible revolution [the march of equality] which has advanced for centuries in spite of every obstacle and which is still advancing in the midst of the ruins it has caused. (1: 6–7)

The image of marching equality, or the ruins it leaves in its path, is accompanied by a sense of urgency and despair at the mindlessness of political actors.

A new science of politics is needed for a new world. This, however, is what we think of least; placed in the middle of a rapid river, we obstinately fix our eyes on the ruins that may still be descried upon the shore we have left, while the current hurries us away and drags us backward towards the abyss. (1: 7)

Unless we grasp the meaning of the change, the rapid river—Chateaubriand's symbol of time—will drag us to our ruin.

Why, as Tocqueville looks at the march of equality, are his eyes turned toward America? He does see equality's Providential march through Europe, but there it has to demolish many obstacles on its way, causing ruin and despair. Yet Providence also gave to equality an empty

25. *Paradise* was known to Tocqueville, most probably, in the translation by Chateaubriand.
26. "A Fortnight in the Wilds," 347–348.

continent to expand into, and in America its march could unfold in harmony, even, perhaps, reaching its goal and ending peacefully. Therefore, when America herself appears to the eyes of the observer (in the introductory chapter on the "Exterior Form of America"), she presents a magnificent "spectacle." Her shape is marvelously easy to discern at first glance; her rivers and mountains are divided in a way that is both simple and majestic. It is a real gift of God. Everything is symmetrical, and the multitude of waters, the confusion of objects, and the extreme variety of "tableaux" are simplified by this symmetry. The description of the majesty of the "central" forest and of the confusion of rivers is identical to the opening forest scene of the "Journey to Lake Oneida," as are the corresponding feelings of religious awe. The work, disorder, and activity of the down-below is contrasted with the calm and symmetry of the above. This marvelous America—America as a marvel—is a spectacle in motion, but no society is visible in this image, only the dying Indian races that, just as in contemporary museums of natural sciences, belong here among the natural elements. Indians were placed in America "as if waiting" for Europeans to arrive. Only the traces of their past are left; in the mini-America of Frenchman's Island, only their name remains attached to the lake. The Indians' tomb is actually the empty cradle of a new civilization.

Whereas the beginnings of European civilization were buried in early, barbaric times, bearers of civilization arrived in America already mature. They were vital and virile, and nature was virginal—an empty continent given to a race that was ready to take it. As Tocqueville looked at America, he saw that it was made for that purpose, that its shape contained is future.[27] He therefore interprets America's emptiness as a sign of God's intention. Here the poetic is joined to the political. The (empty) *cradle, tomb, trace*—the "everyday" words of Romantic poetic language—now are used for political justification. America is likened to René's *château:* the *cradle,* where he lay, newborn; the *tomb* of his mother who died giving birth to him; and an *empty place,* a *trace* or *ruin* of a former life, from which René, like the Indians, was chased away.

Tocqueville felt a profound sympathy with the Indians: he and Beaumont truly identified with this "exiled nation." He included them in the brotherhood of victims by applying to them a Romantic vocabulary. But it was also easy for him to accept their exodus and extinction as

27. Myra Jehlen, *American Incarnation* (Cambridge: Harvard University Press, 1986), 40.

inevitable and logical, a consequence of their nature that prevented them from ever truly possessing their land and therefore doomed them to certain death. Here French Romantic nostalgia used the vocabulary of American practicality; in fact, Tocqueville's ideas about America's emptiness and destiny can be found in many of his American sources.[28]

The conquest and colonization of the Americas were accompanied by genocide. The enormity of this *fact,* if one may use such a word to describe it, was known and acknowledged, as we can see from, among other sources, Montaigne's *Essays* (1588). In two of them, "On the Coaches" and "On the Cannibals," Montaigne expressed the same attitude that was to characterize *Democracy in America.* He believed Western civilization to be corrupt and decadent; its superiority, however, made its expansion obvious and inevitable. Tocqueville was equally critical of Western culture and equally convinced of the essential link between culture and power, of the relationship between "lumières" and the spread of European dominion.[29] "Lumières" meant for Tocqueville not only ideas and culture but also material goods and comforts, which resulted from and accompanied these ideas. In a memorandum about the French expansion in Algiers, he expressed this conviction very clearly. After the initial military conquest, the French would be wise to use other forms of persuasion: "It will be easier to win [the colonized] with our riches and our arts than with our cannons."[30] The sorrow he felt at the extinction of the Indians did not prevent him from actively supporting the politics of French and Western colonization. He is aware that the Indian and the Algerian are corrupted and destroyed by contact with "civilization," but he holds it against them. He thought that contact between superior and inferior races corrupts the inferior not so much because the superior is itself corrupted but because of the inability of the inferior to grow and mature. "Their implacable prejudices, their uncontrolled passions, their vices, and still more, perhaps, their savage virtues consigned them to inevitable destruction."[31] It is their race that

28. Especially in Thomas Jefferson's *Notes on the State of Virginia* (1785). The image of the Indian as vulnerable to destruction by civilization because of his inability to possess and cultivate land can be found in C. F. Volney's *Observations générales sur les Indiens ou Sauvages de l'Amérique du Nord,* published as an appendix to his *Tableau du climat et du sol des Etats-Unis* (1803). It was one of Tocqueville's sources. See F. Furet, "From Savage Man to Historical Man," in *In the Workshop of History,* 153–156, and James Schleifer, *The Making of "Democracy in America,"* 40, 78.

29. See *Democracy in America,* 1: 5.

30. "Première lettre sur l'Algérie," *Oeuvres Complètes,* 5: 30. Chateaubriand was convinced that it was Church music that converted Indians, not the dogmas of the faith.

31. *Democracy in America,* 1: 7.

makes them unable to adapt to civilization; so it is, in a way, their race that kills them. Civilization had to expand, so Indians had to die. To highlight the inevitability and, so to speak, the involuntary character of this phenomenon, Tocqueville used the image of Indian races "vanishing daily like the snow in sunshine, and disappearing from view over the land."[32] This sun, "les lumières," was European civilization. "The ruin of these tribes began from the day when Europeans landed on their shores; it has proceeded ever since, and we are now witnessing its completion." The Indians were not subjects of history; they have been allowed by Providence to enjoy the riches of the New World "for a season" (1: 7), and now they are being removed. History may begin.

The Frenchman was also an (unsuccessful) explorer and settler whose presence was pushing back the Indians. Chateaubriand, Tocqueville, and Beaumont actively supported French colonial expansion, not only in their writing but also in their political practice. As a political man, Tocqueville supported (one may even say, implemented) French colonial expansion in Algiers, as well as many French government actions directed against the urban lower classes; he also advocated repressive prison methods.[33] Like Madame de Sévigné, whom he quotes so critically in the second volume of *Democracy*, he understands human suffering but does not apply this understanding to certain groups of people. He is more able to commiserate with the Indians, "the race that is dying out" and is distant in space, than with Parisian workers whom he meets everyday. His politics are governed by convictions but also by fears.

Paradise

This very active political attitude is expressed in the language of nostalgia for the idyllic past. (Rationally, Tocqueville did not see this past as idyllic.) The "Journey to Lake Oneida" is a text in which

32. "A Fortnight in the Wilds," 329.

33. They were repressive in relation to other methods proposed at the same time. He believed in prisoners' continuous isolation in solitary confinement and in strict discipline. It is difficult to detect any pity in his attitude—such was the distance he felt from the criminals. See his summary of his conversations with prisoners in a model Philadelphia prison; the class origin of the prisoner is always noted (*Oeuvres Complètes* [1984], 4: 329–341). See also Jardin, *Tocqueville*, 183. Although prison was a place where he thought he was likely to find himself, as his *Voyage en Sicile* attests, it was a different kind of imprisonment. The criminals were, in his opinion, morally defective, and there was little that could be done but to isolate them.

one can observe the hidden, nonexplicit terms of this nostalgia. Its protagonist is a noble exile, a chivalrous figure from the past. Such a figure, although present already in Sophie von La Roche's novel, was statistically very unlikely.[34] But the encounter between the exiled aristocrat and the new continent was particularly fertile. In spite of Tocqueville's conviction that because of its empty attachment to forms the French aristocracy was, together with the state, largely responsible for the Revolution, the aristocrat of Lake Oneida was simply a victim. He embodied everything that was noble and pure in France's past. His escape to the United States made his solitude and vulnerability extreme. It was a place in which his aristocracy of spirit could and did come into conflict with fate, the violence of nature, and the strangeness of the new human world. René, the first of these aristocrats, finds in America the ultimate exile, the great Gothic château of the forest; as his château was his cradle and the place of the first exile, so America became his tomb enclosed by the forest and transformed now into a cathedral.

In the "Journey to Lake Oneida," as well as in "A Fortnight in the Wilds" (although to a lesser degree), we can see Tocqueville's "American unconscious." In rewriting *René*, he expressed this side of himself which he banished from *Democracy in America*. It was an important part, so important that it steals back into *Democracy* and can be found in Tocqueville's overwhelming ambiguity toward things American. Beaumont makes his attitude clearer; *Marie* is, on one of its levels, an appeal against emigration to the United States. The two friends agreed on that matter, but Tocqueville expressed his attitude in a more complicated way, which can be, for the purpose of analysis, divided into two aspects: one rational, another unconscious. The Frenchman belonged to the latter.

The island on Lake Oneida is a little paradise. One arrives at it through the veils and domes of the forest-cathedral, in religious awe and in total silence. On the way, the drama of life and death is played out. Isolated from the world by spotless, innocent, sky-reflecting water, the island has an apple tree in the middle, just like Eden. The first and only couple's place was under that tree. The vine may be an image of the

---

34. See Massimo Boffa, "Emigrés," *Dictionnaire Critique de la Révolution Française*, 346–362. According to the statistical data, the aristocracy constituted only 17 percent of the entire emigration due to the Revolution—approximately 26,000 people. Of these, many were military men residing in Europe. Emigration to America was very small and short-lived, although distinguished. Talleyrand was the best known of the American exiles.

serpent, or quite the opposite, of the Church—God being the Keeper of the Vineyard. The final metamorphosis of the story—the half-dead tree—has powerful religious symbolism.[35] The Frenchman, like Christ, is dead but alive, a symbol of martyrdom. The meaning of his life is now clear, his death is a sacrifice.

The story of the young exile is purified of all external elements; even his marriage (presumably childless) is terminated by his wife's death. In fact, marriage in the literature of the time had a powerfully socializing meaning,[36] and the defeat in love which dooms the Romantic hero is a metaphor for his inability to be integrated. Chateaubriand, whose work is the source of this image and who was able, as always, to unite political with poetic,[37] characterized the Indians as *unwed* to the land of America: they did not cultivate the land, which therefore bore no fruit.[38] Tocqueville later called America empty for the very same reason: possession of the land civilized peoples, and uncivilized ones were doomed to perish on contact with civilization. The story of the Frenchman can also be translated into terms of possession: he failed to "marry" the island.

The Christian terminology and allusions were not accidental. They were shared with Chateaubriand, as a way of domesticating a landscape, a continent, and a fate. The seated man was transformed here into the Man of Sorrows, the traditional figure of Jesus sitting in distress, with his head on his hand. The place that was beautiful but otherwise uninteresting, as Beaumont said, became very understandable. The ease with which Tocqueville accepted the news of the Frenchman's disappearance was the result of translating the social situation into a religious framework: the Frenchman was doomed right from the start. His death was not a failure of adjustment to the social world but an act of sacrifice, of martyrdom. In this way the Frenchman was purified and so was America.

Christianizing the island, fitting it into the known categories of low and high, dead and alive, prosaic and noble is a way to attach this new territory to the continent of one's own culture. The tree is one of the main symbols in Western culture, even more, one of the main forms of Western thought. The tree and its roots are the symbols of unity, hierar-

35. "The tree is a symbol of either life or death, depending upon whether it is healthy and strong, or poorly nourished and withered." George Ferguson, *Signs and Symbols in Christian Art* (Oxford: Oxford University Press, 1954), 39.

36. Barbéris, 107.

37. In the already-quoted words of Pierre Michel, *Les Barbares: Un mythe romantique 1789-1848* (Lyon: Presses Universitaires, 1981), 83.

38. François-René de Chateaubriand, *Atala,* in *Atala, René,* 55. It was an explanation present as well in the American writings about the origin of American society.

chy, continuity, and transcendence and are found in all branches of Western science, including linguistics and psychology.[39] The image of a tree that is half-dead and half-alive is particularly dramatic: it is the very symbol of contradiction, of rupture. Tocqueville had this contradiction within himself—hence the final transformation of the Frenchman into the half-dead tree. The tree, planted on the island, made it the center, the capital of this other America. This is the meaning of the tree in Beaumont's drawing: like a flag, it shows what type of territory one is about to enter. It is a real tree but, separated from other trees, it becomes a tree of meaning.

We are not accustomed to looking for an image of purely asocial America in the work of the author of *Democracy in America*. Tocqueville moved between two Americas: one rational, the other poetic. His "esprit lucide" dwelt in the political institutions, his "âme troublée" in American nature.[40] These two Americas were in conflict: one, Tocqueville thought, was Anglo-Saxon and Protestant, the other French and Catholic; one was political, the other social; one was the land of freedom, the other of slavery; one was acceptable, the other was not. The island of Lake Oneida was poetic, natural America in miniature, the pure America, the unlivable land of spiritual exile.

Of course, these divisions are neither exclusive nor convincing; they represent, however, the way Tocqueville perceived America. The religious imagery of "Journey to Lake Oneida" makes the island quite Catholic. Chateaubriand expressed surprise that America had no tall, imposing churches, and he explained it as the result of Protestantism. Domes, veils, religious awe, and martyrdom are part of the splendor and mystery of the Catholic rite. Tocqueville makes this side of the island totally unintelligible to the fisherman's wife, who represents social, Protestant America in his text. It is the feeling of the sublime, of tragedy, of high spirituality which characterizes the island in opposition to the Protestant practicality of the mainland. For Tocqueville, it is like being in a church, and this is one of the reasons for his feeling that he has already been there.

Tocqueville associated Catholicism with French character and mores, and with French political influence. The island of Lake Oneida was a

---

39. Gilles Deleuze and Félix Guattarii, "Rhizome," in *Mille Plateaux: Capitalisme et schizophrénie* (Paris: Editions Minuit, 1984), 9–29. "The binary logic," they write, "is the spiritual reality of the tree-root" (p. 11).

40. It is Pierre Michel who said that Tocqueville had "l'esprit lucide, l'âme troublée" (in his *Les Barbares: Un mythe romantique,* 269).

French island, a symbol of the former French control over the territory. It was also a fantasy of exile—the tentative, imaginary emigration by Tocqueville and Beaumont. "Literary texts play the role of fictive solutions to problems that have been displaced and couldn't find real solution in that moment," P. Barbéris has written (p. 6). The insistent repetition of the image of empty America, of the impossible paradise, of *le mort-vivant* was an effort on the part of Tocqueville to face the problems he could not quite formulate in the vocabulary of his everyday realities. America was a space in which to experiment, to face the fear of the future, of expansion and exile. It was the place to transport, literally and figuratively, the untenable social tensions of Western Europe. The little paradise on Lake Oneida was a place where Tocqueville tried and failed in his imaginary emigration. (In his "Letter" he openly writes that his health would not permit him to survive on the island; this is only one of the signs of how much he identified with the Frenchman.) Having experimented with that, he was now able to turn toward the America of political institutions. It was a country he had already rejected, that he did not plan to live in, and, in a sense, he had already died in. Now he was able to look at it as a model, to conceptualize it and find out what it meant.

10

Social America

The America of Many Oneidas

Empty, sublime America was devoid not only of Indians; it also had no Europeans. In a striking retelling of the Oneida episode in *Democracy in America,* the Frenchman loses whatever identity he had before, even his nationality. "Sometimes the progress of man is so rapid that the desert reappears behind him," writes Tocqueville, and he develops this image in a paragraph that ends with nature covering man's ephemeral traces. In the following paragraph he adopts a very personal tone and, as if to illustrate the truth of his observation, tells the story that we know so well.

I remember that in crossing one of the woodland districts which still cover the state of New York, I reached the shores of a lake which was encircled by forests coeval with the world [paradise]. A small island, covered with woods whose thick foliage concealed its banks, rose from the center of the waters. Upon the shores of the lake no object attested to the presence of man except a column of smoke which might be seen on the horizon, rising from the tops of the trees to the clouds and seeming to hang from heaven rather than to be mounting to it. An Indian canoe was hauled up on the sand, which tempted me to visit the islet that had first attracted my attention, and in a few minutes I set foot upon its banks. The whole island formed one of those delightful solitudes of the New World, which almost led civilized man to long for the haunts [life] of the savage. A luxuriant vegetation bore witness to the incomparable fruitfulness of the soil. The deep silence, which is common to the wilds of North America, was broken only by the monotonous cooing of the wood-pigeons and the tapping of the woodpecker on the bark of trees. I was far from supposing that this spot had ever been inhabited, so completely did nature seem to be left to herself; but when I reached the center of the isle, I thought that I discovered some traces of man. I then proceeded to examine the surrounding objects with care, and I soon perceived that a European had undoubtedly been led to seek refuge in this place. Yet what changes had taken place in the scene of his labors! The logs that he had hastily hewn to build himself a shelter had sprouted afresh; the very props were intertwined with living verdure, and his cabin was transformed into a bower. In the midst of these shrubs a few stones were to be seen, blackened with fire and sprinkled with thin ashes; here the hearth had no doubt been, and the chimney in falling had covered it with debris. I stood for some time in silent admiration of the resources of Nature and the littleness of man; and when I was obliged to leave that solitude [enchantés lieux], I was still repeating with sadness: "Are ruins, then, already here?" (1: 295–296)

All the basic elements of the story are here. Although we have no revolution to expel the European from his country, he had to seek refuge and was defeated by nature; the island, centered on a surface of water, is a little paradise; the scene is of nature resurrecting the tree-logs and covering man's traces. The traveler passes through the island to contemplate this sublime spectacle of life and death, and of ruin in the midst of an empty continent.

There is, however, a slight shift of accent in this version of the Oneida story. The forest in "Journey" was, in a manner of speaking, baptized, and the Frenchman was made a martyr. Here the forest is exotic, and instead of the Frenchman's story we have a description of luxuriant vegetation and birds. That change shows that the Frenchman is unessential in the "colonization" of the island, that it is enough for Tocqueville to find there a trace of any European. America—a spectacle of human frailty exposed to the saddened eyes of the observer—became part of the new, Romantic "Grand Tour."

The many Oneidas of this tour were all covered with forest. The forest, like the tree, has a special place in Tocqueville's mental geography. In empty America, the tree is a symbol of civilization, of man, and the forest is a cathedral, a tomb, a cradle; but there is still another America, and a different tree. It is the one that is cut out by the pioneer and used by him in his fight against nature. Tocqueville wrote:

In Europe people talk a great deal of the wilds of America, but the Americans themselves never think about them; they are insensible to the wonders of inanimate nature and they may be said not to perceive the mighty forests that surround them till they fall beneath the hatchet. Their eyes are fixed upon another sight: the American people views its own march across these wilds, draining swamps, turning the course of rivers, peopling solitudes, and subduing nature. This magnificent image of themselves . . . [is] always flitting before his mind.

This march of a people, as irresistible as the march of equality, has a poetic grandeur to it; but it is contrasted with the everyday life of the United States, which is "inconceivably petty, insipid, crowded with paltry interests, in a word, anti-poetic" (2: 74). There is a poetic greatness about the tree in the forest but also a practical utilitarian aura.

The same opposition can be found in Beaumont. In writing about Indians, he complains that the forests are taken away from them to be cut down, not made into poetry.

These beautiful forests, magnificent solitudes, splendid palaces of wild nature, need a divine bard! They cannot fall beneath the ax of the industrialist without having been celebrated by the lyre of the poet. That poet is not to be found in America. . . . Atala, René, the Natchez, were born in America, children of the wilderness. The New World inspired them, old Europe alone has understood them. When the Americans read Chateaubriand, as when they see the marvel of Niagara, they say, "And what does that prove?" (*Marie*, 116)

The last sentence is the one spoken by the fisherman's wife: she could not comprehend why the travelers wanted to go to an island that was "too far from the market." The tragedy of Lake Oneida consists in the fact that a man who might have been Tocqueville's and Beaumont's equal died there, misunderstood and rejected by the New World as well as the Old. In still another duality, there was the America of poetry and the America of industry, and the forest was where they met.

This symbolic meeting place was of utmost importance for the internal equilibrium of various elements in *Democracy in America*. America was for Tocqueville like a forest: a confusion, but one that could be mastered. "One could compare America to a great forest," he wrote, "with a myriad of straight roads built through it, all of them leading to the same point. One need only find the crossroads and everything will become visible at a single glance."[1] The disorder and chaos could be overcome with clear thinking. The division into two Americas (poetic and prosaic) and two systems (aristocratic and democratic) had as its objective the reintegration, the healing, the reunification of Tocqueville's world. This division was an intellectual tool but also a projection,

---

1. Quoted from Tocqueville's letter to the Count Molé, *Ouevres Complètes* vol. 5, pt. 1, 26. See also Furet, "The Conceptual System," 172.

in the intellectual sense of the word, of the rupture in the world Tocqueville inhabited. Impossible to heal at home, it was easier to overcome in a place that was like Europe but was also its negation.

Poetic, empty America contained traces and vestiges of Europe's past but not its feudal social institutions. The past, therefore, was no obstacle in the functioning of the second, "practical" America—the free and prosperous democracy that foretold Europe's future. In this tension between past and future, today's practical America becomes intelligible and, therefore, nonthreatening: a spectacle of continuous activity, of symmetry and meaning, of (relative) freedom. Here equality ends peacefully its march. "Yes, it is certain that in the New World the French traveller found reasons to hope, while in Europe, and especially in France, he found only motives to fear."[2] Tocqueville took what was best in America and projected it onto Europe's future.

The little world of Lake Oneida, poetic and limited as it was, contained all the elements of the universe called America. Its persistent reappearance in the writings of Tocqueville served a very important function. Tocqueville's acceptance of democracy did not come from his heart. "I have for democratic institutions *un goût de tête*," he wrote, "while I am an aristocrat in my instincts and opinions."[3] In his life, in his friendships, in his writing style, and in his political activity he belonged to the aristocratic milieu and its mores. (The only exception may have been his marriage to a commoner.) The attraction of democracy, strong as it was, had little to do with everyday living. The analysis of the working of democracy was meant to show the way, to indicate the future for the French. Therefore Tocqueville needed only a general view of American society; he was interested in the behavior and peculiarities of Americans only insofar as they had bearing on the future of democracy. Americans as such were of no interest to him; he was not a travel writer. In that sense François Furet's already-quoted remark is strikingly true: Tocqueville did not "learn" anything outside of the framework of his theory. Yet he did notice and interpret many little facts that led him to new ideas.

During his journey, Tocqueville often found Americans difficult to bear. Their manners were coarse; they were too loud; they did not keep

2. Pierre Manent, "Commentaire," *Revue Tocqueville* (1981), 23-30, esp. 25.

3. Quoted in J. P. Mayer, *Alexis de Tocqueville: A Biographical Essay in Political Science* (New York: Harper and Row, 1960), 28–29. A similar Tocqueville statement is quoted by Boesche: "I have an intellectual taste for democratic institutions, but I am an aristocrat by instinct. Which means that I scorn and fear the crowd." In Boesche, *The Strange Liberalism of Alexis de Tocqueville,* 169. The quotation comes from an unpublished fragment and is reported by Boesche after Edward Gargan, *Alexis de Tocqueville* (1955).

enough physical and social distance between themselves and their guest; their conversations were devoid of charm and were "argumentative"— concentrated uniquely on exhausting whatever topic they discussed; they chewed tobacco and continuously spat it around them, with the more elegant among them using spitoons. (This custom seriously damaged the image of nineteenth-century Americans: no traveler could avoid noticing it.) One of the most irritating customs of the Americans, Tocqueville observed, was that they continuously boasted about their country:

Nothing is more embarrassing . . . than this irritable patriotism of the Americans. . . . America is a free country in which, lest anybody should be hurt by your remarks, you are not allowed to speak freely of private individuals or of the state, of the citizens or of the authorities, of public or of private undertakings, or, in short, of anything at all except, perhaps, the climate and the soil; and even then Americans will be found ready to defend both as if they had cooperated in producing them. (1: 244)

If the foreigner does not respond to the incessant harassment of their efforts to incite praise, they resort to praising themselves.

This peculiarity of American behavior is frequently described in the travel literature of the time. Everybody complained about it, except for travelers who did not know English. British authors were particularly irritated, as they not only understood what was said but also took it personally (as it was certainly meant to be taken). Mrs. Trollope and Charles Dickens ridiculed this habit a great deal. It was variously interpreted as violent republicanism, a sense of national insecurity in a young nation, as tyranny of the majority; but always it was considered a sign of bad manners and abominable taste. Tocqueville's analysis is, as usual, truly original. In the age of democracy, he said, an aristocratic, disinterested love of one's country is dying out; we therefore need to offer people a practical reason to be attached to their fatherland. That can happen only if

everyone takes an active part in the government of society. . . . As the American participates in all that is done in his country, he thinks himself obliged to defend whatever may be censured in it; for it is not only his country that is then attacked, it is himself. The consequence is that his national pride resorts to a thousand artifices and descends to all the petty tricks of personal vanity. (1: 243–244)

This observation is doubly useful. It satisfactorily explains a strange bit of behavior, and, disregarding its unpleasant side-effects, it points to still another reason why democracy is the necessity of the new age.

This intelligent (and valid) explanation was possible because, while writing *Democracy in America,* Tocqueville was examining social facts only in their relation to problems of equality and the future of France. Mrs. Trollope and Dickens used the criterion of good taste as they considered the United States, and they judged this country by how closely it imitated England, whereas Tocqueville came to it looking for solutions to problems that interested him. Here was a nation of people with no common past, no reason for "instinctive" love of country, and yet they were truly patriotic. Even if its expression irritated, it was a phenomenon worth drawing lessons from. This cool distance characterizes Tocqueville's way of looking at Americans throughout his book. He disregards what he considers their vulgarity and concentrates on what makes them and their manners useful for democracy.

Tocqueville's attitude toward social America was totally *de tête.* Facts and observations had meaning only in their relationship to equality, and to social and political democracy. He linked manners to institutions, as he did literature and religion—all constituted separate surfaces of the same crystal at whose heart was the functioning of the democratic system. Each facet offered a different plane, creating a complicated pattern of interdependence. The light these surfaces reflected came from another crystal at whose center was the French aristocratic system. The interaction of these two crystals created this brilliant, mobile spectacle, which could be described with the sentence, quoted earlier, that Heine used to characterize Tocqueville's *discours:* they have, he said, "a frozen brilliance like cut ice."

The admiration Tocqueville feels is for ideas, for the beauty of the spectacle of the forever changing and moving symmetries of various facets of these ideas. Their complicated relationships were kept in place by the all-embracing vision of the march of equality and by the sense of urgency due to the rapid decline of the old world around him. "Tocqueville's journey was a search for the essence, for the nature of democracy; it is an effort to overcome, by intellectual clarity, the 'religious terror' [he felt]: knowing the nature of democracy, he will know what to hope for and what to fear from it."[4] The march of history, although it crushes individuals, also enlarges human liberty; the crushed man belonged to the poetic America of the past, whereas the practical American belonged to the America of social relations. In such a way, yesterday's nightmare made way for tomorrow's hope.

4. Pierre Manent, *Tocqueville et la nature de la démocratie* (Paris: Julliard, 1982), 9.

The Discovery of America

It is paradoxical that Tocqueville found hope in America, which may have been the source of the problems he was seeking the remedy for. Although the history of modern Europe cannot be reduced to a single motif, the discovery—or invention—of America certainly had a formidable influence on Europe's fate. America was a projection and extension of Europe, but its existence radically changed the old continent, so that another voyage of discovery was needed—Tocqueville's.

The fundamental change, the one that underlay all the others, was in the realm of sheer space. America was discovered by a world that had no place in its scheme for such a continent. It is because of this, argues Mexican historian Edmundo O'Gorman, that America was not in reality discovered but rather "invented": the stumbling upon the previously unforeseen continent was interpreted by the Western world as a discovery. That term implies a conscious, direct effort rewarded by finding something already "there." Its use had profound consequences for how America was understood.

In his inspiring book, *The Invention of America* (1961), O'Gorman analyzes the writings of Christopher Columbus, Amerigo Vespucci, and other explorers and geographers to show that they had no previous idea of the new land and had not been looking for what they found; quite the opposite: once they found America, they attempted to integrate the new continent into the shape of the world they knew. That world, founded on religion, consisted of the Island of the Earth, composed of three continents—Europe, Asia, and Africa—enclosed by the Ocean, which defined the Island's borders. The self-enclosed world was given by God for people to inhabit. The very existence of new inhabited territories undermined the integrity of this image. In O'Gorman's interpretation, Christopher Columbus oscillated between the conviction that the land he came upon was an Asiatic peninsula (the geographic world thus remaining basically the same) and the conviction that it was a Terrestrial Paradise (thus maintaining the world's spiritual integrity). But the facts had to be reinterpreted, and soon a new vision appeared in which the Ocean was no longer seen as a boundary, and the Island of the Earth, through the addition of the "island" of America, now became a globe.

If we designate Columbus's first voyage, which took place in 1492, as the starting moment, the process of reshaping the world took a mere fifteen years. In 1507, the name "America" appeared on the map illustrating the first commentary in which the newly discovered island was called the "fourth part" of the world.[5] The name of the "land of Amerigo" was feminized to show that its nature was identical to that of Europe, Asia, and Africa. The change was not of size but of space. "The moment that the *Orbis Terrarum* was conceived as transcending its ancient insular bounds," writes O'Gorman, "the archaic notion of the world as a limited space in the universe assigned to man by God wherein he might gratefully dwell lost its *raison d'être*" (pp. 128–130).

This statement describes well the impact of the discovery of America. To accommodate the existence of the new continent, the world changed its shape, and, since the globe's surface now had no center, Europe lost her geographic supremacy. This meant a psychological *decentrement,* a process of which 1492 marked only the beginning. As Europe's size diminished, these gigantic American territories opened to her for expansion: they could be annexed, manipulated, or colonized, extending Europe, it seemed, almost endlessly. Unlike Asia or Africa, America was considered empty: the invading Europeans disregarded the civilizations they found there and even denied their existence. America was a space, a gigantic space, that demanded to be settled. The pull of this space, the force of attraction that this "emptiness" exerted, had a profoundly destablizing effect on Europe.

The medieval Europe of the Island of the Earth was a continent in which people's identity depended on the place they were from. Some other cultures named people with the name of their fathers, but in the center of Europe people were identified by geographic names: Leonardo from Vinci, Chrétien from Troyes, Michel Eyquiem from Montaigne. One was born to a place in the same way one was born to a mother: it was a natural occurrence that did not require acceptance. Psychologically and culturally speaking, exile and emigration were not options; only banishment. The attachment to place was so fundamental that banishment threatened one's identity (which was ultimately guaranteed by God). Dante's *Divine Comedy* was born of this attachment to and identification with the place of birth of the poet.

Of course, there were exceptions, escapes, and movements of popula-

5. This is the 1507 publication by the Academy of St. Dié of *Cosmographiae Introductio,* which contained the *Lettera* by Amerigo Vespucci, the Martin Waldseemüller world map with what is today called South and North America (in distorted shapes), and a commentary. (See Edmundo O'Gorman, *The Invention of America* [Bloomington: Indiana University Press, 1961], 123.) The same cartographer later reversed himself and reattached the new land to Asia. More time and exploration were clearly needed to complete this process of realization.

tion; medieval Europe had its pilgrims and explorers, and also vaga-
bonds, itinerant scholars, and wandering Jews. In the last thirty years
since O'Gorman wrote his book, social and demographic historians
have shown that late-medieval and early modern European population
was more geographically mobile than previously thought. Still, these
movements were enclosed within a clearly delineated, finite, flat world,
and for the vast majority of the population the next village was already a
new world. The old Greek and Roman dreams of colonization lived
only in port-cities, which sent their emissaries to sea until, finally, they
found the New World.

Once this world became known, it needed to be conquered—named,
partitioned, and then settled. The people of Europe, theoretically all the
people of Europe, were no longer locked in their continent but instead
had a new, open space to go to. The political and spiritual meaning of
that opportunity was parallel to the "spatial unlocking": people did not
have to stay still and endure their fate anymore, and even the very
concept of fate was put in doubt. The reaction of a young Californian
friend of mine, when first hearing the story of King Oedipus, was:
"Why didn't he move?"

The discovery or invention of America unlocked also the flow of
time: the New World replaced the End of the World. Before the Americas were found, Europe lived in religious, ritualistic time, which had a
very clear beginning—the moment of creation—and was running out
as the Day of Judgment approached. Dante's way of talking about
history was that of prophecy: events were already written down, they
just needed to unfold as time was running out. But the encounter with
other worlds and other populations which seemed to have been created
on the side, so to speak, destabilized this concept of time as well. Here
were lands outside history, whose very existence undermined the linear-
ity and purposefulness of time's movement. America was empty both in
space and in time.

"The conquest of America heralds and establishes our present identity," wrote Tzvetan Todorov. "Even if every date that permits us to
separate any two periods is arbitrary, none is more suitable, in order to
mark the beginning of the modern era, than the year 1492. . . . We are
all the direct descendants of Columbus."[6] Some historians believe that
the sixteenth century—the period of expansion into the Americas—was
the moment of the creation of modern capitalism. In Karl Marx's fa-

6. Tzvetan Todorov, *The Conquest of America*, 5.

mous saying, with the appearance of the world market and of world-wide commerce in the sixteenth century commenced the modern biography of Capital. Several phenomena that destabilized the old order and brought forward the world of today were due to readjustments made to swallow the Americas. Whereas Spain projected onto South America her system of hierarchy and privilege—transplanted herself as she was—in North America a new social model was soon created.[7] Latin America was conceived of as a providential gift to the mother country. North America, though, was to fulfill the "providential opportunity to exercise religious, political, and economic liberty, so hindered and fettered in the Old World," wrote O'Gorman with the optimist's vision of history quite outdated today.

It was the Spanish part of the invention of America that liberated Western man from the fetters of a prison-like conception of his physical world, and it was the English part that liberated him from subordination to a Europe-centered conception of his historical world. In these two great liberations lies the hidden and true significance of American history.[8]

The unlocking of space and time had a liberating influence on Europe: its hungry and discontented populations had somewhere to go. It also rendered the "old order" liable to questioning if confronted with the society created *ex nihilo* by human will. The existence of this new society undermined the conviction that the world is as it should be—the best of all possible worlds. It therefore must have been one of the indirect causes of the French Revolution, which itself performed for the French society a similar operation of unlocking the (already weakened) old social hierarchies and political space. The appearance of a country in which "the king" was elected every four years was an expression of the same movement of history that brought Louis XVI's death by guillotine.

Moreover, there was definitely a link between the American Declaration of Independence and the French Revolution. The images and ideas of the French Revolution are directly traceable to independent America, which offered, for the French,

from La Fayette to Chastellux, from Mirabeau to Brissot, from Malby to Condorcet, from subtle argument to polemic . . . a new discourse on human equal-

7. The difference in founding principles of the two hemispheres can be seen in their attitude toward nature: North Americans set themselves right from the beginning as pioneers, subjugating the forests and marshes, whereas the South Americans adapted to the land and did not colonize "the immense deserts." For a comparison of these two attitudes, see Jehlen, *American Incarnation*, 29–40.

8. O'Gorman, 144–145.

ity and on the right way to govern societies. . . . American independence crystallized the idea of a history-as-origin, by means of which society would once again conform to nature and reason. That is the deep connection between the two revolutions. *The idea of revolution in its 1789 sense originated for the French in the birth of the United States.* (Italics added)[9]

It was only one of the ways in which America returned to Europe to shake her very hard.

The link between the two revolutions, intuitively perceived by the Romantics, was openly acknowledged by Tocqueville. In a letter to his brother Hippolyte, he described the circumstances that prevented the French from establishing their control over America. "Had we been successful," he writes, ". . . the Americans of the United States would not have revolted against their mother country. . . . There wouldn't have been any American Revolution, and perhaps no French Revolution—or at least the circumstances would not have been the same."[10] He did not, however, identify the beginning of the modern era with the discovery of America. The march of equality starts, for him, in the twelfth century, with the growth and establishment of the clergy, with the weakening of the nobility, the acceleration of commerce, and the ripening of civilization. The march of equality was a European phenomenon. Tocqueville goes to America because equality attained there its "extreme limit" (1: 3), the state he expects will soon come to Europe as well. In fact, if he thought in these terms, Tocqueville would think the discovery of America and her Constitution as brought in by equality. For him, to paraphrase the famous Soviet postrevolutionary slogan—Communism equals the power of soviets plus electrification—America equaled equality plus space. His voyage to America is propelled by the worry that equality and freedom may not go together. When he comes back, the two are *precariously* reconciled.

Tocqueville's America

Tocqueville's journey was thoroughly prepared, and so was his "second journey," that is, his writing. He had read many travel accounts, and his itinerary was influenced by one of them. He had read

9. Furet, "From Savage Man to Historical Man," 157, 160.
10. Letter dated November 26, 1831, quoted in Jardin, *Tocqueville*, 165.

Volney's *Tableau,* the *Federalist Papers,* many histories of American states, books about Indians, and so on.[11] As we have seen, there was also another source for the images and themes in his perception of America—Romantic literature. He oscillated between the two sources, which were not complementary: Romanticism interrupted the orderliness of his thought. What is striking and can now be seen is that the themes and terms in which Tocqueville conceived of America were well within the bounds of the tradition that dates from Columbus. America, even before it was found, was a dream of Europeans—a New Eden. It was therefore logical to see America as a paradise (or its opposite: hell). In this sense, too, Tocqueville knew America before he went there.

Unlike Russia, America was in some way considered to be an extension and part of Europe. I would like to remind the reader of the description, quoted in this book's first part, of Custine's arrival in Saint Petersburg. Custine contrasted there the watery surroundings of this city with the Roman countryside. Although the vicinity of Saint Petersburg was a "dull, muddy mirror," a ruinless wasteland that reminded Custine of nothing, the Roman countryside, he said, evoked endless reminiscences. I suggested that difference stemmed from the fact that in Western travel descriptions, among "general views" of cities, there is no scene of arrival in Saint Petersburg and that therefore the "desert" around this city was historical or cultural rather than geographic. But this interpretation does not go far enough.

In the already-quoted version of the Oneida-like episode from *Democracy in America* itself, Tocqueville-the-narrator, while approaching the island, notices the virginal nature of his surroundings: "Upon the shores of the lake no object attested the presence of man except a column of smoke which might be seen on the horizon rising from the tops of the trees to the clouds and seeming to hang from heaven rather than to be mounting to it." He then goes on to find the traces of the European and ends the episode with the question, "Are ruins, then, already here?" (1: 295–296). The column of smoke reminded this reader of the comment René makes while sitting and gazing at the Roman countryside: "Sometimes a tall column rose up solitary in a wasteland [*un désert*], as a great thought may spring from a soul ravaged by time and sorrow" (*René,* 90). The architectural similarity between the two landscapes indicates that one did not need to find a ruin to

11. See Schleifer, *The Making of Tocqueville's "Democracy in America,"* which refers many of his ideas to their sources, and Jardin, *Tocqueville,* 95.

"recognize" the new place. Convinced that Russia was (mostly) a part of Asia, Custine made no effort to "civilize" its landscape. Tocqueville's America functioned as the extension of Europe and was, therefore, known to him, or at least adaptable.

Although Tocqueville's political and philosophical analysis was strikingly modern, it was enmeshed in attitudes toward the natives, the land, and the essence of America that stemmed directly from convictions present already when the country was being created, interpreted, and "invented." The belief, expressed by Tocqueville, that the "savages," even if noble, are fundamentally inferior to "civilized" men predated, attended, and was built into the "formation" of America. As O'Gorman has written,

If the new lands were the fourth part of the world, their inhabitants, in spite of their strangeness, shared in the same nature as that of the Europeans, Asians, and Africans . . . they too were descended from Adam and were beneficiaries of Christ's redemption. . . . The consequence was that the native cultures of the newly-found lands could not be recognized and respected in their own right, as an original way of realizing human ideals and values, but only for the meaning they might have in relation to Christian European culture, the self-appointed judge and model of human behavior. (P. 139)

Christopher Columbus, when told by the inhabitants of Cuba that despite his wishes it was an island and not a continent, wrote in his journal:

And since these are bestial men who believe that the whole world is an island and who do not know what the mainland is, and have neither letters nor long-standing memories, and since they take pleasure only in eating and being with their women, they said that this was an island.[12]

In his analysis of Columbus's writings Todorov establishes this fundamental truth of the conquest: "Columbus has discovered America but not the Americans. The entire history of the discovery of America . . . is marked by this ambiguity: human alterity is at once revealed and rejected" (pp. 49–50).[13]

12. In the Bernaldez transcription of the journal of the second voyage. Quoted after T. Todorov, *The Conquest of America*, 21–22.
13. The year 1492 also saw the Spanish victory over the Moors in Granada and the expulsion of the Jews. Columbus sees a deep connection between these facts and his "discovery of the Indias," which, for him, means the spread and victory of the Christian faith. "But we can also see," comments Todorov, "[these] actions as directed in opposite, and complementary, directions: one expels heterogeneity from the body of Spain, the other irremediably introduces it there" (p. 50).

Tocqueville's attitude toward the continent of North America also continues the traditional way of looking for meaning in its very shape. His already-quoted description—the "Exterior Form of North America"—is written as if it were a commentary on a map: in a gesture analogical to that of the explorers, Tocqueville bends over the continent he wants to re-discover. With this "bird's-eye view" he is able to *perceive* the wisdom of God as expressed in the symmetry and providential emptiness of the continent. (We can appreciate now the multiple use Tocqueville makes of the verbs denoting visual assessment of American reality: he is an observer and a visionary at the same time.)

The map he sees contains religious and geographic components, and this combination determines what he will find. Like Columbus, Tocqueville saw America in religious dimensions, and he found many traces of the Terrestrial Paradise on the continent: the Little Island in the middle of the Virginal Forest where time repeats always the same drama. In that way the past is continuously replayed as present. But America was also the land of the future, of destiny. Here, too, the geographic dimension meets the religious. America is a continent—a self-enclosed, self-sufficient entity, with "coasts so admirably adapted for commerce and industry." Tocqueville sees a providential offering of an empty continent to civilized man when he denies the discovery of America: "l'Amérique se découvre"—discovers herself—he writes (1: 239). Discovery is made by itself, almost involuntarily, so ripe and ready is its object. Such an offering of a continent cannot but be meaningful: the land here incorporates the idea of future. Tocqueville is emphatic about this right at the beginning of *Democracy in America,* establishing the uniqueness of his project. And he finishes the mental map of the continent with this stirring sentence: "In that land the great experiment of the attempt to construct society upon a new basis was to be made by civilized man; and it was there, for the first time, that theories hitherto unknown, or deemed impracticable, were to exhibit a spectacle for which the world had not been prepared by the history of the past" (1: 25). Here geography becomes an expression of destiny, and from the shape of America one can see that it was predestined to fulfill human fate.[14]

The establishment, right at the beginning of his book, of the exceptional and, in a way, supernatural character of America has an all-important meaning for the argument of Tocqueville. What he was look-

---

14. For the functioning of the idea of incorporation see again Myra Jehlen's *American Incarnation: The Individual, the Nation, and the Continent.*

ing at and describing was not an accidental development in capricious human history but a profound expression of mankind's destiny. The effort of understanding was directed toward the future because only understanding of the future could satisfactorily explain the present. And the future, if one looked at it from the American point of view, could be somewhat reassuring. In France, the future implied final destruction and replacement of aristocratic culture and freedoms. In America, where the forest and the noble Indian race were already almost totally destroyed, the future held in it mostly harmonious social development. Perhaps in this development human freedom could be preserved.

There is still another column of smoke, mentioned earlier: the smoke that symbolized the fate of René's family, blown away by the wind. In that image the oak tree—steady, rooted—was surrounded by its family, while René wandered aimlessly, space his enemy—a void. We have seen that in his American journey Tocqueville often encountered René and these "islands" of void. But as he came across them, he reinterpreted them in religious terms and saw them as surrounded by another kind of space, equally empty but hospitable: into this space human freedom could expand. The tomb could become a cradle.

Empty America was covered by a forest—symbol of freedom—and by the islands the forest was covering. The two traditional ways of seeing America—as Eden or as the land of (religious) freedom—are here precariously united to overcome the void. The European's peeling away of the forest introduces the image of social America with its "continuous activity" that Tocqueville admires *de tête*. But this other America, the America of personal discovery, cannot be exorcised. Poetic, marginally expressed, even suppressed, it is a mirror image, reflected in the waters of the lake, of this other, social worry that forced Tocqueville to travel. In "Journey to Lake Oneida," René's exile and death are reenacted. In *Democracy in America,* by a prodigious effort, Tocqueville convinced René that everything would be all right.

11

Conclusions

America, Russia, and Freedom

Tocqueville and the "aging René"—Custine—went to two countries on the edges of Europe. Both Russia and the United States were semi-European entities: European forms of social life were used and transformed there. Both were "new" countries. Russia, although present in European life at the beginning of the millennium, disappeared later under the "Tartar yoke"; her reappearance was approximately contemporary with the discovery of America.[1] Although the "discoverers" of Russia—Herberstein, Olearius, Fletcher—did not find the country "empty," that is, ready for colonization, both America and Russia were characterized by enormous space that was, by European standards, unoccupied. (Siberia was Russia's America.) In the eighteenth century, both countries became gigantic social laboratories: Peter the Great introduced radical reforms in Russia, and the American Revolution marked the beginning of a new political system. These social experiments defied Europe's traditionalist attitude in which historical continuity was preferred to rupture as a matter of course. Europe's reaction to these radical changes was one of interest mixed with disgust, not only because the experiments expressed a lack of respect for tradi-

1. Depending on the historical school, the end of Mongol rule over Muscovy was in 1452, the year Moscow stopped paying tribute to the Great Horde, or in 1480, with the Great Horde's unsuccessful attempt to invade Muscovy.

tion but, above all, because of the slavery present in both countries. The slavery itself was shocking, but even more shocking was its copresence with the egalitarian ethos. The serfdom of peasants in Russia and the slavery of blacks in the United States were despised by the French as non-European.[2]

When Tocqueville and Custine were writing their books, comparisons of the two countries were quite new.[3] For a European, there were striking similarities between the countries. In the travel descriptions of the nineteenth century, for example, American cities were often compared to Russian ones.[4] Most Russian and American cities were new by European standards, and that made them "modern." They were monotonous, with straight, broad streets; their separation from the countryside was not complete; they were similar to each other, with few distinguishing characteristics. With the exception of Moscow, Saint Petersburg, New York, Baltimore, Boston, and Philadelphia, the American and Russian cities consisted of people living *closer* to one another but not living an altogether different type of life. American cities were even less urban than Russian ones, since they often did not even have a central square—only a main street. Yet although Custine, as I have said, was profoundly bored and depressed by Russian cities, Tocqueville often found American cities charming. "Arrival at Utica," he writes cheerfully in his notebook. "Charming city of ten thousand souls. Very pretty shops. Founded since the War of Independence. In the middle of a pretty plain."[5] In a letter to his mother he described Auburn as a "small city of two thousand people with all the houses and all the shops

2. Nineteenth-century France and England "banished" slavery to the colonies. In "young" Russia the serfdom was considered an early sign of decay; in "free" America, of hypocrisy. (In a striking coincidence, both slavery and serfdom were abolished at approximately the same time—in the 1860s; Tocqueville and Custine did not live to see this happen.) Both countries were profoundly divided internally by a chasm that was much deeper than the usual class differences.

3. René Rémond lists five authors who did compare the future of the two countries before Tocqueville, but none of them did it in any extended form. See René Rémond, *Les Etats-Unis devant l'opinion française, 1815–1852* (Paris: Colin, 1962), 379, fn. Later on, such comparison was more common; in an 1854 article, "La société russe et la société américaine" (in *La Revue des Deux Mondes*), Gustave de Beaumont contrasted the freedom of America to the serfdom and lack of private property in Russia. The article was a review of August von Haxthausen's book about Russia, which was written in a polemic with Custine.

4. Patricia Herlihy, "Visitors' Perceptions of Urbanization: Travel Literature in Tsarist Russia," 132, 135.

5. In "Pocket Notebook Number 1," *Journey to America*, 126.

very well furnished."[6] "Pretty shops" and "houses well furnished" are criteria that Tocqueville applied to the American cities: what was likable about them was their spontaneous growth and the useful arrangements put together by their inhabitants. The Russian cities, in contrast, were founded and organized by central authorities, each of them the implementation of a decree, rather than the expression of a free (commercial) will.

But the America that truly interested Tocqueville was neither urban nor rural; the political organization of democracy resided somewhere in between and was personified by the pioneer who, in alliance with others like himself, lived a temporary life in the wilderness, informed by his newspapers about the business of the republic in which he actively participated. For Custine, by contrast, the Russians he met in the provinces were pale copies of the courtiers he met at court, none of them having any say over the governance of their country. Tocqueville found America decentered and decentralized, and therefore vital; Custine discovered that one man held all power in Russia, and that this man's main function was that of a jailer. This is why Custine was despairing over what he saw as the mute tranquility of the Russian people in the face of their suffering. But for Tocqueville, who perceived in each American an expression of democratic power, their imperturbability in facing difficulties was a sign of their sense of responsibility. Where Custine was driven to anguish by what he understood as the acquiescence to enslavement, Tocqueville rejoiced at the spectacle of freedom.

The comparisons made by both men were presented in terms that expressed anxiety: did either country suggest the coming shape of Europe? In his book about Russia, Custine answered this question affirmatively, giving Russia as much or even more influence over Europe's future than America would have (1: 147). In his celebrated ending of the first volume of *Democracy*, Tocqueville considered both countries to be the ones that represent the future:

All other nations seem to have nearly reached their natural limits, and they have only to maintain their power; but these [Russia and America] are still in the act of growth. All the others have stopped, or continue to advance with extreme difficulty; these alone are proceeding with ease and celerity along a path to which no limit can be perceived. (1: 434)

6. Letter to Madame de Tocqueville, July 17, 1831. In *Oeuvres Complètes* (B), 7: 32–38; 38.

Although perhaps agreeing with the diagnosis, Custine rejected both "futures." Russia was for him a gigantic Siberia, a concentration camp, if one may borrow this term from the future. America offered no consolation.

Boring America, with its commercial anxieties . . . can she comfort us after the decomposition of Italy? Those who praise incessantly the material prosperity of the United States without indicting the weight of the sacrifices needed to obtain such advantages are people of great theories but very shortsighted.[7]

America is for Custine an English society, but more mercantile and therefore boring. He feels threatened by the horrors of despotism and uninterested in the prosaic practicalities of democracy.

Tocqueville used different terms in his comparison, and to him there was a gigantic difference between America and Russia. He summarizes this difference in a simple and poignant way:

The American struggles against the obstacles that nature opposes to him; the adversaries of the Russian are men.

And he goes on to develop this opposition:

The former combats the wilderness and savage life; the latter, civilization with all its arms. The conquests of the American are therefore gained by the plow-share; those of the Russian by the sword. The Anglo-American relies upon personal interest to accomplish his ends and gives free scope to the unguided strength and common sense of the people; the Russian centers all the authority of society in a single man. The principal instrument of the former is freedom; of the latter, servitude. Their starting-point is different and their courses are not the same; yet each of them seems marked out by the secret will of Heaven to sway the destinies of half the globe. (1: 434)

In this juxtaposition, the terms of comparison are clear; America was a country of freedom (and therefore of peace and labor), whereas Russia was one of enslavement (and war). In America, men fought against nature; in Russia, against other men. And, although Custine did not care much for American freedom, his description of Russia would con-

---

7. Letter to Marquis de Dreux-Brézé, May 14, 1831, quoted in René Rémond, *Les Etats-Unis devant l'opinion française, 1815–1852,* 725. The real opposition was, for him, between Italy and England: "It is necessary to study Italy to know humankind; but to know the future, one needs to study England." (Custine, *Mémoires et Voyages,* 2 vols. [Paris: Vézard, 1830], 2: 453.) Although this comparison served to "round off" the book that placed side-by-side descriptions of a journey to Italy and of a much later trip to England, the opposition is nevertheless consistent in his work.

firm the Russian side of that comparison. The political systems of both countries, different as they were, were based on equality; but whereas in Russia all were slaves of one master, in America nobody had any master at all. (Custine would say that Americans were enslaved by the almighty dollar.) This difference made Tocqueville approve of things that drove Custine to desperation.

The difference between the countries was in part responsible for the difference between *La Russie en 1839* and *Democracy in America*. But not entirely—the authors were different as well. Although the two men shared many emotions, owing to their aristocratic heritage, they used them differently in their work. Custine did not strive to write an orderly treatise; quite the opposite: he looked for telling detail, description, image. He let his emotions flow freely and infused every page of his book with them. Not so Tocqueville. Because of his character and intellectual tastes, but also because America offered a more acceptable face to him, he was able to separate somewhat his emotions from his political thinking. He accepts America, although not for himself. Custine rejects Russia for everybody.

That difference can be seen through the attitude of both men to space. The vocabulary and images they started with were the same: if we compare Custine's description of Siberia with Tocqueville's poetic islands interrupting the monotony of the American wilderness, we can see that both places are, at first, tombs. But whereas in America the tomb changes into a cradle, in Russia there is no transformation, and the tomb is an eternal prison. In the many quotations reproduced here, Custine spoke of Siberia as a gigantic graveyard, where death is, as it were, useless: the graveyard continues to hold people prisoners. In America, the dying out of the Indian race readies the continent for the birth of a new civilization. Even the Frenchman's death—the death of an unsuccessful colonizer—has the effect of a catharsis, as if this human sacrifice compensated for the "melting away" of the Indians. The American tomb is not leaden or silent like the Siberian, it is active, full of trees that are half-dead but also half-alive. The leaden veil of Siberia is juxtaposed to the poetic veil of the American forest, and "cet enfer russe" is the opposite of the little paradise in the middle of the wilderness. In Russia, death does not lead to resurrection. In America, death reintroduces the Frenchman into nature's life cycle, a rebirth is possible, new generations are coming; therefore death is understandable (in religious terms), and life may go on.

Custine, Tocqueville, and René

Before his death in American exile, René wandered the world, gazing at volcanoes, sunsets, and ruins. He was an embodiment of what Bakhtin would call outsideness—he was uprooted, floating in indefinite social space. His gaze, although fixed on the outside world, was in reality turned inward. He was assessing damage, taking stock of the situation. The following generations of Renés turned more to the outside. As Custine and Tocqueville traveled, they looked at themselves but also at the surrounding world. The defeat of their class, the end of their world, was already understood and absorbed. They now tried to figure out the future.

But first, Custine attempted to reaffirm the past, and this is why he went to Russia. There, it seemed, tradition was still intact, and revolution kept in abeyance. Upon closer examination, however, it turned out that the past he found there was not his. As if in a distorted mirror, all social relations and realities were caricatures of what he had dreamed of. The tsar was a tyrant who enslaved everybody; the enslaved nobility was oppressing the rest of society; violent revolt against this state of affairs was just a matter of time. Custine returned to France reconciled with the limitations of his own society. The past he saw in Russia predicted a future he definitely did not want to become part of.

Tocqueville was pushed abroad by the same worries, but in going to America he looked not at the past but at the future. Younger than Custine, he acknowledged that the seeds of the defeat of their class were contained in their past. He therefore tried to keep his thinking separate from his feelings. He did not *like* America, but he found there a future at the sight of which he did not recoil in horror. America was a privileged place, given to mankind to fulfill its destiny. Since this future did not include him or his class, he, too, returned to France. But he returned reconciled and reassured that the future is not one of unmitigated violence and tyranny.

We can now return to the Bakhtin sentence quoted in the preface at the beginning of this book. "Without *one's own* questions one cannot creatively understand anything other or foreign (but, of course, the questions must be serious and sincere)." Both Custine and Tocqueville went abroad with their own questions—questions that were certainly as serious and sincere as can be. They tried to understand the future of their world and to find a place in it for themselves. The terms in which their questions were asked stemmed from the turbulence and violent social change that afflicted their country and shook their class. Since they associated freedom with aristocracy, they feared that the ascendance of equality would render individual freedom impossible. Both men asked how to preserve freedom; both considered it their sacred duty to apply their thinking to the task of finding an answer to this question. "A man is under the same obligation," wrote Tocqueville, "to offer up his mind in the service of society as he is, in time of war, his body."[8] The two Frenchmen went abroad in the service of their society.

What we are looking at, while observing Custine and Tocqueville, is a transformation of noblemen into intellectuals. The aristocracy of birth had to be replaced by an aristocracy of the spirit. From now on, their identity would not be defined by their origins but by their social responsibilities. Only by fulfilling these responsibilities would they maintain their membership in the group that is defined by merit. They therefore go on to reformulate the concept of individual freedom. The political system of a country was not given once and for all: there was a mutual responsibility of the governing and the governed, and man was a citizen—his freedom depended on his efforts. Limited but protected by his historical circumstances, he should strive to preserve and enlarge his freedom within the framework of family, private property, and his native political system. The scope of the duties and the rights of all individuals is enlarged.

Both Custine and Tocqueville feared violent change, and both found a remedy in social involvement and a sense of responsibility on the part of all citizens. Custine found the nightmare of violence realized in Russia; Tocqueville discovered in America the many new possible shapes of social engagement, with violence deflected toward "nature" (Indians and the forest). This is why Tocqueville saw in America so many lakes reflecting, crystal-like, the sky, trees, and his own face. The crystal reframed many forms in many configurations, each of them new and spontaneous. And this is why the waters on which Custine approached Saint Petersburg seemed to him a dull, muddy mirror. They reflected nothing.

There is a tendency in treating political writings to stick to their declarative side. This approach assumes that what is important is spelled out. But the political ideas I summarize here were conveyed to us in many complex ways. Custine and Tocqueville were immersed in a culture that

8. *Ouevres Complètes,* vol. 13, pt. 1, 373, letter no. 117. Quoted in Jardin, 94.

made them express some things but imply others. Certain strong influences were at work on both of them, notably aristocratic origin, Catholicism, and the whole French Romantic sensibility symbolized by Chateaubriand. In my study I looked for the undeclared, the suggested, the implied. The images that both authors used showed their ambivalence, although none was declared, and their nostalgia, which they dismissed because it seemed to lead nowhere. To understand these images, to understand the choices of sources, I looked at the traditions both men came from and continued. Their works, as is obvious, were formed in a cultural context that they reacted to, used, and prolonged. To understand them, we needed to visit the library at which they were the center.

Although their methods and styles are dissimilar, their writings are parallel both in their main topics and in their conclusions. The threat they reacted to was the threat of extinction. Interpreting the French Revolution, they saw the threat as being directed against not only themselves but also the world as they knew it. The apocalyptic terms in which they saw violence came not only from experience but also from the Catholic tradition, which supplied them with the most fundamental terms of their world-view. These terms seemed so obvious as to function unacknowledged, and therefore unquestioned.

In response to the threat of extinction, these aristocratic writers looked for the ways to reassert themselves and the values they believed in. They "sat down" to avoid being swept away, but, as soon as the tempest rolled over, they insisted on the supremacy of the seated man. Equality notwithstanding, *la classe pensante* was necessary to continue civilization. But the way in which la classe pensante was integrated was paradoxical. Custine, Tocqueville, and René were to remain outsiders. By their common effort they made that position a point of advantage. They convinced themselves and us that only a view from outside can penetrate our world and predict the future. And that, if we let them do this, it might turn out that the future is not going to be bad.

Custine, Tocqueville, and René went abroad to find a place for themselves. They were successful. We can observe in them the creation of modern intellectuals, and the process through which they carved out for themselves a place in their own society. We are painfully interested in that process because we are their descendants, and because the river that is dragging us to our ruin seems swifter than ever. We inherited their responsibilities, uncertainties, and ridiculous poses. But most of all, we inherited their outsideness. And we are still seated at the foot of our volcanoes, and don't know where to go.

Bibliography

Angelot, Jacques. *Six mois en Russie*. Bruxelles: Wahlen, 1827.

Bakhtin, Mikhail M. *Problems of Dostoevsky's Poetics*. Ann Arbor, Mich.: Ardis, 1973.

———. *Speech Genres and Other Essays*. Trans. Vern W. McGee. Austin: University of Texas Press, 1986.

Balzac, Honoré de. *Cousine Bette*. Paris: Garnier, 1962.

Barbéris, Pierre. *"René" de Chateaubriand*. Paris: Larousse, 1973.

Beaumont, Gustave de. *Lettres d'Amérique (1831-1832)*. Ed. André Jardin and G. W. Pierson. Paris: Presses Universitaires de France, 1973.

———. *Marie ou L'Esclavage aux Etats-Unis*. Paris: Charles Gosselin, 1842 (5th ed.).

———. *Marie or Slavery in the United States*. Trans. Barbara Chapman; Introduction by Alvis L. Tinnin. Stanford, Calif.: Stanford University Press, 1958.

———. *Notice sur Alexis de Tocqueville*. Paris: Calmann Lévy, 1897.

Beauvoir, Simone de. *The Second Sex*. New York: Knopf, 1953.

Benjamin, Walter. *Moscow Diary*. Cambridge: Harvard University Press, 1986.

Bien, David D. "Aristocratie." In *Dictionnaire Critique de la Révolution Française*, 647–651. (American edition: "Aristocracy," 616–628.)

Boesche, Roger. *The Strange Liberalism of Alexis de Tocqueville*. Ithaca, N.Y.: Cornell University Press, 1987.

Boffa, Massimo. "Emigrés." In *Dictionnaire Critique de la Révolution Française*, 346–362. (American edition: "Emigrés," 324–331.)

Brand, C. P. *Italy and the English Romantics: The Italianate Fashion in Early Nineteenth-Century England*. Cambridge: Cambridge University Press, 1957.

Brodsky, Joseph. *Less Than One: Selected Essays.* New York: Farrar, Straus, Giroux, 1986.

————. "Why Milan Kundera is Wrong About Dostoyevsky." *The New York Times Book Review,* February 17, 1985.

Cadot, Michel. *La Russie dans la vie intellectuelle française (1839–1856).* Paris: Fayard, 1967.

Chateaubriand, François-René. *Atala, René.* Paris: Garnier-Flammarion, 1964.

————. *Atala, René.* Trans. Irving Putter. Berkeley: University of California Press, 1952.

————. *Mémoires d'outre-tombe,* 2 vols. Paris: Gallimard, 1958.

————. *Oeuvres romanesques et voyages.* Preface by Maurice Regard, 2 vols. Paris: Gallimard, 1969.

————. *Travels in America.* Trans. Richard Switzer. Lexington: University of Kentucky Press, 1969. (Translation of *Voyage en Amérique.*)

————. *Voyage en Amérique.* Prepared for publication by C. A. Sainte-Beuve. Paris: Calmann-Lévy, n.d.

Chateaubriand Today. Ed. Richard Switzer. Madison: University of Wisconsin Press, 1968.

Chaurand, Jacques. *Histoire de la langue française.* Paris: Presses Universitaires de France, 1969.

The City in Russian History. Ed. Michael F. Hamm. Lexington: University Press of Kentucky, 1976.

Compagnon, Antoine. *De la Seconde Main ou le travail de la citation.* Paris: Seuil, 1979.

Considérant, Nestor. *La Russie en 1856: Souvenirs de voyages,* 2 vols. Bruxelles and Leipzig: Auguste Schnée, 1857.

Corbet, Charles. *L'opinion française face à l'inconnue russe, 1799–1894.* Paris: Didier, 1967.

Cronia, Arturo. *La conoscenza del mondo slavo in Italia. Bilancio storico-bibliografico di un millennio.* Venezia-Padova: Istituto di Studi Adriatici, 1958.

Cross, A. G. *N. M. Karamzin: A Study of His Literary Career 1783–1803.* Carbondale: Southern Illinois University Press, 1971.

Custine, Astolphe de. *Aloys ou le Religieux du Mont Saint-Bernard.* Presentation by Philippe Sénart. Paris: Union Générale d'Editions, 1971.

————. *Empire of the Czar: A Journey Through Eternal Russia.* Foreword by Daniel J. Boorstin; Introduction by George F. Kennan. New York: Doubleday, 1989. (American edition of *La Russie en 1839.*)

————. *Journey for Our Time: The Russian Journals of the Marquis de Custine.* Ed. and trans. Phyllis Penn Kohler; Introduction by General Walter Bedell Smith. Chicago: Henry Regnery Company, 1951. (Shortened American edition of *La Russie en 1839.*)

————. *La Russie en 1839,* 4 vols. Paris: Librairie D'Amyot, 1843.

————. *L'Espagne sous Ferdinand VII,* 4 vols. Paris: Ladvocat, 1838.

————. *Lettres à Varnhagen D'Ense.* Presentation by Roger Pierrot. Genève: Slatkine Reprints, 1979.

———. *Lettres de Russie: La Russie en 1839*. Ed. and with a Preface by Pierre Nora. Paris: Gallimard, 1975. (Shortened French edition of *La Russie en 1839*.)

———. *Mémoires et Voyages*. Paris: Vézard, 1830.

Deleuze, Gilles, and Félix Guattari. "Rhizome." In *Mille Plateaux: Capitalisme et Schizophrénie*. Paris: Editions Minuit, 1980.

Dictionnaire Critique de la Révolution Française. Ed. François Furet and Mona Ozouf. Paris: Flammarion, 1988. (American edition: *A Critical Dictionary of the French Revolution*. Ed. François Furet and Mona Ozouf; trans. Arthur Goldhammer. Cambridge: Harvard University Press, 1989.)

Doran, Eva. "Two Men and a Forest: Chateaubriand, Tocqueville, and the American Wilderness." *Essays in French Studies*, no. 13 (Nov. 1976): 44–61.

Dumas, Alexandre (père). *Voyage en Russie*. Paris: Hermann, 1960.

Fayard, Jean-François. *La Justice révolutionnaire: Chronique de la Terreur*. Preface by Pierre Chaunu. Paris: Robert Laffont, 1987.

Ferguson, George. *Signs and Symbols in Christian Art*. Oxford: Oxford University Press, 1961 (1954).

Fletcher, Giles. *Of the Rus Commonwealth*. Ed. and with an Introduction by Albert J. Schmidt. Ithaca, N.Y.: Cornell University Press, 1966.

Fournière, Xavier de la. *Alexis de Tocqueville: Un monarchiste indépendent*. Paris: Librairie Académique Perrin, 1981.

Frank, Waldo. *Dawn in Russia: A Record of a Journey*. New York: Charles Scribner's Sons, 1932.

Furet, François. "L'Ancien Régime." In *Dictionnaire Critique de la Révolution Française*, 627–637. (American edition: 604–615.)

———. *In the Workshop of History*. Trans. Jonathan Mandelbaum. Chicago: Chicago University Press, 1984. First published as *L'Atelier de l'Histoire*. Paris: Flammarion, 1982.

Gassouin, Olivier. *Le marquis de Custine: Le courage d'être soi-même*. Preface by Hugo Marsan. Paris: Lumière & Justice, 1987.

Gautier, Théophile. *Russia*. Trans. Florence MacIntyre Tyson, 2 vols. Philadelphia: John C. Winston Co., 1905.

———. *Voyage en Russie*, 2 vols. Paris: Chapentier, 1866, 1867.

Gooch, G. P. *History and Historians in the Nineteenth Century*. Boston: Beacon Press, 1959 (1913).

Grössing, Helmuth. *Humanistiche Naturwissenschaft. Zur Geschichte der Wiener mathematischen Schulen des 15. und 16. Jahrhunderts*. Baden-Baden: Koerner, 1983.

Harrauer, Christine. "Die Ziegenössischen Lateinischen Drucke der *Moscovia* Herbersteins und Ihre Entstehungsgeschichte. (Ein Beitrag zur Editionstechnik um 16.Jh)." *Humanistica Lovaniensia* 31 (1982): 141–163.

Haxthausen, August von. *Studies on the Interior of Russia*. Chicago: Chicago University Press, 1972.

Herberstein, Sigismund von. *Description of Moscow and Muscovy* (1557). Ed. Bertold Picard; trans. J. B. C. Grundy. London: J. M. Dent and Sons Limited, 1969. (Translation of *Rerum Moscoviticarum Commentarii*.)

————. *Notes Upon Russia: Being a Translation of the Earliest Account of that Country, Entitled "Rerum Moscoviticarum Commentarii."* Trans. and ed., with Notes and an Introduction, by R. H. Major, 2 vols. New York: Burt Franklin Publisher, n.d.

————. *Rerum Moscoviticarum Commentarii.* Sigismundi Liberis Baronis in Herberstein. Basilea: Ioannis Oporinus, 1551.

Herlihy, Patricia. "Visitors' Perceptions of Urbanization: Travel Literature in Tsarist Russia." See *The Pursuit of Urban History,* 125–137.

Hingley, Ronald. *The Russian Mind.* New York: Charles Scribner's Sons, 1977.

Hittle, J. Michael. "The Service City in the Eighteenth Century." See *The City in Russian History,* 53–68.

Hoffman, Léon-François. *Le nègre romantique; personnage littéraire et obsession collective.* Paris: Payot, 1973.

Honour, Hugh. *The New Golden Land: European Images of America from the Discoveries to the Present Time.* New York: Pantheon, 1975.

————. *Romanticism.* New York: Harper and Row, 1979.

Jardin, André. *Tocqueville: A Biography.* Trans. Lydia Davis and Robert Hemenway. New York: Farrar, Straus, Giroux, 1988.

Jehlen, Myra. *American Incarnation: The Individual, the Nation, and the Continent.* Cambridge: Harvard University Press, 1986.

Karamzin, N. M. *Memoir on Ancient and Modern Russia.* See Pipes.

Kennan, George. *Siberia and the Exile System.* Chicago: University of Chicago Press, 1958. (A shortened edition of the 1891 original.)

Kennan, George Frost. *The Marquis de Custine and His "Russia in 1839."* Princeton, N.J.: Princeton University Press, 1971.

Krizhanich, Iurii. *Russian Statecraft: The "Politika" of Iurii Krizhanich.* An analysis and trans. by John M. Letiche and Basil Dmytryshyn. London: Basil Blackwell, 1985.

Kundera, Milan. "An Introduction to a Variation." *The New York Times Book Review,* January 6, 1985.

Lange, Victor. "Visitors to Lake Oneida. An Account of the Background of Sophie von La Roche's Novel *Erscheinungen am See Oneida." Symposium* 2 (1948): 48–78.

Leitsch, Walter. "Herberstein's Impact on the Reports About Muscovy in the 16th and 17th Centuries: Some Observations on the Technique of Borrowing." *Forschungen zur Osteuropäischen Geschichte,* no. 24 (1978): 163–177.

Levi, Carlo. *Il futuro ha un cuore antico.* Turin: Einaudi, 1956.

Levin, Harry. *Refractions: Essays in Comparative Literature.* Oxford: Oxford University Press, 1966.

Lortholary, Albert. *Le Mirage russe en France au XVIIIe siècle.* Paris: B. Boivin, 1951.

Lotman, Iurii M. "The Decembrist in Daily Life (Everyday Behavior as a Historical-Psychological Category)" and "Binary Models in the Dynamics of Russian Culture (to the End of the Eighteenth Century)." In *The Semi-*

otics of Russian Cultural History, Essays by Iurii M. Lotman, Lidiia I. Ginsburg, Boris A. Uspenskii. Ithaca, N.Y.: Cornell University Press, 1985.

————. *Sotworenije Karamzina.* Moscow: Kniga, 1987.

Lubomirski, Jozef. *Scènes de la vie militaire en Russie. Le Prince Soldat. Superstitions russes. Impressions de voyage.* Paris: Didier, 1873.

Manent, Pierre. "Commentaire." *Revue Tocqueville* (1981): 23–30.

————. *Tocqueville et la nature de la démocratie.* Paris: Julliard, 1982.

Mayer, J. P. *Alexis de Tocqueville: A Biographical Essay in Political Science.* New York: Harper and Row, 1960.

McFarland, Thomas. *Romanticism and the Forms of Ruin: Wordsworth, Coleridge, and Modalities of Fragmentation.* Princeton, N.J.: Princeton University Press, 1981.

Mellon, Stanley. *The Political Uses of History.* Stanford, Calif.: Stanford University Press, 1958.

Michel, Pierre. *Les Barbares: Un mythe romantique 1789–1848.* Lyon: Presses Universitaires, 1981.

Montesquieu, Charles Louis Sécondat de la Brède. *De l'esprit des loix.* Ed. Jean Brethe de la Gressaye, 3 vols. Paris: Société Les Belles Lettres, 1958.

————. *The Spirit of the Laws.* Trans. and ed. Ann M. Cohler, Basia Carolyn Miller, and Harold Samuel Stone. Cambridge: Cambridge University Press, 1989.

Newby, Eric. *Big Train Ride: Ride on the Trans-Siberian Railway.* Middlesex, Eng.: Penguin Books, 1978.

O'Gorman, Edmundo. *The Invention of America.* Bloomington: Indiana University Press, 1961.

Olearius, Adam. *The Travels to Muscovy and Persia.* Trans., ed., and with an Introduction by Samuel H. Baron. Stanford, Calif.: Stanford University Press, 1967.

Perlina, Nina. *Varieties of Poetic Utterance: Quotation in "The Brothers Karamazov."* Lanham, Md.: University Press of America, 1985.

Pierson, George W. *Tocqueville and Beaumont in America.* New York: Oxford University Press, 1938.

Pipes, Richard. *Karamzin's Memoir on Ancient and Modern Russia: A Translation and Analysis.* Cambridge: Harvard University Press, 1959.

Possevino, Antonio, S. J. *The Moscovia.* Trans. and with an Introduction by Hugh F. Graham. Series in Russian and East European Studies, No. 1. Pittsburgh: University of Pittsburgh Press, 1977.

Praz, Mario. *Il mondo che ho visto.* Milan: Adelphi Edizioni, 1982.

The Pursuit of Urban History. Ed. Derek Fraser and Anthony Sutcliffe. London: Edward Arnold Publishers, 1983.

Pushkin, Alexandr. *A Journey to Arzrum.* Trans. Birgitta Ingemanson. Ann Arbor, Mich.: Ardis, 1974.

Reconsidering Tocqueville's "Democracy in America." Ed. Abraham S. Eisenstadt. New Brunswick, N.J.: Rutgers University Press, 1988.

Rémond, René. *Les Etats-Unis devant l'opinion française, 1815–1852.* Paris: Librairie Armond Colin, 1962.

Riasanovsky, Nicholas V. "Asia Through Russian Eyes." In Wayne S. Vucinich, ed., *Russia and Asia: Essays on the Influence of Russia on the Asian Peoples*, 3–29.

Riffaterre, Michael. "Chateaubriand et le monument imaginaire." In *Chateaubriand Today*, ed. Richard Switzer, 63–81.

Russia and Asia: Essays on the Influence of Russia on the Asian Peoples. Ed. Wayne S. Vucinich. Stanford, Calif.: Hoover Institution Press, 1972.

Russian Intellectual History: An Anthology. Ed. Marc Raeff; Introduction by Isaiah Berlin. New York: Harcourt, Brace, and World, 1966.

Said, Edward. *Orientalism*. New York: Pantheon, 1978.

Schiller, Friedrich von. *Two Essays: Naive and Sentimental Poetry; On the Sublime*. Trans., with Introduction and Notes, by Julius A. Elias. New York: Ungar, 1966.

Schleifer, James T. *The Making of Tocqueville's "Democracy in America."* Chapel Hill: University of North Carolina Press, 1980.

———. "Tocqueville as Historian." In *Reconsidering Tocqueville's "Democracy in America,"* ed. A. S. Eisenstadt. New Brunswick, N.J.: Rutgers University Press, 1988, 146–167.

Schnitzler, J.-H. *La Russie, la Pologne et la Finlande: Tableau statistique, géographique et historique*. Saint Petersburg and Paris: Jules Renouard, 1835.

Sédillot, René. *Le coût de la Révolution française*. Paris: Librairie Académique Perrin, 1987.

The Semiotics of Russian Cultural History: Essays by Iurii M. Lotman, Lidiia I. Ginsburg, Boris A. Uspenskii. Ed. A. and A. Nakhimovsky; Introduction by Boris Gasparov. Translated from the Russian. Ithaca, N.Y.: Cornell University Press, 1985.

Simpson, Colin. *This Is Russia*. Sydney, Australia: Hodder and Stoughton, 1965.

Staël, Madame de. *Madame de Staël on Politics, Literature, and National Character*. Trans., ed., and with an Introduction by Morroe Berger. New York: Doubleday, 1964.

Taine, Hippolyte. *Italy, Rome and Naples*. Trans. J. Durand. New York: Henry Holt and Co., 1889.

Tarn, Julien-Frédéric. *Le Marquis de Custine ou Les Malheurs de l'exactitude*. Paris: Fayard, 1985.

Tocqueville, Alexis de. *De la démocratie en Amérique*. Introduction by Harold J. Laski: Vols. 1–2 of *Oeuvres Complètes*. Paris: Gallimard, 1961.

———. *Democracy in America*. The Henry Reeve translation, rev. by Francis Bowen; 2 vols. New York: Knopf, 1945.

———. *Journey to America*. Trans. George Lawrence; ed. J. P. Mayer. New York: Doubleday (Anchor Books), 1971. (Here we find "Journey to Lake Oneida," "A Fortnight in the Wilds," and Pocketbooks 1 and 2.)

———. *The Old Régime and the Revolution*. Trans. Stuart Gilbert. New York: Doubleday, 1955.

———. "Quinze jours dans le désert." In vol. 5 of *Oeuvres Complètes*. Paris:

Gallimard, 1957; pp. 343–387. In the same volume "Cahier Portatif no. 1" (pp. 153–162) and "Cahier non-alphabétique no. 1" (pp. 59–86).

———. *Recollections*. Trans. George Lawrence; ed. J. P. Mayer and A. P. Kerr; Introduction by J. P. Mayer. New York: Doubleday, 1970. (Translation of *Souvenirs*.)

———. *Souvenirs*. Introduction by Luc Monnier. Vol. 12 of *Oeuvres Complètes*. Paris: Gallimard, 1964.

———. "Voyage au Lac Onéida." In vol. 5 of *Oeuvres Complètes*. Paris, Gallimard, 1957; pp. 336–341.

Todd, William M. *The Familiar Letter as a Literary Genre in the Age of Pushkin*. Princeton, N.J.: Princeton University Press, 1976.

Todorov, Tzvetan. *The Conquest of America*. New York: Harper and Row, 1984.

Torunczyk, Barbara. "Kings and Spirits in the Eastern European Tales." *Cross Currents* 7 (1988): 183–206.

Virtanen, Reino. "Tocqueville and the Romantics." *Symposium* 13 (1959): 167–185.

Voyce, Arthur. *Moscow and the Roots of Russian Culture*. Norman: University of Oklahoma Press, 1964.

Walicki, Andrzej. *A History of Russian Thought: From the Enlightenment to Marxism*. Trans. Hilda Andrews-Rusiecka. Stanford, Calif.: Stanford University Press, 1979.

———. *The Slavophile Controversy: History of a Conservative Utopia in Nineteenth-Century Russian Thought*. Trans. Hilda Andrews-Rusiecka. Oxford: Clarendon Press, 1975.

Wallach, Erica. *Light at Midnight*. New York: Doubleday, 1967.

Waller, Margaret. "*Cherchez la Femme*: Male Malady and Narrative Politics in the French Romantic Novel." *PMLA* 104, 2 (March 1989): 141–151.

Wittram, Reinhard. *Russia and Europe*. Trans. Patrick and Hanneluise Doran. New York: Harcourt, Brace, Jovanovich, 1973.

White, Hayden. *The Content of the Form: Narrative Discourse and Historical Representation*. Baltimore: Johns Hopkins University Press, 1987.

Index

Académie des Sciences Morales et
  Politiques, 2
Académie Francaise, 2
Adolphe (Constant), 19 n. 10
Adventures in Czarist Russia. See *Voyage en
  Russie* (Dumas)
Aglaia, 35
Alexander II, Tsar, 48, 51, 86
*Alexis de Tocqueville: A Biographical Essay
  in Political Science* (Mayer), 149 n. 3
*Alexis de Tocqueville: Un monarchiste
  indépendant* (Gargan), 105 n. 9, 149
  n. 3
Allemands et Francais (Heine), 3 n. 4
*Aloys ou Le Religieux du Mont Saint-
  Bernard* (Custine): Custine's first
  novel, 13; description of Alps in, 137
  n. 24; as psychological novel, 19 n.
  10; secret of, 14
Les amants exilés en Sibérie, 20
America: aristocratic vs. democratic, 148;
  compared to cradle, 139; continent of,
  159; as decentralized, 163; as described by Chateaubriand, 102–103;
  as described by Tocqueville, 106, 108
  n. 15, 148–158; destiny of, 138–140,
  149; division into two, 125, 144, 148,
  160; emotional vs. rational attitude toward, 101, 122–125; as empty in
  space and time, 143, 145, 154; imag-

ery of, 103, 142, 160, 165; impact of,
  152–153, 155, 163–164; politics in,
  99; as Protestant, 126; racism in, 122;
  vs. Russia, 162–165; as seated young
  woman, 130 n. 9; as semi-European
  entity, 161; Siberia compared to, 83
American Declaration of Independence,
  155
American English, 74
*American Incarnation: The Individual, the
  Nation, and the Continent* (Jehlen),
  139 n. 27, 155 n. 7, 159 n. 14
American Indian: Chateaubriand on, 140
  n. 30, 143; vs. civilization, 141; de-
  scription of, 112; genocide of, 139,
  140, 165; as symbol of individual free-
  dom, 103; Tocqueville on, 158
American Revolution, 156, 161
American travel notes (Tocqueville), 115–
  118
Ancien Régime, 13, 133
"L'Ancient Régime" (Furet), 133 n. 15
Anecdotes, as genre, 75
Anecdotes et Curiosités italiennes (Valéry),
  56
Angelot, Jacques, 43
Anglo-Saxon America, 144
Aniello, Tommaso, 18
Antiheroic description, 81
Antonio, 1

177

on Volney's influence on Tocqueville, 140 n. 28
Future, search for, 166

Gallimard, Gaston, 10
Gargan, Edward, 149 n. 3
Gasparov, Boris, 53 n. 21
Gassouin, Olivier, 63–64
Gaston, 123–124
Gautier, Théophile: on Cathedral of Saint Basil, 44 n. 12, 48–49; plagiarized Custine, 81 n. 7; on Russia, 86; on Siberia, 81
Génie du Christianisme (Chateaubriand), 128
Genocide, 140
Genre: anecdotes as, 75; caractères as, 75; définition as, 75 n. 17; histoires as, 75; réflexions as, 75; souvenirs as, 75; tableaux as, 75 n. 17
Geography, imaginative vs. positive, 78
Gerasimov, Dmitrii, 30 n. 7
Gibbon, Edward, 18
Gide, André-Paul-Guillaume, 73
Gillies, John, 34
Giovio, Paolo, 29 n. 5, 30
Goethe, Johann Wolfgang von, 13, 88, 130
Goethe in the Campagna (painting by Tischbein), 130
Gombrowicz, Witold, 61
Gooch, G. P., 17 n. 6, 35 n. 23
Graham, Hugh F., 30 n. 6
Grech, Nikolai Ivanovich, 72
Greece. *See* Russia
Greek-Orthodox Church, 91
Greek war. *See* War of liberation
Guagnini, Alessandro, 30
Guattarii, Félix, 144 n. 39
Guicciardini, Francesco, 26
Guicciardini, Ludovico, 26
Gurowski, Ignacy, 1, 10, 65

Hall, Basil, 74
Hamm, Michael F., 90 n. 18
Hanska, Madame, 66
Harrauer, Christine, 27 n. 3
Haxthausen, August von: on Cathedral of Saint Basil, 42–43, 48–49; on image of Siberia, 81–83; in praise of Russian

cities, 90; uses comparative labeling for Russia, 56
Hegel, George Wilhelm Friedrich, 37
Heine, Heinrich, 3, 121
Herberstein, Sigismund von: basis for historical tradition of Russia, 25–33; biography of, 26–27; criticism of Muscovy, 33–34; as discoverer of Russia, 161; influence on Custine, 40; literary influence on, 27; as major influence in Asiatic geography and cartography, 20 n. 5; on Russia, 28, 28 n. 4, 29–30; Russian travels of, 72
"Herberstein's Impact on the Reports about Muscovy in the 16th and 17th Centuries: Some Observations on the Technique of Borrowing" (Leitsch), 30 n. 8
Herlihy, Patricia, 90, 162 n. 4
Herzen, Aleksandr, 92
Hesse, Wilhelm, 65
Hingley, Ronald, 68 n. 8
Histoire de la langue francaise (Chaurand), 70 n. 10
"Histoire de Telenef" (Custine), 20
Histoires, as genre, 75
Historian, vs. role of courtier, 36
Historical cycle of revolution, 16
Historiography, 36, 39
History: as action of writing, 37; as éloge, 35; as formula, 100; themes in, 18; theory of continuity in, 59; used as explanation and expression of Revolution, 15
History and Historians in the Nineteenth Century (Gooch), 17 n. 6, 35 n. 23
A History of Russian Thought: From the Enlightenment to Marxism (Walicki), 34 n. 21, 59 n. 31
History of the Italian Republics (Sismondi), 18
History of the Russian State (Karamzin): on action of writing history, 37–38; as influence on Custine, 33; as influence on Herberstein, 27; as major literary work, 35; supervised by Tsar Alexander I, 36; on Western character of Russia, 51
Hittle, J. Michael, 90 n. 18
Hodeoporicon Ruthenicum; De bello Mosovito (Moscoviticum?) commentariorum libri (Jacob the Dane), 32 n. 16

Designer: UC Press Staff
Compositor: Huron Valley Graphics
Text: 10/13 Galliard
Display: Galliard
Printer: Thomson-Shore, Inc.
Binder: Thomson-Shore, Inc.